THREEFOLD LOTUS KWOON PRESS

Prajna Paramita Sutra

On the Buddha-Mother's Producing the Three Dharma Treasures, Spoken by the Buddha

Rev. Sylvain J. Chamberlain
12/1/2016

ISBN: 978-1-365-56125-2

The Prajna Paramita Sutra

Chapter 1: The Practice of the Knowledge of All Modes

INTRODUCTION

Thus I now hear at this time. The Lord, dwelling at Rajagriha, on the Vulture Peak, together with a great gathering of 1,250 beings, all of these Arhats, - their outflows being dried up, undefiled, fully controlled, quite free in heart, well free and wise, thoroughbreds, great Serpents, their work being done, their task getting accomplished, their burdens laying down, their own weal becoming accomplished, with fetters which bound these to becoming extinguished, hearts quite free by right understanding, in perfect control of whole mind with the exception of one single person, i.e., the Venerable Ananda.

The Lord says to the Venerable Subhuti, the Elder: "Make it clear now, Subhuti, to Bodhisattvas, the great beings, starting from perfect wisdom, how Bodhisattvas, the great beings go forth into perfect wisdom!"

Herein the Venerable Sariputra thinks to himself: Will this Venerable Subhuti, the Elder, expound perfect wisdom of himself, through the operation and force of own-power in revealing wisdom, or through the Buddha's might?

The Venerable Subhuti, knowing through the Buddha's might, the Venerable Sariputra to be in such wise discoursing, says to the Venerable Sariputra: "Whatsoever, Venerable Sariputra, the Lord's Disciples teach, all this is to be known as Tathagata's work. In dharma which Tathagatas demonstrate, the devoted ones train and realize true nature and hold this in mind. Herein nothing which these teach contradicts true nature of dharma. Whatsoever these sons and daughters of good family may expound as nature of dharma, this these do not bring into contradiction with actual nature of dharma.

THE EXTINCTION OF SELF

Herein the Venerable Subhuti, by the Buddha's might, said to the Lord: "The Lord says, 'Make it clear now, Subhuti, to Bodhisattvas, the great beings, starting from perfect wisdom, how Bodhisattvas, the great beings go forth into perfect wisdom!'" As one speaks of a 'Bodhisattva', which dharma does this word 'Bodhisattva' denote? Lord, I see neither this dharma 'Bodhisattva', nor any dharma called 'perfect wisdom'. Since I neither find, nor apprehend, nor see this dharma 'Bodhisattva', nor any dharma called 'perfect wisdom', what Bodhisattva do I instruct and admonish, in what perfect wisdom? And yet, O Lord, as this is pointed out, a Bodhisattva heart is known as neither cowed, nor stolid...neither despairing nor despondent, as one neither turns away nor is dejected or trembling, neither is frightened or terrified, it is just this Bodhisattva, this great being which comes to be instructed in perfect wisdom. It is precisely this which is recognized as the perfect wisdom of any Bodhisattva, as one's instruction in perfect wisdom. As one thus stands firm, this is one's instruction and admonition. As a Bodhisattva courses in perfect wisdom and is developing such...this one so trains oneself, as one does not pride oneself on or with any thought of enlightenment [with which one begins one's career]. Any thought is no thought, since in its essentially aware nature thought is transparently luminous.

Sariputra: This thought which is no thought, is this something which is?

Subhuti: Is here existing, or can one apprehend in this state of absence of thought either a 'here is' or a 'here is not'?...

Sariputra: No, not this.

Subhuti: Is this now a suitable question which the Venerable Sariputra asks whether this thought which is no thought is something which is?

Sariputra: So, what is this absence of thought?

Subhuti: It is without modification or discrimination.

Sariputra: Well do you expound this, Subhuti, you whom the Lord declares to be foremost of any who dwell in Peace. And for this is seen to be foremost of any who dwell in Peace. And for this reason [i.e. as one does not pride oneself on any thought of enlightenment] is a Bodhisattva considered as incapable of turning away from full enlightenment, and as one who never ceases from taking perfect wisdom to heart. Whether one perseveres in training on the level of Disciple, or Pratyekabuddha, or Bodhisattva, - does one listen to this perfection of wisdom, take this up, bear this in mind, recite this, study this, spread this among others, and in this very perfection of wisdom does one train and exert oneself. In this very perfection of wisdom does one endowed with skill in means exert oneself, concentrating on procuring any and all dharmas which constitute a Bodhisattva. In just this perfection of wisdom any and all dharmas which constitute a Bodhisattva, and in which one trains and exerts oneself, are indicated in full detail. Any being which aspires to train for full enlightenment also listens, takes up, bears in mind, recites, studies and spreads this perfection of wisdom. Any being which is endowed with skill in means exerts oneself in just this perfection of wisdom, with the aim of procuring any and all dharmas which constitute a Buddha.

Subhuti: As I who do not find anything to correspond to the words 'Bodhisattva', or 'perfect wisdom', -which Bodhisattva do I now instruct and admonish in which perfect wisdom? It is truly regrettable as I, while unable to find either thing itself, merely in words might cause a Bodhisattva to arise and to pass away. Even so, this, thusly designated, is neither continuous nor not-continuous, neither discontinuous nor not-discontinuous. And why? Simply...this does not exist. This is why this is neither continuous nor not-continuous, neither discontinuous, nor not-discontinuous. A Bodhisattva, being as unafraid as this unfathomable and perfect wisdom is indicated can be recognized as not lacking in perfect wisdom, and, as one in this irreversible stage of Bodhisattva, standing firmly in consequence of not taking one's stand anywhere. So too, a Bodhisattva coursing in perfect wisdom and developing as such, neither does nor even can stand in form, feeling, perception, impulse and consciousness, due to this fact...as one stands in, or is set in view regarding form, etc., as such, one courses only in its formative influence, and one can neither gain perfect wisdom, exert oneself upon nor fulfill this. As one does not fulfill perfect wisdom, neither can one go forth to all-knowledge, so long as one remains trying to appropriate the essentially elusive. In perfect wisdom form, feeling, perception, impulse and consciousness is/are not appropriated. So, the non-appropriation of form, etc., is not form, etc. [the 5 skandhas], and perfect wisdom also cannot be appropriated. It is thus which a Bodhisattva courses in perfect wisdom. This concentrated insight of a Bodhisattva is called 'the non-appropriation of all dharmas'. It is vast, noble, unlimited and steady, not shared by any of the Disciples or Pratyekabuddhas. All-knowledge cannot be taken hold of, as it cannot be seized through any sign. Could all-knowledge be seized through a sign, Srenika the Wanderer could not gain faith in this our doctrine and tradition. Srenika the Wanderer believes resolutely in cognition of all-knowing, and as a faith-follower he enters cognition with a limited scope. He does not take hold of these skandhas. Nor does he review cognition with joyful zest and pleasure. He views this neither as from inside form, etc., nor as from outside, nor as from both inside and outside, nor as from other than form, etc. In this scripture passage, Srenika the Wanderer, as one who always resolutely believes in cognition of the all-knowing, is called a faith-follower. He takes true nature of dharmas as his standard, and resolutely believes in signlessness such as he neither takes hold of any dharma, nor apprehends any dharma which he even might appropriate or release. He does not even care about Nirvana. This also can be known as a Bodhisattva's perfect wisdom, as he does not take hold of form, etc., and he does not enter Nirvana midway before he realizes ten powers of Tathagatas, his four grounds of self-confidence, and the eighteen dharmas peculiar to a Buddha. Herein too is known as a Bodhisattva's perfection of wisdom. Further, any Bodhisattva coursing in perfection of wisdom and developing this, considers and meditates on what perfection of wisdom is, on one demonstrating perfect wisdom, and on perfect wisdom as dharma which does not exist, which cannot be apprehended. Only as these considerations make a type of wordless sense, and do not make one doubtful or afraid, can be one be known as, or come to be known as a Bodhisattva taken hold of by perfect wisdom.

Sariputra: How can a Bodhisattva become known as 'taken hold of by perfect wisdom', as form does not possess the own-being of form, and as well the other skandhas; as perfect wisdom does not possess own-being of perfect wisdom; and as all-knowledge does not possess own-being of all-knowledge?

Subhuti: It is so, Sariputra. Form does not possess own-being of form, and as well the other skandhas. Perfect wisdom does not possess any mark (of being) 'perfect wisdom'. A mark does not possess own-being of a mark. Any 'thing' whatsoever as 'marked' does not possess own-being as [or for] being marked, and this which is seen or thought of as own-being does not possess any mark of [being] own-being, neither as any of vision, sound, thought, word nor concept, nor subject or object.

Sariputra: Even so, the Bodhisattva training in this goes forth to all-knowledge?

Subhuti: Such a one does. As any and all dharmas are unborn, and do not go forth. As a Bodhisattva courses thus, one comes nearer all-knowledge. To such and any extent as one comes nearer all-knowledge, one's body, thought and marks are known as exceedingly pure, for the sake of maturing beings, and one meets with Buddhas. It is thus any Bodhisattva coursing in perfect wisdom comes nearer all-knowledge.

Subhuti speaks further concerning the Bodhisattva: One courses in a sign as one courses in any form, feeling, perception, impulse, or consciousness, or, in the sign of any of these skandhas, or in ideas such as 'form is a sign', or in production of form, or in the stopping or destruction of form, or in the idea that 'form is empty', or 'I course', or 'I am a Bodhisattva'. For one actually courses in the idea 'I am a Bodhisattva' as a basis. Or, as it occurs to one 'one coursing thus, courses in perfect wisdom and develops it', one courses only in a sign. Such a Bodhisattva is known as unskilled in means.

Sariputra: So, how does a Bodhisattva course as one coursing in perfect wisdom?

Subhuti: One does not course in skandhas, nor in any sign of such skandas, nor in ideas such as 'skandhas are signs', nor in production of skandhas, nor in any stopping or destruction of such, nor in any idea such as 'skandhas are empty', or 'I course', or 'I am a Bodhisattva'. And, this also doesn't occur to this one, 'one coursing thus courses in perfect wisdom and develops it'. One courses but one does not entertain such ideas as 'I course', 'I do not course', 'I course and I do not course', 'I neither course nor do I not course', and the same [four] with 'I will course'. One does not go near any dharma at all as all dharma are unapproachable and unappropriatable. So, a Bodhisattva purely cognizes and is as undifferentiated concentrated insight 'Not grasping at any dharma' by name or appearance, and regardless whether vast, noble, unlimited and steady, not shared by any of the Disciples or Pratyekabuddhas. As one dwells as this concentrated insight, a Bodhisattva quickly realizes full enlightenment which Tathagatas of this time predict for one such as this. But as one dwells in such concentration, one neither reviews nor thinks 'I am collected', 'I will enter concentration', 'I am entering into concentration', 'I have entered into concentration'. All these thoughts or notions in any and all ways do not exist for one such as this.

Sariputra: Can one show forth such concentration?

Subhuti: No, Sariputra. Because any one of these ones born of good family neither knows nor perceives it.

Sariputra: You say one neither knows nor perceives it?

Subhuti: I do, for such concentration does not exist.

The Lord: Well said, Subhuti. And thus a Bodhisattva trains herein, as one trains in perfect wisdom.

Sariputra: As one thus trains, one trains in perfect wisdom?

The Lord: As one thus trains, one trains in perfect wisdom.

Sariputra: As one thus trains, which dharmas does one train in?

The Lord: One does not train in any dharma whatsoever. Dharmas do not exist in such a way as people without such training are accustomed to suppose.

Sariputra: So, how do these exist?

The Lord: As these do not exist, so these exist. And so, since these do not exist [avidyamana], these are called [result of] ignorance [avidya]. People not diligent and untrained in such have settled down in these. Although these do not exist, these people nonetheless have constructed all dharmas. Having constructed these, yet attached to two extremes, these people neither know nor see dharmas in their true reality. So these beings construct all dharmas which yet do not exist. Having constructed these, people settle down in two extremes. Depending on this link as a basic fact, beings now construct past, future and present dharmas. Now, once constructed these settle down in name and form. Thusly constructed are any and all dharmas, which yet do not exist, and these beings as such neither know nor see any path as it truly is. In consequence these ones do not go forth from any triple world, and do not wake up to any reality limit. For this reason ones such as these come to be styled as 'fools'. Such ones as these reveal faith neither to self nor others in the true nature of dharma. But a Bodhisattva does not settle down in any dharma.

Sariputra: As one trains thus, is a Bodhisattva trained in all-knowledge?

The Lord: As one thus trains oneself, a Bodhisattva does not even train in all-knowledge, and yet one trains in all dharmas. As one thus trains oneself, a Bodhisattva trains in all-knowledge, comes near to this and goes forth to it.

Subhuti: As, O Lord, someone asks, -- "Does this illusory one train in all-knowledge, does one come near this, does one go forth to it?" --How does one explain it?

The Lord: I ask you a counter-question which you may answer as best you can.

Subhuti: Well said, O Lord. And the Venerable Subhuti listened to the Lord.

The Lord: Do you think, Subhuti, form, feeling, perception, impulse and consciousness, is one thing, and illusion another?

Subhuti: No Lord, it is not so illusion being one thing, and these skandhas, another; this very form is illusion, this very illusion is form.

The Lord: Do you think, Subhuti, this notion 'Bodhisattva', this denomination, this concept, this conventional expression, - is the five grasping skandhas?

Subhuti: Yes, it is. A Bodhisattva training oneself in perfect wisdom trains oneself as an illusory person for full enlightenment. One bears in mind these five grasping aggregates are this illusory person as well. The Lord says form is as an illusion. And as this is true of form, this is true also of six sense organs, and of five grasping aggregates.

Subhuti: Do Bodhisattvas newly set out in this vehicle not tremble, hearing this exposition?

The Lord: These ones tremble getting into hands of bad friends, but not getting into hands of good friends.

Subhuti: Who are a Bodhisattva's good friends?

The Lord: The ones instructing and admonishing these in the perfections. The ones pointing out to Bodhisattvas deeds which are seen as being of Mara, and saying, 'this is how faults and deeds seen as being of Mara come to be recognized. These are faults and deeds seen as being of Mara. Get rid of these as you recognize these.' These ones are known as good friends of a Bodhisattva, as great beings, armed with great armor and set out in this great vehicle, and mounted on this great vehicle.

THE MEANING OF 'BODHISATTVA'

Subhuti: Regarding what the Lord is saying, as speaking of 'Bodhisattva', what is meant by this word 'Bodhisattva'?

The Lord: Nothing real is meant by this word 'Bodhisattva'. A Bodhisattva trains oneself in non-attachment to any and all dharmas. The Bodhisattvas, great beings, awake in non-attachment to full enlightenment in a sense in which one understands any and all dharmas. As one has enlightenment as one's aim, this 'enlightenment-being' [Bodhisattva], this great being, is so called.

THE MEANING OF 'GREAT BEING'

Subhuti: So, as the Lord is speaking of a Bodhisattva as 'great being', --for what reason is a Bodhisattva called 'great being'?

The Lord: Any Bodhisattva is called 'great being' through understanding such as any of these reveal to countless masses and collections of beings' access to their own unlimited awareness.

Sariputra: It is clear also to me this understanding through which a Bodhisattva is called 'great being'.

The Lord: Make it clear what you think now!

Sariputra: Any Bodhisattva is called 'great being' through understanding such as any of these demonstrate dharma as truly as it is, and great errors are forsaken and dissolved - such erroneous views as any assumption of a self, a being, a living soul, a person, of becoming, of not-becoming, of annihilation, of eternity, of individuality, etc. - erroneous views or notions of things or beings of any intrinsically non-dependent inherencies, or as such may lose any or all attributes assumed of such inherencies.

Subhuti: It is clear also to me this understanding through which any Bodhisattva is called 'great being'.

The Lord: Make clear, Subhuti, what you think now!

Subhuti: Any Bodhisattva is called 'great being' as being simply unattached to and uninvolved in any thought of enlightenment, any thought of all-knowledge, any thought without outflows, any unequalled thoughts or any thought of equaling the unequalled, or thoughts as either shared or unshared by any of the Disciples or Pratyekabuddhas. Any thought of all-knowledge is without outflows, and unincluded [in any empirical world]. Respecting all-knowledge, and regarding any thought which is without outflows and unincluded, one remains unattached and uninvolved. In coming to understand this as such, any Bodhisattva comes to be styled as 'great being'.

Sariputra: For what reason is one unattached even to this thought, and uninvolved in such?

Subhuti: As such, this is no thought.

Sariputra: Is this thought, which is no thought, something which is?

Subhuti: Is here existing now, or can one apprehend in this state of absence of thought, either a 'here is' or 'here is not'?

Sariputra: No, not even this.

Subhuti: So...how can Venerable Sariputra ask, or even say, 'is such thought, which is no thought, something which is'?

Sariputra: Well do you expound this, Subhuti, whom the Lord announces as foremost, as dwelling in Peace.

Herein the Venerable Purna, son of Maitrayani, says to the Lord: 'Great being' is one thus called, armed in great armor is such a being, one set out in this great vehicle, such is mounted on this great vehicle. This is why one comes to be styled as 'great being'.

Subhuti: How great is this which entitles one to be called 'armed in great armor'?

The Lord: Here the Bodhisattva, the great being, thinks thus: 'countless beings do I lead to Nirvana yet here is neither one leading to Nirvana, nor any being led thus'. However many beings one may lead to Nirvana, yet neither has any being been led to Nirvana, nor had any led others to it. As such is this true nature of dharmas, seeing this nature as such, is illusory. Subhuti, just as a clever magician, or magician's apprentice conjures up at these crossroads a great crowd of people and makes these vanish again... What do you think, Subhuti, is anyone killed by anyone, or murdered, or destroyed, or made to vanish?

Subhuti: No indeed, Lord.

The Lord: Even so a Bodhisattva, great being, leads countless beings to Nirvana, and yet not any being has been led to Nirvana, nor has one led others to it. Hearing this exposition without fear is a great thing which entitles this Bodhisattva to be known as 'armed with the great armor'.

Subhuti: As I understand the meaning of the Lord's teaching, as certainly not armed with an armor this Bodhisattva, this great being, is known.

The Lord: So it is. As all-knowledge is not made, not unmade, not affected. Such beings also for whose sake one is armed with great armor are not made, not unmade, not effected.

Subhuti: So it is. For form, feeling, perception, impulse, consciousness, is neither bound nor freed. And such is true also of Suchness of form, Suchness of feeling, Suchness of perception, Suchness of impulse or Suchness of consciousness

Purna: But what now is the form of which you say is neither bound nor freed, and what this Suchness of form, etc.?

Subhuti: The form of any illusory being is neither bound nor freed. Suchness of form of an illusory being is neither bound nor freed. In reality it is not here at all, it is isolated, it is unproduced. This is the great armor, the great non-armor of a Bodhisattva, a great being, armed as the great armor, set out in this great vehicle, mounted on the great vehicle.

After these words the Venerable Purna is silent.

THE MEANING OF 'GREAT VEHICLE'

Subhuti: It is thus, O Lord, a Bodhisattva, great being, is armed with great armor, and is set out in the great vehicle, is mounted on the great vehicle. But what is this great vehicle? How does one know any one thus set out in this great vehicle? Whence does it go forth and whither? Who or what being sets out in it? Where does it stand? Who or what being goes forth by means of this great vehicle?

The Lord: 'Great vehicle' is a synonym of immeasurableness. 'Immeasurable' is infinite, and as such nothing by which to determine any measurement either by name nor number, saying this is as such or this many. By means of perfections a Bodhisattva sets out. From this triple world one goes forth. One sets out to where is no objective support whatsoever. Such is a Bodhisattva, a great being going forth, -but not going forth to anywhere. Nor does one set out in this as one does not stand anywhere, yet stands on all-knowledge by way of making a stand nowhere. And finally, by means of this great vehicle no one goes forth, no one has gone forth, no one will go forth. As neither of these dharmas exist, - one going forth, and this by which one goes forth - neither can these be got at. Since any and all dharmas do not exist, what dharma could go forth by what dharma? It is thus Subhuti, a Bodhisattva, a great being, is armed with great armour, and is mounted on the great vehicle.

Subhuti: The Lord speaks of the 'great vehicle'. Surpassing the world with its Gods, beings and Asuras, such a vehicle goes forth. It is the same as space, and exceedingly great. As in space, so in this vehicle is room for immeasurable and incalculable beings. Such is this great vehicle of the Bodhisattvas, these great beings. One neither sees its coming, nor going, and its abiding as such, does not exist. Thus one cannot get at any beginning of this great vehicle, nor at any end, nor at any middle. Yet, such is self-identical everywhere. Thus, hereof one speaks of a 'great vehicle'.

The Lord: Well said, Subhuti. So it is. It is thusly the great vehicle of the Bodhisattvas, the great beings. Trained herein Bodhisattvas reach all-knowledge, have reached it, will reach it.

Purna: This Elder Subhuti, as asked about perfect wisdom, fancies the great vehicle is something which can be pointed out.

Subhuti: Have I, O Lord, spoken of the great vehicle without transgressing against perfect wisdom?

The Lord: You have. In agreement with perfect wisdom you point out the great vehicle.

ATTAINMENT

Subhuti: Through the Buddha's might O Lord, moreover, a Bodhisattva setting out on this journey does not approach the goal of full Bodhisattvahood from any beginning, nor any ending, nor from any middle either. Bodhisattvas are as boundless as form, feeling, perception, impulse and consciousness are boundless. One does not approach any idea such as 'a Bodhisattva is form', etc. This also does not exist, and is not apprehended. Thus in each and every way neither do I get at any of the dharmas which constitute a Bodhisattva, nor do I see any dharma which the word 'Bodhisattva' denotes. Perfect wisdom also is neither seen nor got at. All-knowledge also neither is seen nor got at. As in each and every way these dharmas are neither seen nor apprehended, -what dharma does one instruct and admonish, through what dharma, in what dharma? 'Buddha', 'Bodhisattva', 'perfect wisdom', all these are mere words. What 'things' being such as these denote is something uncreated? It is as with any self or notion hereof. Although we speak of a 'self', yet absolutely any self is some 'thing' uncreated. Since herein all dharmas are without own-being, what is form, etc., which cannot be seized, and which is something uncreated? Thus any fact -such as all dharmas are without own-being ...is the same as any fact that these are uncreated. Yet non-creation of any and all dharmas differs from these dharmas. How do I instruct and admonish non-creation in perfect wisdom which is also non-creation? And yet, one cannot apprehend as other than uncreated all dharmas, regardless whether these are thought of as constituting a Buddha, or a Bodhisattva, or one marching to enlightenment. If any Bodhisattva as this is being taught is not afraid, one can know 'this Bodhisattva, this great being courses in perfect wisdom, develops, investigates, and meditates on and as such.' At such a time as a Bodhisattva investigates these dharmas in perfect wisdom, at such a time one does not approach form and other skandhas, nor go to any of these. Nor does one review any production of form, etc., nor any stopping. For non-production of form, etc., is not form, etc. Any non-passing-away of form, etc., is not form, etc. Non-production and form are herein neither two nor divided. Inasmuch as one calls any thing 'form', etc., one makes a count of what is not two. Thus, Bodhisattvas investigate in perfect wisdom any and all dharmas in any and all modes as such may merely indicate, yet one does not at any time approach form, feeling, perception, impulse, or consciousness.

Sariputra: As I understand the teaching of the Venerable Subhuti, a Bodhisattva also is non-produced. Yet, as a Bodhisattva is non-produced, how does one go on this difficult pilgrimage, and how can one possibly endure any experience of sufferings which one is said to undergo for the sake of beings?

Subhuti: I do not look for a Bodhisattva going on any difficult pilgrimage. In any case, one coursing in perception of difficulties is not a Bodhisattva. One generating a perception of difficulties is unable to work the weal of countless beings. On the contrary, one forms the notion of ease, one forms this notion of all beings, whether men or women, are one's parents and children, and thus one goes on pilgrimage of a Bodhisattva. A Bodhisattva identifies all beings with one's parents or children, yes, even with one's own self, like this: "As I myself aspire to be quite free from all sufferings, just so all beings aspire to be quite free from all sufferings." In addition regarding all beings, one forms the notion: "I do not desert all these beings. I aspire to set these free from any measureless heap of sufferings! And I do not produce towards any a thought of hate, even though I might be dismembered a hundred times!" It is thus a Bodhisattva lifts up one's heart. As one dwells as one whose heart is this way, one neither courses nor dwells as one perceiving difficulties. And further a Bodhisattva produces the thought, "as in each and every way a self does not exist, and so not got at, so in each and every way all dharmas do not exist, and are not got at." Such a one applies this notion to all dharmas, inside and outside. As one dwells as one whose heart is as such, one neither courses nor dwells as one perceiving difficulties. But as the Venerable Sariputra said, "non-produced is the Bodhisattva,"...indeed it is so, "non-produced is any Bodhisattva."

Sariputra: Further, is just such a Bodhisattva non-produced, or dharmas also which constitute one?

Subhuti: Dharmas which constitute a Bodhisattva are also non-produced.

Sariputra: Are only dharmas which constitute a Bodhisattva non-produced, or also any state of all-knowledge?

Subhuti: Any state of all-knowledge is also non-produced.

Sariputra: Is just the state of all-knowledge non-produced, or also any and all dharmas which constitute it?

Subhuti: Dharmas which constitute all-knowledge are also non-produced.

Sariputra: Are just dharmas which constitute all-knowledge non-produced, or also any common people?

Subhuti: Any common people are also non-produced.

Sariputra: Are just any common people non-produced, or also dharmas which constitute these?

Subhuti: Dharmas which constitute any common people are also non-produced.

Sariputra: If, Venerable Subhuti, the Bodhisattva is non-produced and also dharmas which constitute one as such, and also the state of all-knowledge, and also dharmas which constitute this, and also any common people, and also dharmas which constitute these, - surely, the state of all-knowledge is reached by a Bodhisattva without any exertion?

Subhuti: I do not wish for any attainment of any unproduced dharma, nor reunion with one. Further, does one attain an unproduced attainment though unproduced dharma?

Sariputra: So is unproduced attainment got at through unproduced dharma, or through produced dharma?

Subhuti: Is unproduced dharma produced, or unproduced?

Sariputra: Is production a dharma which is a non-production, or is non-production dharma which is production?

Subhuti: To talk of production as non-production-dharma is not intelligible.

Sariputra: To talk of non-production is also not intelligible.

Subhuti: Non-production is just talk. Non-production just appears before the mind's eye. Non-production is just a flash in the mind. Absolutely it is nothing more.

Sariputra: In the first rank of preachers of dharma should the Venerable Subhuti be placed. For in whatever way he may be questioned, he finds a way out; he does not swerve from the correct teaching about true nature of Dharma, and he does not contradict true nature of Dharma.

Subhuti: This is the Lord's Absolute...the essence of Disciples without any support, so in whatever way these are questioned, these find a way out, do not contradict true nature of dharmas, nor depart from such. This is such as this, as these do not rely on any dharmas.

Sariputra: Well said, Subhuti. And what is this perfection of the Bodhisattvas which allows these to not lean on any dharmas?

Subhuti: Perfection of wisdom, beneficial to all the three vehicles, is also perfection which allows these to not lean on any dharma, due to it showing all dharmas as having no support and can thus give none. As any Bodhisattva remains unafraid as this deep perfection of wisdom is being taught, one can know such a one is adjusted to perfection of wisdom, and one is not lacking in this attention to true facts about dharmas.

Sariputra: How is it a Bodhisattva does not lack in attention being adjusted to perfect wisdom? For if a Bodhisattva is not lacking in attention, one automatically lacks in adjustment to perfection of wisdom. And if one does not lack in adjustment to perfection of wisdom, one is lacking in attention. But if in a Bodhisattva the two facts that one is not lacking in attention, and one is not lacking in dwelling in perfection of wisdom belong together, then all beings also will not be lacking in dwelling in perfection of wisdom because these also dwell not lacking in attention.

Subhuti: Well said, and yet I must reprove you, although the Venerable Sariputra has taken hold of the matter correctly as far as the words are concerned. One knows attention is without own-being in the same way in which beings are without own-being; attention has no real existence in the same way in which beings have no real existence; attention is isolated in the same way in which beings are isolated; attention is unthinkable in the same way in which beings are unthinkable; acts of mental attention do not undergo any process which leads to enlightenment in the same way in which beings do not undergo any process; acts of attention do not in any real sense undergo any process which leads to enlightenment, any more than beings do. It is through attention of such a character as this I wish a Bodhisattva, a great being, may dwell in this dwelling.

Chapter 2: SAKRA

PREAMBLE

At this time, many Gods are coming to the assembly and taking their seats: Sakra, Chief of Gods, with forty thousand Gods of the Thirty-three; the four world-guardians, with twenty thousand Gods belonging to the retinue of the four Great Kings; Brahma, ruler of this world system, with ten thousand Gods belonging to the company of Brahma; and five thousand Gods of the Pure Abode. And yet...the might of the Buddha with his majesty and authority surpasses even the splendor of these Gods, a reward for the deeds these have done here, even in this past.

Sakra: These many thousands of Gods, Subhuti, have come to this assembly, and taken seats, as we want to hear about perfect wisdom from the Holy Subhuti, and to listen to his advice to the Bodhisattvas, to his instruction and admonition how these Bodhisattvas stand in perfect wisdom, how train in it, how one devotes oneself to it?

Subhuti: Let me now explain it to you, through the Buddha's might, majesty and authority. The Gods, not yet aspiring to full enlightenment should do so. Any however, being certain to have got safely out of this world [i.e., the Arhats having reached their last birth, and thinking to have done with it all] are unfit for full enlightenment as these are not willing to go, from compassion, back into birth-and-death. And why? The flood of birth and death hems these ones in. Incapable of repeated rebirths, these ones are unable to aspire to full enlightenment. And yet, these may still aspire to full enlightenment, and I confirm such as these also. I do not obstruct their wholesome root. For one should uphold distinguished dharmas above all others.

The Lord: Well said, Subhuti. You well encourage Bodhisattvas.

Subhuti now says to the Lord: We are grateful to the Lord, and not ungrateful. For the Lord, in presence of Tathagatas leads for our sake the holy life with enlightenment as his view. Even as he definitely develops Bodhisattva realization [as being dedicated to a thought of enlightenment], disciples still instruct and admonish him in these perfections, and by his coursing herein is revealing utmost cognition, to and for beneficence of unlimited beings. So also do we help, champion, aid and sustain Bodhisattvas, as these Bodhisattvas we help, champion, aid and sustain, soon come to know full enlightenment.

HOW TO STAND IN EMPTINESS, OR THE PERFECTION OF WISDOM

So, now Subhuti says to Sakra: Listen now, Kausika, and attend well as I teach you how a Bodhisattva stands in perfect wisdom. Through standing in emptiness, one stands in perfection of wisdom. Armed with great armor, the Bodhisattva thus develops so one does not take one's stand on any of these: not on form, feeling, perception, impulses, consciousness; not on eye, ear, nose, tongue, body, mind; not on forms, sounds, smells, tastes, touchables, mind-objects; not on eye-consciousness, etc., until we come to: not on mind-consciousness, etc., until we come to: not on the elements, i.e., earth, water, fire, wind, ether, consciousness: not on the pillars of mindfulness, right efforts, roads to psychic power, faculties, powers, limbs of enlightenment, limbs of the Path; not on the fruits of Streamwinner, Once-Returner, Never-Returner, or Arhatship; not on Pratyekabuddhahood, nor on Buddhahood. One does not take one's stand on the idea, 'this is form', 'this is feeling', etc., to: 'this is Buddhahood'. One does no
t take one's stand on any ideas like 'form, feeling, perception, impulse, or consciousness, is permanent, or impermanent'; 'form, etc., is ease or ill'; 'form, etc., is self, or not self', 'form, etc., is lovely or repulsive', or even that 'form, etc., is empty, or apprehended as something'. One does not take one's stand on any notion such as the fruits of the holy life derive their dignity from something called 'Unconditioned'. Or this - a Streamwinner is worthy of gifts, and will be reborn seven times at the most. Or, a Once-Returner is worthy of gifts and, as one has not yet quite realized through to any end, one makes an end of ill after one has once more come into this world. Or, a Never-Returner is worthy of gifts and, without once more returning to this world, realizes Nirvana elsewhere. Or, an Arhat is worthy of gifts and just here in this very existence will win Nirvana in the realm of Nirvana leaving nothing behind. Or, a Pratyekabuddha is worthy of gifts, and will win Nirvana after rising above the level of a Disciple, but without having attained any level of a Buddha. Or even, a Buddha is worthy of gifts, and will win Nirvana in the Buddha-Nirvana, in the realm of Nirvana leaving nothing behind, once one rises above the levels of a common being, of a Disciple, and of a Pratyekabuddha, wroughts the weal of countless beings, leads to Nirvana countless hundreds of thousands of niyutas of kotis of beings, assures countless beings of Discipleship, Pratyekabuddhahood and full Buddhahood, is standing [!] on the stage of a Buddha and does a Buddha's work, -even now on this a Bodhisattva does not take one's stand.

Hereupon the Venerable Sariputra thought to himself: If even here upon this one does not take one's stand, how does one stand, and train oneself? The Venerable Subhuti, through the Buddha's might, read his thoughts and said: What do you think, Sariputra, where does Tathagata stand?

Sariputra: Nowhere does Tathagata stand. A Tathagata mind neither seeks nor relies upon support. Ones such as these stand neither in what is conditioned, nor in what is unconditioned, nor do these emerge from such.

Subhuti: Even so a Bodhisattva stands and trains oneself. One decides this, "as the Tathagata does not stand anywhere, nor not stand, nor stand apart, nor not stand apart, so also I stand." Just so one trains oneself, "as Tathagata is stationed, so also I stand, and train myself." Just so one trains oneself, "as the Tathagata is stationed, so do I stand, well in place as without a place to stand upon." Even so Sariputra, a Bodhisattva stands and trains oneself. As one trains thus, one adjusts oneself to perfection of wisdom, and never ceases from taking it to heart.

THE SAINTS AND THEIR GOAL ARE ILLUSIONS

So, now here comes this thought to some of the Gods in this assembly: "What the fairies talk and murmur, we understand this though mumbled. But, Subhuti is just telling us what we do not understand." Subhuti read these thoughts, and said: "Here is no-thing to understand, nothing at all to understand. Nothing in particular is indicated, nothing in particular is explained."

Hereupon the Gods thought: "May the Holy Subhuti enlarge on this! May the Holy Subhuti enlarge on this! What the Holy Subhuti here explores, demonstrates and teaches, is remoter than remote, subtler than subtle, deep beyond depth." Subhuti read these thoughts, and said: "No one can attain any fruit of holy life or keep it, - from the Streamwinner's fruit to full enlightenment - unless one patiently accepts this... - the elusiveness of dharma."

Now these Gods thought: "What could one wish any beings to be like who are worthy to listen to the doctrine from the Holy Subhuti?" Subhuti read these thoughts, and said: "These learning doctrine from me one might wish to be like an illusory magical creation, for these neither hear my words nor experience the facts which are here and now expressed."

Gods: Beings like a magical illusion, are these not in truth just an illusion?

Subhuti: Like a magical illusion are these beings, like a dream. For not two different things are magical illusion and beings are dreams and beings. Any and all objective facts also are like a magical illusion, like a dream. The various classes of saints, from Streamwinner to Buddhahood, also are like a magical illusion, like a dream.

Gods: A fully enlightened Buddha also, you say, is like a magical illusion, is like a dream? Buddhahood also, you say, is like a magical illusion, is like a dream?

Subhuti: Even Nirvana, I say, is like a magical illusion, is like a dream. How much more so anything else?!

Gods: Even Nirvana, Holy Subhuti, you say, is like an illusion, is like a dream?

Subhuti: If perchance here could be anything even more distinguished, of such too I say is like an illusion, like a dream. For not two different things are illusion and Nirvana, are dreams and Nirvana.

Hereupon the Venerable Sariputra, the Venerable Purna, son of Maitrayani, the Venerable Mahakoshthila, the Venerable Mahakatyayana, the Venerable Mahakashyapa, and the other Great Disciples, together with many thousands of Bodhisattvas, said: "Who, Subhuti, are these grasping this perfect wisdom as here explained?"

Hereupon the Venerable Ananda said to these Elders: "Bodhisattvas incapable of falling back grasp this, or beings, persons reaching sound views, or Arhats in whom the outflows are realized as dried up."

Subhuti: No one grasps this perfect wisdom as here explained [i.e. explained in such a way as really no explanation at all]. For no dharma at all is being indicated, lit up, or communicated. So here too, is not even one grasping it.

SAKRA'S FLOWERS

Now this thought comes to Sakra: Let me now, in order to do worship to this discourse on dharma which is being taught by the Holy Subhuti, conjure up some flowers, and scatter them over the Holy Subhuti. Sakra conjured up flowers, and scattered them over the Venerable Subhuti. The Venerable Subhuti thought to himself by the way of reply: These flowers which [now] appear among the Gods of Thirty-three I had not noticed before. These flowers, which Sakra scatters, are magical creations. They are not issued from trees, shrubs or creepers. These flowers which Sakra is scattering are mind-made. Sakra replied: "These flowers are not issuing forth at all. For here are really no flowers whether they issue forth from mind, trees, shrubs, or creepers." So, Subhuti now says to him: "As you say, Kausika, 'these flowers do not issue forth at all, neither from mind, nor from trees shrubs or creepers', for this which never issues forth is not a flower."

Note to interpolation: [any numbers appearing in square brackets refer to the versified version of Perfection of Wisdom in 8,000 Lines.]

TRAINING IN PERFECT WISDOM

So now the thought occurs to Sakra, Chief of Gods: Profoundly wise, surely, is the Holy Subhuti, as he explains this merely nominal existence [of all separate things], and yet even so does not bring it into conflict with any norm of truth, but enlarges on such and quite simply expounds it. Sakra now says to the Venerable Subhuti: "So it is. The Bodhisattva so trains oneself [in this insight] as Holy Subhuti points out."

Subhuti: Truly one so dedicated does. As one thus trains, one does not train to achieve any results of a Streamwinner, nor in any other fruits of the holy life, even up to Buddhahood. For as one trains oneself on any of these stages, one trains oneself in, or as buddha-nature, or toward pure and undifferientiated cognition of all-knowledge; and so in the immeasurable and incalculable Buddha-dharmas. So in this, one trains oneself neither for the increase of form, feeling, perception, impulse, or consciousness, nor yet for their decrease; [43] neither to appropriate form, etc., nor to let them go. Nor does one train oneself to get hold of any other dharma even up to all-knowledge, nor to produce one, or make one disappear. As one thus trains, a Bodhisattva trains in all-knowledge, and dedicated thusly, goes forth to all-knowledge.

Sakra: Does a Bodhisattva go forth to all-knowledge, even though one does not train oneself to get hold of any dharmas, -even of all-knowledge, -nor to produce one, or make one disappear?

Subhuti: One such as this does. [44]

Sakra now says to Sariputra: How or where does a Bodhisattva search for perfect wisdom?

Sariputra: In the exposition of the Venerable Subhuti.

Sakra: Through whose might, and on whose authority, does the Holy Subhuti teach perfect wisdom?

Sariputra: Through the Tathagata's might, and on his authority.

Subhuti: It is indeed the Tathagata's might, Sakra, by which such perfect wisdom is taught. And as you ask, ¡®How or where does a Bodhisattva search for perfect wisdom?', the answer is: One should not search for such in form, nor in any other skandhas; nor in any thing which is other than form, or other than any other skandhas. Because, perfect wisdom is not one of these skandhas, nor yet other than these. [45]

THE INFINITUDE OF PERFECT WISDOM

Sakra: This perfection of wisdom, Subhuti, is a great perfection, unlimited, measureless, infinite.

Subhuti: So it is. And why? Perfect wisdom is great, unlimited, measureless and infinite because form, feelings, etc., are so. Hence one does not settle down in any such conviction that this is a ¡®great perfection,' and ¡®unlimited perfection,' a ¡®measureless perfection,' or ¡®infinite perfection.' This is how and why perfect wisdom is a great perfection, unlimited, measureless and infinite. [46] Perfect wisdom is an infinite perfection because objects as well as [individual] beings are infinite. Perfect wisdom is an infinite perfection because one cannot get at the beginning, middle, or end of any objective fact [since as a dharma, such have no own-being]. Moreover, perfect wisdom is infinite perfection as all objective facts are endless and boundless, and any beginning, middle, or end are not apprehended. For one cannot apprehend the beginning, middle and end of form, or any such skandhas. In such a way as this perfect wisdom is infinite perfection by reason of this infinitude of objects. And further still, any being is endless and boundless as one cannot get at any beginning, middle or end. Thus perfect wisdom is infinite perfection by reason of this infinitude of beings.

Sakra: How is it, Holy Subhuti, this perfect wisdom is an infinite perfection by reason of this infinitude of beings?

Subhuti: It is not so because of their exceedingly great number and abundance.

Sakra: So, how now Holy Subhuti, is perfect wisdom an infinite perfection by reason of the infinitude of beings? [47]

Subhuti: Well Kausika, what factual entity does the word ¡®being' denote?

Sakra: The word ¡®being' denotes no dharma or non-dharma. It is a term which is added on [to any of this which is really here]...as something adventitious, groundless, as no-thing in itself, unfounded in any objective fact whatsoever.

Subhuti: Is herein [i.e., by uttering this word ¡®being'] any being showing up [as an ultimate fact]?

Sakra: No indeed, Holy Subhuti!

Subhuti: So, as no being whatsoever is showing up, how is herein an infinitude of these beings? For, if any Tathagata, with a voice of infinite range, with this deep thunder of a voice, pronounces, for aeons countless as the sands of the Ganges, this word ¡®being,' ¡®being,' ¨C would this Tathagata hereby produce or stop any being whatsoever, either in this past, future or present?

Sakra: No indeed, Holy Subhuti! Because any being is pure from beyond even any beginning, perfectly pure.

Subhuti: In this way also perfect wisdom is this infinitude of perfection by reason of this identical infinitude of beings. In this manner also any infinitude of perfect wisdom can be known from this infinitude of beings. [48]

CONFIRMATION

Hereupon these Gods around Indra, Brahma and Prajapati, and these hosts of men and women around Rishis as well thrice shouted forth in triumph: Hail the Dharma! Hail the Dharma! Hail the Dharmahood of Dharma! Also these added: Beautifully does Subhuti the Elder even just now indicate, demonstrate, show and clarify how thusly any Tathagata comes to be manifest. As potential Tathagatas we henceforth regard any Bodhisattva possessing fullness of this perfection of wisdom and who here so dwells within.

The Lord now speaks: So it is, O Gods! So do I, as I met a Tathagata, Dipankara, in the bazaar of Dipavati, the royal city, possess the fullness of this perfection of wisdom, so Dipankara, a Tathagata predicted one day I am to be fully enlightened, and said to me: "You, young Brahmin, in this future period, after incalculable aeons, become a Tathagata, Sakyamuni by name, - endowed with knowledge and virtue, Well-Gone, a world-knower, unsurpassed, tamer of beings to be tamed, teacher of Gods and people, a Buddha, a Blessed Lord!"

The Gods replied: This is wonderful, O Lord, this is exceedingly wonderful, O Well-Gone, how much all-knowledge is nourished and promoted in these Bodhisattvas, these great beings, by this perfection of wisdom!

Chapter 3: REVERENCE FOR THE RECEPTACLE OF THE PERFECTIONS, WHICH HOLDS

IMMEASURABLE GOOD QUALITIES

WORLDLY ADVANTAGES OF PERFECT WISDOM

The Lord sees these Gods assembled and seated, and the monks, nuns, laymen and laywomen assembled and seated, and he speaks thus to these Gods: Mara and his hosts are unable to harm anyone taking up this perfection of wisdom, bearing this in mind, teaching, studying or spreading this. Humans and ghosts alike are unable to harm these. Nor do these die untimely deaths. Any deities setting out for full enlightenment, but not yet having hold of this perfection of wisdom, as these approach any person who does so and listen, these also take up, bear in mind, teach, study, and spread this perfection of wisdom. A person devoted to this perfection of wisdom certainly experiences no fear, one certainly never becomes stiff with fright, - whether one be in a forest, at the foot of a tree, in an empty shed, an open place, a road, a highway, or the woods, or on any ocean.

The Four Great Kings: It is wonderful, O Lord, any beings taking up, bearing in mind, etc., this perfection of wisdom, for these discipline beings in the three vehicles, and yet do not perceive any being. We, O Lord, do protect such a person.

Sakra, Brahma and other Gods likewise promise to protect any follower of perfect wisdom.

Sakra: It is wonderful, O Lord, by taking up, etc., this perfection of wisdom, one gains many advantages even here and now. Does one, taking up perfection of wisdom, take up all the six perfections?

The Lord: Yes. And further, by taking up, etc., perfection of wisdom, one gains advantages even here and now. Listen attentively, as I now teach you which ones these are.

So be it, Lord, replied the Gods.

The Lord: The quarrels, contentions and contradictions of any opposing this dharma simply vanish away; the intentions of opponents remains unfulfilled. It is a fact for any followers taken hold of by perfect wisdom such disputes simply vanish away, and do not abide. This is one advantage even here and now. Here, we have an herb, Maghi by name, which is a cure for all poison. Suppose a viper, famished, is to see a creature and pursue it, following the scent, in order to eat it; but now, this creature goes to a patch of Maghi and stands here, we know the smell of the herb causes the snake to turn back. As the healing quality of this herb is so powerful it overpowers the viper's poison, just so do quarrels, contentions and contradictions to which any follower of perfect wisdom is exposed, become stilled, appeased through this piercing flame of perfect wisdom, through its power, its strength, through impregnation with its power. These simply vanish, and neither grow, nor abide. And why? It is perfect wisdom which appeases all evil, - from [ordinary] greed to seizing on Nirvana (?) - and does not increase it. And these Gods and all these Buddhas, and all these Bodhisattvas, protect this follower of perfect wisdom. This is an advantage even here and now. And further, the speech of any follower of perfect wisdom is acceptable, soft, measured and adequate. Wrath and conceit do not overpower such as these. As one concentrates with diligence to reveal such facts in one's life, perfect wisdom tames and transforms this one. Wrath and conceit does not increase. Neither enmity nor ill will take hold of one such as this, not even a tendency towards these. One turns mindful and friendly. Such a one reflects: "As I foster ill will in myself, my faculties go to pieces, such that any features beneficial to any and all beings are consumed, and it is in any case quite illogical as I, being set out for full enlightenment and aspiring to train myself for such, might allow myself to come under the sway of wrath." In this way one quickly regains one's mindfulness. This is another advantage even here and now.

Sakra: It is wonderful how this perfection of wisdom is set up for the control and training of the Bodhisattvas.

The Lord: Well, even further Kausika, as any follower of perfect wisdom may go into battle, even to the very front of it, one such could not possibly lose one's life in it. It is impossible for one to lose one's life from the attack of somebody else. If someone strikes this one, with sword, or stick, or clod of earth, or anything else - one's body cannot be hit.

As, a great lore is this perfection of wisdom; a lore without measure, a quite measureless lore, an unsurpassed lore, a lore which equals the unequalled is this perfection of wisdom. As one trains oneself in this lore, one is intent neither on disturbing one's own peace nor others. The Bodhisattva, the great being training in this lore, uncovers and reveals full enlightenment, gains the gnosis of all-knowing. This is another advantage here and now.

Further, as here or wherever this perfection of wisdom is written down in a book, and is put up and worshipped, where it is taken up, borne in mind, etc., any beings so engaged can come to no harm, except as inclined toward such for past deeds. This is another advantage even here and now.

Just the same too, Kausika, humans and ghosts go to the terrace of enlightenment, or to its neighborhood, or its interior, or to the foot of the tree of enlightenment, and cannot be hurt by humans or ghosts, or be injured by these, or taken possession of, even with the help of evil animal beings, except for in compensation for former deeds. In this, these past, future, and present Tathagatas come to uncover and reveal their enlightenment, and in this, promoting and revealing to these beings fearlessness, lack of hostility, lack of fright. Just so Kausika, any place in which one takes up, bears in mind, etc., perfection of wisdom, in it beings cannot be hurt by beings. Perfection of wisdom makes any spot of earth wherever it is into a true shrine for beings, - worthy of being worshipped and adored, - into a shelter for beings coming to it, a refuge, a place to rest and final relief. This is another advantage here and now.

THE CULT OF PERFECT WISDOM COMPARED WITH THE CULT OF THE BUDDHAS

Sakra: Suppose here are two persons. One of these two, a son or daughter of good family, has written down this perfection of wisdom, made a copy of it; this one now puts it up, and honors, reveres, worships, and adores this with heavenly flowers, incense, perfumes, wreaths, unguents, aromatic powders, strips of cloth, parasols, banners, bells, flags, with rows of lamps all round, and with manifold kinds of worship. The other deposits in Stupas relics of the Tathagata, having gone to Parinirvana; this one takes hold of these and preserves these; honors, worships and adores these with heavenly flowers, incense, etc., as the other does. Which one of these two, O Lord, would beget greater merit?

The Lord: I question you on this point, and you may answer to the best of your ability. The Tathagata, as acquiring and knowing full enlightenment or all-knowledge, in which practice does the Tathagata train in order for such an all-knowledge-personality to have been revealed?

Sakra: It is in just this perfection of wisdom the Tathagata acquires and knows full enlightenment or all-knowledge.

The Lord: So, the Tathagata does not derive any name from the fact one acquires this physical personality, but from the fact one acquires all-knowledge. And this all-knowledge of Tathagatas comes forth as a result of taking up just this perfection of wisdom. The physical personality of Tathagatas, on the other hand, is the result of the skill in means of perfection of wisdom. And this very sameness is a sure foundation for [acquisition of] cognition of all-knowing by others. Supported by this foundation the revelation of cognition of all-knowing takes place, the revelation of Buddha-body, of Dharma-body, and of Sangha-body. Acquisition of the physical personality is thus the cause of cognition of all-knowing. As a sure foundation of whatever cognition, it has for all beings, become a true shrine, worthy of being saluted respectfully, of being honored, revered and adored. Once thus gone to Parinirvana my relics also are worshipped. It is for this reason the person copying and worshipping perfection of wisdom begets a different type of merit. For, in doing so, this one worships cognition of all-knowing. The son or daughter of good family, having made a copy of the perfection of wisdom, and worshipping it, begets different merit. For by worshipping the perfection of wisdom one worships cognition of all-knowing.

Sakra: How can it be...people of Jambudvipa, who do not copy this perfection of wisdom, nor take it up, nor study it, nor worship it, do not know the Lord is teaching such as the cultivation of the perfection of wisdom is greatly profitable! How is it these ones are not aware what the Lord teaches supports the cultivation of the perfection of wisdom and brings great advantages, fruits and rewards! But these do not know this, these are not aware of this! These have no faith in it!

The Lord: What do you think, Kausika, how many of the people of Jambudvipa are endowed with perfect faith in the Buddha, the Dharma, the Sangha? [60]

Sakra: Only a few.

The Lord: So it is, Kausika. Only a few people of Jambudvipa are endowed with perfect faith in the Buddha, the Dharma and the Sangha. Fewer than these few are ones attaining the fruits of a Streamwinner, and, after this, the fruit of a Once-Returner, or of a Never-Returner. Fewer still are any attaining Arhatship. Fewer still realize Pratyekabuddha-enlightenment. Fewer still raise any thoughts to full enlightenment. Fewer still are any, purifying by removing obstacles, and hereby raising thoughts to full enlightenment, and even now continuously strengthening such thoughts. Fewer still are any who, raising these thoughts thusly to full enlightenment, and strengthening such thoughts, now in addition dwell with vigor exerted. Fewer still are any who pursue meditation on perfection of wisdom. Fewer still are any coursing and applying perfection of wisdom. Fewer still are any who, coursing and striving toward perfection of wisdom, abide on any irreversible Bodhisattva-stage. Fewer still, coursing and striving steadily in perfection of wisdom, are any who come to know full enlightenment. Fewer still, coursing and striving in perfection of wisdom, do actually know full enlightenment. Now, as to any Bodhisattvas standing on any irreversible Bodhisattva-stage, knowing and revealing full enlightenment, these expound perfection of wisdom to other sons and daughters of good family who are earnestly intent, who train themselves and strive in perfection of wisdom. And these in their turn take up perfection of wisdom, study and worship it. Here are, on the other hand, countless beings who raise thoughts to enlightenment, who strengthened such thoughts of enlightenment, which course towards enlightenment, -- and perhaps just one or two of these can abide on any irreversible Bodhisattva-stage! For full enlightenment is difficult to reveal, and indeed is hard to come up to if one has inferior vigor, is slothful or displays characteristics defined as an inferior being, allows inferior thoughts, notions, intentions and wisdom. So, if someone wants quickly to know full enlightenment, one indefatigably and continually hears and studys this very perfection of wisdom. One comes to understand this...as Bodhisattvas Tathagatas train in perfection of wisdom; also oneself need train in such; for she is Tathagatas Teacher. In any case, upon any Tathagata's disappearance into final Nirvana, Bodhisattvas run back to this very perfection of wisdom. Here and now, Kausika, if someone builds, for the worship of the Tathagata once having disappeared into final Nirvana, many kotis of Stupas made of the seven precious things, enshrining herein such relics of Tathagatas, and all one's life honor these with flowers, etc., does this one on the strength of such actions, beget a great deal of merit?

Sakra: Indeed, such a one does, O Lord.

The Lord: Vastly different is any merit of someone truly believing in this perfection of wisdom; who, trustingly confiding in this, resolutely intent on this, serene in one's faith, with one's thoughts raised to enlightenment in earnest intent...hears this, learns this, bears this in mind, recites and studies this, spreads, demonstrates, explains, expounds and repeats this, illuminates this in detail to others, uncovers this meaning, investigates this with one's mind; and who, using wisdom to one's fullest extent, thoroughly examines this; who copies this, and preserves and stores away the copy so this good dharma lasts long, so this guide of the Buddhas might not be annihilated, so the good dharma might not disappear, so the Bodhisattvas, great beings might continue being assisted since this guide does not give out, - and who, finally, honors and worships this perfection of wisdom...well Kausika, vastly different is any merit of any devotee of perfection of wisdom compared not only with a person building many kotis of Stupas made of seven precious things, enshrining the relics of Tathagatas...it is even more vastly different than any merit of one completely filling the entire Jambudvipa with such Stupas. It is vastly different than any merit produced by all beings in a four-continent world system even as each single one of these built such a Stupa. Or, equally, as all beings in a small chiliocosm, or in a medium dichiliocosm, or in a great trichiliocosm were to do likewise. Or if, to put an imaginary case forth...all beings in any great trichiliocosm simultaneously became human beings, and each one of these built such a Stupa; and if each one of these, having built all such Stupas, and honoring such for an aeon or the remainder of an aeon; still, any devotee of perfection of wisdom has vastly different merit than any kind or amount of merit resulting from the effect of the meritorious deeds of all such beings as were to erect and worship those countless Stupas.

Sakra: So it is, O Lord. For any person honoring perfection of wisdom...in an absolute sense...such a one honors any and all past, future and present Buddhas in all world systems, which can all be simultaneously comprehended by only the cognition of a single Buddha. Such a one's merit is different than any kind or amount of merit of all beings in great trichiliocosms countless like the sands of the Ganges, even if each single being in these built a Stupa, and if each one of these having built all such Stupas, and were to honor these for an aeon or the remainder of an aeon.

PERFECT WISDOM, A GREAT SPELL

The Lord: So it is, Kausika. The merit of any devotee of perfection of wisdom is entirely different; such is immeasurable, incalculable, inconceivable, incomparable, illimitable. From perfection of wisdom all-knowledge of Tathagatas comes forth; from all-knowledge has come forth the cult of the relics of Tathagata. Here the difference in merit of any devotee of the perfection of wisdom bears no proportion at all to the accumulation of merit born from building Stupas, made of the seven precious things, enshrining the relics of Tathagatas.

Herein forty thousand gods in the assembly are saying to Sakra, the Chief of Gods: Sir! Do take up perfection of wisdom! The perfection of wisdom, Sir, take this up, recite such, study such and explain such for unlimited benefit of any and all beings!

The Lord: Kausika, do take up perfection of wisdom, recite, study and explain it! If the Asuras form any idea of fighting with the Gods of the Thirty-three, and if you, Kausika, have studied, and then recite and explain perfection of wisdom by bringing this to mind, the Asuras will drop such ideas.

Sakra: A great lore is this perfection of wisdom, a lore without measure, a quite measureless lore, an unsurpassed lore, an unequalled lore, a lore which equals the unequalled.

The Lord: So it is, Kausika. For it is due to this lore, i.e. perfection of wisdom, Buddhas of any and all times come to reveal and know full enlightenment. Due to this, Buddhas of any future know it. Thanks to this, Buddhas of any present know it. Thanks to this is it known and revealed. Thanks to just this lore ten wholesome ways of acting are revealed in the world, the four trances associated with the limbs of enlightenment, the four Unlimited associated with the limbs of enlightenment, the four formless attainments upheld by the limbs of enlightenment, the six super-knowledges associated with the limbs of enlightenment, in short the eighty-four thousand articles of dharma, cognition of Buddha, cognition of self-existent, inconceivable cognition. However, as at times it -seems- no Tathagatas are in the world...it is Bodhisattvas, -endowed with skill in means as a result of hearing the outpouring of perfection of wisdom in any past (whenever here are Buddhas), full of pity for beings, come into this world out of pity, -who foster in the world the ten wholesome ways of acting, the four trances as dissociated from the limbs of enlightenment, etc. to: the five super-knowledges as dissociated from the limbs of enlightenment. Just as thanks to the disk of the moon all the herbs, stars and constellations are illuminated according to their power and strength, so, as Tathagata -seem- to pass beyond and this good dharma -seems- to have disappeared, in any seeming absence of Tathagatas, whatever righteous, upright, outstanding, or wholesome life is conceived and manifested in worlds, all coming forth from the Bodhisattva, is brought forth by one, is spread from one's skill in means. But skill in means of Bodhisattvas is known as coming forth from perfection of wisdom. Moreover, any such as are devoted to perfection of wisdom, expect herein many advantages here and now.

Sakra: Which are these advantages?

The Lord: These devotees do not die any untimely death, nor from poison, or sword, or fire, or water, or staff, or violence. As these bring to mind, repeat, and apply this perfection of wisdom, the calamities which threaten these from kings and princes, from king's counselors and king's ministers, do not take place. As kings, etc., may try to do harm to these who again and again bring to mind, repeat and apply perfection of wisdom, such kings, etc., do not succeed; for perfection of wisdom upholds such devotees. Although kings, etc., may approach these ones with harmful intent, they instead decide to greet these, and to converse. For this perfection of wisdom entails an attitude of friendliness and compassion amongst and within all beings. Herein, even though any devotee of the perfection of wisdom may be in the middle of a wilderness infested with venomous vipers, neither beings nor ghosts can harm these, except as in a return for past deeds.

Hereupon one hundred Wanderers of other sects approached the Lord with hostile intent. Sakra, Chief of Gods, perceived these Wanderers from afar, and he reflected: Surely, these Wanderers of other sects are approaching the Lord with hostile intent. Let me now recall as much of this perfection of wisdom as I have learned from the Lord, bring it to mind, repeat, apply and spread it, so these Wanderers cannot approach the Lord, and the preaching of this perfection of wisdom may not be interrupted.

Hereupon, Sakra, Chief of Gods, recalls as much of this perfection of wisdom as he is learning from the Lord, brings it to mind, repeats, applies and spreads it. The Wanderers of other sects hereupon reverently saluted the Lord from afar, and went off on their way.

So, now it occurred to the Venerable Sariputra: For what reason do these heretical Wanderers reverently salute the Lord from afar, and now depart on their way?

The Lord: As Sakra, Chief of Gods, perceived the thoughts of such hostile Wanderers of other sects, he recalled this perfection of wisdom, brought it to mind, repeated, applied, and spread it, with the object of turning back the Wanderers of other sects who wanted to quarrel, dispute and obstruct, and prevented these from approaching this place the perfection of wisdom is being taught. And I have granted permission to Indra, Chief of Gods. I saw not even one pure dharma in these Wanderers. They all wanted to approach with hostile intent, with thoughts of enmity.

Hereupon it occurred to Mara, the Evil One: The four assemblies of Tathagata are assembled, and seated face to face with Tathagata. Face to face with Tathagata these Gods of the realm of sense-desire and of the realm of form are sure to be predicted in this assembly as Bodhisattvas to full enlightenment. Let me now approach to blind them. - Herein Mara conjured up a fourfold army, and is moving towards the place the Lord is.

Now, again it occurs to Sakra, chief of gods: Surely, I can see this is Mara, the Evil One, who has conjured up a fourfold army moving towards the place the Lord is. But the array of this army is not the array of King Bimbisara's army, nor of King Prasenajit's army, not of the army of the Sakyas or of the Licchavins. It is seen for a long time Mara the Evil One pursues the Lord, looking for any chance to enter, searching for a chance to enter, intent on hurting beings. I now recall this perfection of wisdom, bring it to mind, repeat, apply and spread it. Hereupon Sakra recalls just this perfection of wisdom, brought it to mind, repeated, applied and spread it. Immediately Mara, the Evil One, is seen as turning back again, and going on his way.

The Gods of the Thirty-three conjured up heavenly Mandarava flowers, flew through the air, and scattered these over the Lord. Now in triumph these cry: "For a long time surely is this perfection of wisdom coming to these people of Jambudvipa!" Seizing more Mandarava flowers, these scattered and strewed these over the Lord, and said: "It is seen how Mara and his host have no chance to enter any beings who preach and develop this perfection of wisdom, or which course in it. Any beings hearing and studying perfection of wisdom are endowed with no small wholesome root. These who come to hear of this perfection of wisdom fulfill duties also under the Jinas of other times. How much more so any studying and repeating it who are trained in Thusness progress to such and make endeavours regarding such; these are people honoring Tathagatas. For it is in this perfection of wisdom one searches for all-knowledge. Just as all jewels are brought forth by a great ocean, and are searched for through it, just so the great jewel of all-knowledge of Tathagatas is searched for through the great ocean of perfection of wisdom."

The Lord: So it is, Kausika. It is from great oceans of perfection of wisdom the great jewel of all-knowledge of Tathagatas comes forth.

PERFECT WISDOM AND THE OTHER PERFECTIONS

Ananda: The Lord does not praise perfection of giving, nor any of the first five perfections; he does not proclaim their name. Only perfection of wisdom does the Lord praise, its name alone he proclaims.

The Lord: So it is, Ananda. For perfection of wisdom controls the five perfections. What do you think, Ananda, can giving - undedicated to all-knowledge be called perfect giving?

Ananda: No, Lord.

The Lord: The same is true of the other perfections. What do you think, Ananda, is wisdom inconceivable which turns over the wholesome roots by the dedication of these to all-knowledge?

Ananda: Yes, it is inconceivable, completely inconceivable.

The Lord: Perfection of wisdom is given it's name by us from supreme excellence [paramatvat]. Through perfection of wisdom these wholesome roots, dedicated to all-knowledge are given the name of 'perfections.' It is due to this dedication of wholesome roots to all-knowledge this perfection of wisdom controls, guides and leads the five perfections. The five perfections are in this manner contained in this perfection of wisdom, and the term 'perfection of wisdom' is just a synonym for the fulfilling of all six perfections. In consequence, as perfection of wisdom is proclaimed, all six perfections are proclaimed. Just as gems, scattered about in the great earth, grow as all conditions are favorable; and the great earth is their support, and these grow supported by the great earth; even so, embodied in perfection of wisdom, the five perfections rest in all-knowledge, these grow supported by perfection of wisdom; and as upheld by perfection of wisdom are these given the name of 'perfections.' So, it is just this perfection of wisdom controlling, guiding and leading these five perfections.

FURTHER ADVANTAGES FROM PERFECT WISDOM

Sakra: So far the Tathagata has not proclaimed all the qualities of perfection of wisdom, qualities which one acquires by learning, studying and repeating perfection of wisdom. For how else could the limited amount of perfection of wisdom which I learned from the Lord, have spread when just now heretics and Mara were turned away?

The Lord: So it is, Kausika. Moreover, not only by learning, studying, and repeating perfection of wisdom does one develop these qualities, but also one who is reverent towards, and concentrating on a copy of this also is taught, and develops advantages here and now. [83]

Sakra: I also protect ones who are reverent towards and concentrating on a copy of this perfection of wisdom, and still more so ones who in addition learn, study and repeat this.

The Lord: Well said, Kausika. Moreover, as anyone repeats this perfection of wisdom, many hundreds of Gods come near, many thousands, many hundreds of thousands of Gods, so as to listen to Dharma. And, as these hear Dharma, these Gods want to induce a readiness to speak in one speaking of Dharma. Even when one may not be willing to talk, these Gods still expect, through their respect for Dharma, a readiness to speak is induced in such a one as this, and this one now feels an urge to expound this. This again is another quality which someone acquires just here and now by learning, studying, and repeating perfection of wisdom. Moreover, the minds of any discoursing on this perfection of wisdom remain uncowed in front of these four assemblies. These have no fear of being plied with questions from hostile persons. For perfection of wisdom protects these ones. Immersed in perfection of wisdom one does not see the hostility, nor any who act with hostility, nor any who want to be hostile. In this way upheld by perfection of wisdom, one remains unaffected by censure and fear. These qualities also someone acquires just here and now while learning, studying and repeating this perfection of wisdom. In addition, one is dear to one's mother and father, to friends, relatives and kinsmen, to Shramanas and Brahmanas. One is competent and capable of refuting, in accordance with Dharma, any counter-arguments which may arise, and is able to deal with counter-questions. These qualities also someone acquires just here and now while learning, studying and repeating perfection of wisdom. Moreover, Kausika, among the Gods of the Four Great Kings, any Gods setting out for full enlightenment make up their minds to come to this place here as someone puts up a copy of perfection of wisdom, and is reverent toward and concentrated in this. These come, look upon the copy of this perfection of wisdom, salute this respectfully, pay homage to this, learn, study and repeat this. So also do these depart again. And this applies to all Gods, up to even the Highest of Gods. And any son or daughter of good family pray the Gods, Nagas, Yakshas, Gandharvas, Asuras, Garudas, Kinnaras, Mahoragas, beings and ghosts, in any ten directions in countless world systems, do, with the help of this book, see perfection of wisdom, salute respectfully, pay homage, learn, study and repeat such as it is; as also these return to their respective worlds; and these ones also give to any ones abiding in these places as well, just this gift of dharma. Do not however think, Kausika, only in this four continent world, the Gods of the realm of sense-desire and of the realm of form, who set out for full enlightenment decide to come to this place. Not so, as well, Kausika, do you view it! No, all the Gods in the great trichiliocosm, setting out for full enlightenment, decide to come to this place. These come, look upon a copy of this perfection of wisdom, salute it respectfully, pay homage to it, learn, study and repeat it. Moreover, the house, room or palace of any devotee of perfection of wisdom is well guarded. No one does harm to such as these, except as in return for past deeds. This is another quality which one acquires just here and now. For very powerful Gods, and even other supernatural beings, decide to come to this place.

Sakra: How does one know these Gods, or even other supernatural beings, have come to this place to hear, etc., perfection of wisdom?

The Lord: As one perceives anywhere a sublime radiance or smells a superhuman odor not smelled before, now one can know for certain a God, or other supernatural being is present, is come near. Further, clean and pure habits attract such Gods, etc., and makes them enraptured, overjoyed, full of zest and gladness. But divinities of minor power, having before occupied such a place as these come to manifest, decide to leave it. For these cannot endure the splendor, majesty and dignity of such very powerful Gods, etc. As these very powerful Gods, etc., decide to come to such a one repeatedly, any such devotee of perfection of wisdom gains an abundance of serene faith. This is another quality which any son or daughter of a good family acquires just here and now. Further on, one does not form any unclean or impure habits within the unbound circumference of this abode of guidance to Dharma; otherwise one's deep respect for it remains incomplete. Moreover, any devotee of the perfection of wisdom does not become fatigued in either body or mind. At ease one lies down, at ease one walks about. In one's sleep one beholds no evil dreams. As one sees anything in one's dreams, one will just see the

Tathagatas, or Stupas, or Bodhisattvas, or Disciples of the Tathagata. As one hears sounds, one hears just the sound of perfections and the wings to enlightenment. One just sees the trees of enlightenment; and underneath these, the Tathagatas, as these awaken to full enlightenment. And likewise one sees how the fully Enlightened turn the wheel of dharma. And many Bodhisattvas one beholds, chanting just this perfection of wisdom, delighted by its chorus, which proclaims how all-knowledge is gained, how the Buddha-field is purified. One is shown this action of skill in means. One hears the sublime sound of full enlightenment of these Buddhas, the Lords: "In this direction, in this part of the world, in this world system, under this name, the Tathagatas demonstrate Dharma, surrounded and accompanied by many thousands of Bodhisattvas and Disciples, nay by many hundreds of thousands of nayutas of kotis of Bodhisattvas and Disciples." As one beholds such dreams, one sleeps at ease, one awakens at ease. Even as food is thrown into it, one's body still feels at ease and exceedingly light. No trend of thought arises in this one from excessive eagerness of food. One takes only a mild interest in food. A devotee of perfection of wisdom has no strong desire for food, and only a mild interest in it, even as a monk, who practices Yoga, and who emerged from trance, -merely as one's thoughts overflow with other interests. For to the extent one gives oneself up to devotion to development of perfection of wisdom, to such extent do heavenly beings provide one with heavenly food. These qualities also does one acquire here and now. But again, Kausika, as someone makes a copy of perfection of wisdom, and is reverent towards and concentrated in it, but does not learn, study, repeat and apply this; and as someone else truly believes in the perfection of wisdom, trustingly confides in it, and, resolutely intent on it, serene in one's faith, one's thoughts raised toward enlightenment, in earnest intent, hears, learns, bears in mind, recites and studies such as this perfection of wisdom provides for, spreads, demonstrates, explains, expounds and repeats such as this is, illuminates it in detail for others, uncovers meaning, investigates with one's mind, and, using one's wisdom to the fullest, thoroughly examines, copies, and preserves and stores away the copy, so such good dharma lasts long, so this guide of Tathâgatas might not be annihilated, so good dharma does not disappear, so Bodhisattvas, these great beings, continue to be assisted, since their guide does not fail, - and finally, honors and is reverent toward and concentrated in this perfection of wisdom; well, Kausika, this latter begets vastly different merit. Any aspiring to acquire these distinguished qualities here and now, will diligently imitate such a one as this, and these truly believe in perfection of wisdom, etc., as their guide does not fail. One resolves to share this with any aspiring to such. So this great eye of this Guide of Buddhas does not fail, neither for one such as this, nor for others in quest of virtue. In addition this perfection of wisdom at all times is honored and held in concentrated reverence.

CHAPTER 4: THE PROCLAMATION OF QUALITIES

RELATIVE VALUE OF TATHAGATA-RELICS AND OF PERFECT WISDOM

The Lord: If, Kausika, on this one hand you are given this Jambudvipa filled up to the top with relics of the Tathagatas; and if, on this other hand, you could share in a written copy of this perfection of wisdom; ...and if now you have to choose between the two, which one do you take?

Sakra: Just this perfection of wisdom, Lord. For I see such as, within my esteem for this Guide of Tathagatas, in true understanding this also is the body of Tathagatas. As the Lord says: "The Dharma-bodies are Buddhas, these are Lords. But of this, noble Sangha, do not think this individual body is my body. Rather, noble Sangha, see me as this accomplishment of Dharma-body." But this Tathagata-body needs be seen as brought about by the reality-limit, i.e. by perfection of wisdom. It is not, O Lord, that I lack in respect for these relics of Tathagata. On the contrary, I have a real respect for them. As come forth from perfection of wisdom are these relics of Tathagatas revered, and herein as one reveres just this perfection of wisdom, now also the reverence of these relics of the Tathagata is brought to fulfillment, as the relics of Tathagata come forth from perfection of wisdom. It is as with my own godly seat in Sudharma, the hall of Gods. As I am seated on it, the Gods come to wait on me. But as I am not, the Gods, out of respect for me, pay their respect to this seat, circumambulate it, and go away again. For these recall as seated on this seat, Sakra, the Chief of Gods, demonstrates Dharma to Gods of the Thirty-three. In this same way, perfection of wisdom is the real eminent cause and condition which feeds and reveals all-knowledge of Tathagatas. The relics of Tathagatas, on this other hand, are true deposits of all-knowledge, but these are neither true conditions, nor reasons for production of such cognition. As the cause of cognition of all-knowingness perfection of wisdom is also revered and concentrated upon through relics of Tathagata. For this reason, of the two lots now mentioned, I choose just this perfection of wisdom. But it is not because I lack in respect for the relics of Tathagata. Even choosing thusly I have real respect for these, for these relics are worshipped as these are pervaded by this perfection of wisdom. And, if I had to choose between a copy of perfection of wisdom on this one side, and even a great trichiliocosm filled to the top with relics of the Tathagata on this other, I still choose just this perfection of wisdom, for the same reasons. For the relics of Tathagata are true deposits of cognition of all-knowingness, but such cognition itself is come forth from perfection of wisdom. So just here, of these two lots I choose just this perfection of wisdom. But it is not due to any lacking in respect for the relics of Tathagata. In choosing thus I have real respect for these. These, however, are worshipped as having come forth from perfection of wisdom, and as such are pervaded by it.

SIMILE OF THE WISHING JEWEL

It is like a priceless jewel with the property of preventing beings and ghosts from entering the place it is put. If someone were possessed by a ghost, one only needs to introduce this jewel, and any ghost departs. If someone oppressed by the wind applies this jewel as one's body is inflated, one holds back that wind, and prevents it from getting worse, appeasing it. It has similar effects applied to a body burning with bile, choked with phlegm, or painful as a result of a disease arising from a disorder of the humors. It illuminates the blackest darkness of night. In the heat it cools the spot of earth it is placed. In the cold it warms it. Its presence drives vipers and other noxious animals from districts which are infested with these. If any woman or man is bitten by a viper, one need only show these this jewel; and its sight counteracts that poison, and makes it depart. Such are the qualities of this jewel. If one has a boil in the eye, or clouded eyesight, or a disease in the eye, or a cataract, one need only place this jewel on the eyes, and its mere presence removes and appeases these afflictions. Such are its qualities. Placed in water, it dyes the water all through with its own color. Wrapped in a white cloth, and thrown into water, it makes the water white. Equally, as wrapped or bound in a black-blue, or yellow, or red, or crimson cloth, or into cloth of any other color, it dyes the water into which it is thrown the color of the cloth. It also clears up any turbidity which may have arisen in the water. Endowed with such qualities is this jewel.

Ananda: Do these jewels, Kausika, belong to the world of the Gods, or to the people of Jambudvipa?

Sakra: These are found among the Gods. The jewels found among the people of Jambudvipa, on the other hand, are rather coarse and small, and not endowed with such qualities. As such these are infinitely inferior to these heavenly jewels. But the ones among the Gods are fine and full of all possible qualities. As this jewel is now put in a basket, or even placed upon it, this basket still is desirable after the jewel had again been taken out. The basket, through the qualities of the jewel, becomes an object of supreme longing. In the same way, O Lord, the qualities of cognition of all-knowing are derived from just this perfection of wisdom. On this account the relics of Tathagatas thus gone to Parinirvana are reverently concentrated upon. For these are true repositories of the cognition of all-knowingness. And as any demonstration of Dharma by Buddhas and Lords in all world systems is venerated and held in reverence as it comes forth from perfection of wisdom, so also the Dharma-discourser's demonstration of Dharma. As a king is revered, as his royal might gives courage to a great body of people, so also the speaker of Dharma, because, through this might of this Dharma-body, one such as this gives courage to a great body of people. But the relics of Tathagatas are revered for this same reason one reveres demonstrations of Dharma, and expositors of Dharma.

SUPREME VALUE OF THE PERFECTION OF WISDOM

So now, O Lord, as here are two lots; and as not only this great trichiliocosm, but as all world systems, countless as the sands of the Ganges, filled with relics of Tathagatas, is established as this first lot; and a copy of perfection of wisdom as this second lot and I am invited to choose either, and to take such, I take just this perfection of wisdom. It is not, O Lord, for any lack of respect for relics of Tathagatas. My respect for these is a real one. But it is perfection of wisdom pervading all-knowledge such as these relics of Tathagatas are revered, as these come forth from all-knowledge. In consequence any reverence for and concentration upon perfection of wisdom is in effect a worship of Buddhas, these Lords past, future and present. Moreover O Lord, anyone who aspires to see, in accordance with Dharma, the Buddha, these Lords who just now exist in immeasurable and incalculable world systems, needs course now in perfection of wisdom, make endeavours in, and develop such as this is.

The Lord: So it is, Kausika. All Tathâgatas owe their enlightenment to just this perfection of wisdom, - whether these live in this past, future or present. I also, Kausika, am just now a Tathagata due to perfection of wisdom.

Sakra: A great perfection is this perfection of wisdom. For it allows Tathagatas to rightly know and behold thoughts and doings of all beings.

The Lord: So it is, Kausika. It is due to a Bodhisattva coursing for a long time in perfection of wisdom by which one rightly knows and beholds thoughts and doings of all beings.

Sakra: Does a Bodhisattva course only in the perfection of wisdom, and not in the other perfections?

The Lord: One such as this courses in all these six perfections. But it is just this perfection of wisdom which controls the Bodhisattva as one gives a gift, or guards morality, or perfects oneself in patience, or exerts vigour, or enters into meditative trance, or has insight into Dharmas. One cannot attain to any distinction or difference between these six perfections, all being upheld by skill in means and dedicated to perfection of wisdom, dedicated to all-knowledge. Just as no distinction or difference is conceived between shadows cast by different trees in Jambudvipa, -though their colors may differ, and their shapes, and their leaves, flowers and fruits, and their height and circumference, but these are all just called-shadows - even so one can neither attain nor ascribe to any distinction or difference between these six perfections, - neither can all of these Bodhisattvas upheld by skill in means, dedicated to perfection of wisdom, dedicated to all-knowledge.

Sakra: Endowed with great qualities is this perfection of wisdom, with immeasurable qualities, with boundless qualities!

CHAPTER 5: THE REVOLUTION OF MERIT

THE PERFECTION OF WISDOM A SOURCE OF GREAT MERIT, AND A DIFFERENT MERIT

Sakra: Let us again consider two people. The one truly believes perfection of wisdom, trustingly confides in such, studies, copies, repeats and discourses regarding such, since their guide does not fail. And as this one hears this exposition, this one also unhesitatingly resolves to not abandon this perfection of wisdom, -surely so greatly profitable, so great an advantage, so great a fruit, so great a reward, endowed of such and great qualities (!) - this one guards and preserves such as this is, for such is exceedingly hard to develop, and by oneself, one honors, reveres and adores this.

Now, the other person first venerates this, and now gives a copy to another son or daughter of a good family who, having aspirations towards this and eager, asks for such. Which one of these two persons begets greater merit...on this one hand the one who intends to give this all away, or on this other hand, the one who does not?

The Lord: I question you on this point, and you may answer to the best of your abilities. If this one person by oneself is to honor the relics of Tathagata after one's Paranirvana, minister, revere, and preserve these relics; and now, if this other not only oneself honors these relics of the Tathagata, ministers, reveres and preserves these, but in addition reveals these to others, gives these away, and shares them knowing hereby the reverence of these relics will become even more widespread, and from compassion and true sympathy for beings; so answer now Kausika, which one of these two persons begets great merit, and which a different kind of merit: The one who, while worshipping them oneself, reveals, gives and shares these with others...or the one who by oneself, singularly worships these?

Sakra: Surely Lord, the one who shares these with others.

The Lord: So it is, Kausika. Any person revealing perfection of wisdom for others to behold and develop as regards inclinations, always seeking to help others, purely intent on revealing such completely, ...anyone on the strength of this begets greater merit, and indeed not merely greater merit, but a different merit all together. For such merit has no limit, and as such is beyond any determinations of lesser and greater, and indeed other than any determinations whatsoever, which might be even recognized as merit. If in addition this one goes to persons who are fit vessels for this perfection of wisdom, and shares this with these, one begets still different merit. And so too, Kausika, is great indeed any merit of someone who instigates all beings in Jambudvipa to observe ten ways of wholesome action, and establishes these in these ways?

Sakra: To be sure Lord, great this seems to be.

The Lord: Different even still is any merit of someone who makes a copy of this perfection of wisdom, believes in and has faith in such, faith serene and firm; who constantly reveals one's thoughts toward enlightenment, and with earnest intention gives this perfection of wisdom to another Bodhisattva who steadily reveals one's thoughts to enlightenment; who does first of all perfect oneself by tireless writing and reciting; and after much zealous labor, one persuades the other Bodhisattva, explaining this perfection of wisdom, instigating to such, filling one with enthusiasm for this, making such a one rejoice in this, and does by one's words, lead one to this, educate one in this, illuminate these benefits to such a one, cleanse one's thought and remove one's doubt; and who addresses such a one as follows: "Come here, you of good family, do train yourself in just this Path of Bodhisattvas, for as a result of this training, this coursing, this struggling you surely and quickly awake to full enlightenment. After this you go on to educate an infinite number of beings in the complete extinction of the substratum begotten of beginningless rebirths, in other words, in the revelation of the reality-limit." As this one intends to reveal this completely, this one's merit is infinite and different still from any worldly merits. And this is true even if it is compared with the merit of someone who establishes in the observation of the ten wholesome ways of acting all the beings in world systems of any size, even in all the world systems in existence or not in existence, numerous as the sands of Ganges River. Or if it is compared with that of someone establishing others in the four trances, the four Unlimited, the four formless attainments, the five super knowledges, in any number of world systems. In each case any person not only writing this perfection of wisdom and reciting it by oneself, but writing such for others and revealing such completely to these, easily begets a different type of merit than merit itself. Moreover, Kausika, one also begets a different merit still as one may be conversant with the meaning while reciting this perfection of wisdom; and having written such for others, still reveals such completely, expounds and lights this up, both in its meaning and letter.

THE COUNTERFEIT PERFECTION OF WISDOM

Sakra: Can anyone now expound this perfection of wisdom?

The Lord: Yes, anyone thus conversant with this meaning can expound such to someone not understanding it. For in any time a counterfeit of perfection of wisdom may arise. As one hears this counterfeit, a person not understanding it as such needs be wary of making obeisance to it, as this one, though not understanding, may want to realize full enlightenment.

Sakra: How might one recognize in any time if and when the counterfeit perfection of wisdom is expounded?

The Lord: In any time here be monks and nuns whose bodies are undeveloped, whose moral conduct, thought and wisdom are undeveloped, who are stupid, dumb like sheep, without wisdom. As these announce to expound perfection of wisdom, these actually expound its counterfeit. These expound the counterfeit perfection of wisdom by teaching impermanence of form, feeling, perception, impulse and consciousness is to be interpreted as destruction of these just mentioned skandhas. To strive for such insight, according to them, is coursing in perfection of wisdom. But on the contrary, do not view impermanence of these skandhas as destruction of such. For to view things in such a way means to course in the counterfeit perfection of wisdom. For this reason, Kausika, does one with understanding expound effortlessly and correctly the meaning of truth and in perfection of wisdom. By so expounding this, one realizes different and limitless merit.

THE PERFECTION OF WISDOM UNLIMITED AND DIFFERENT THAN ANY OTHER SPIRITUAL GIFT

And any such merit is quite different than if one even thought of oneself as, or even attempted to accept responsibility for, any ability whatsoever to establish any beings in, say, any number of world systems, even in the fruit of a Streamwinner. And such holds good also for the fruit of any Once-Returner, of any Never-Returner, and of any Arhat. Any Bodhisattva of true and right intention merely recognizes this goaless goal, indicates such, and puts before themselves this path for the beneficence of any and all limitless beings. For it is perfection of wisdom which brings about any fruit of any Once-Returner, of any Never-Returner, and of any Arhat. And any Bodhisattva increases one's endurance by reflecting this way, for, as by training oneself in perfection of wisdom, one comes to obtain dharmas which sooner or later constitute a Buddha, and one comes ever nearer to revealing for the benefit of any and all beings, full enlightenment. For one knows by training oneself in this training, coursing in and struggling in such, one brings forth any and all fruits of holy life, from fruits of a Streamwinner to Buddhahood. Any merit of any person sharing perfection of wisdom also is vastly different from any one establishing in Pratyekabuddhahood any number of beings in any number of world systems. Moreover, Kausika, as someone reveals any such thing as is for full enlightenment to the hearts of as many beings as are in Jambudvīpa; and someone else not only indicated how it is possible for these to reveal their very hearts to full enlightenment, but also in addition gives these a copy of this perfection of wisdom; or, as one such as this presents a copy of this perfection of wisdom to an irreversible Bodhisattva, in consideration of any possibility that this Bodhisattva may allow oneself to be trained in such, make endeavours about and develop such, and as a result of any growth, increase or abundance of the perfection of wisdom, fulfill the Buddha-dharmas; now, compared with the former person, one begets a vastly different type of merit, for certainly once one is awakened to full enlightenment, one cannot help but to indicate the end to the sufferings of countless beings. Thus, one's merit is vastly different, even as the other person thinks to raise to full enlightenment the hearts of any number of beings in any number of world systems. Or, let us again compare two persons: The first presents a copy of this perfection of wisdom to any number of beings in any number of world systems, beings which are irreversible from full enlightenment, who definitely set out for such; yet, the second person, in addition expounds this to these ones according to the meaning and according to the letter. Does this one not on the strength of this beget much great merit?

Sakra: One's merit is indeed great. One can neither easily calculate this heap of merit, nor count it, nor find anything even similar to, or resembling, or with which it can be compared.

The Lord: Still, Kausika, vastly different is any merit of someone who in addition instructs and admonishes in this perfection of wisdom these irreversible Bodhisattvas aspiring to quickly realize full enlightenment. And further, still another Bodhisattva may arise, saying one may realize full enlightenment even more quickly than they. As someone instructs and admonishes in the perfection of wisdom this Bodhisattva of even quicker understanding, one begets a still vast and different type of merit.

Sakra: To the extent any Bodhisattva comes nearer to full enlightenment, to such an extent one is instructed and admonished in the perfection of wisdom, for such brings one nearer and nearer Suchness. As one comes nearer Suchness, one confers many fruits and advantages on any having done services for one, i.e., on the ones through whom one enjoys one's robes, alms-bowl, lodging, and medicinal appliances for sickness. One's merit now becomes still larger, in consequence of the fact one comes nearer to full enlightenment.

Subhuti: Well said, Kausika. You fortify these belonging to the Bodhisattva-vehicle, help these, and stand by these. Even so do you act. Any holy disciple wanting to give help to all beings, as such, fortifies Bodhisattvas in their attitude to full enlightenment, helps these, and stands by these. In this same way does one in diligence act. For begotten of perfection of wisdom is full enlightenment of Bodhisattvas. Just so, as Bodhisattvas do not produce any thought of enlightenment, such do not train themselves in full enlightenment, nor in any six perfections, and as a consequence these do not awaken to full enlightenment. But as the Bodhisattvas do train themselves in the Bodhisattva-training, in these six perfections, so now do these produce this thought of enlightenment, so even now do these awaken to full enlightenment.

Chapter 6: DEDICATION AND JUBILATION

The Supreme Merit of Dedication and Jubilation

Maitreya: On the one side we have on the part of a Bodhisattva, meritorious work which is founded on this Bodhisattva's rejoicing at the merit of others, and on one's dedication of merit to the utmost enlightenment of all beings; on the other side is, on the part of all beings, the meritorious work founded on giving, on morality, on meditational development. Among these the meritorious work of a Bodhisattva founded on jubilation and dedication is declared to be vastly different, excellent, sublime, unequalled, and equaling the unequalled.

The Range of Jubilation

Subhuti: A Bodhisattva, a great being, considers the world with its ten directions, in every direction, extending everywhere. One such as this considers the world systems quite immeasurable, quite beyond reckoning, quite measureless, quite inconceivable, infinite and boundless.

Such ones consider in each of three time periods, in each single direction, in each single world system, the Tathagatas - as quite immeasurable, quite beyond reckoning, quite measureless, quite inconceivable, infinite and boundless, fully revealing final Nirvana in the realm of Nirvana and leaving nothing behind, - their tracks cut off, their course cut off, their obstacles annulled and dissolved, guides through the world of becoming, their tears dried up, with all their impediments crushed, their own burdens laid down, with their own weal reached, in whom any fetters of becoming are extinguished, whose thoughts are well freed by right understanding, and who have attained and maintain completely equanimous perfection in control of their entire hearts.

One considers these from right here, beginning with an appearance of this thought of enlightenment, proceeding throughout and beyond any time and any realization of full enlightenment through finally entering, or a revelation of Nirvana, as Suchness and a totality of Nirvana which leaves nothing behind, and a dissolution of any spans of time beyond even any thought in considerations of some vanishing of good Dharma as exposited by each of these Tathagatas.

One considers this mass of morality, this mass of concentration, this mass of wisdom, this mass of emancipation, this mass of vision and cognition of emancipation of such Buddhas and Lords.
In addition, one considers any store of merit associated with six perfections, with achievement of qualities of Buddha and nature, and with perfections of self-confidence and of powers; and also anyone associated with any perfection of superknowledges, of comprehension, of vows; and any store of merit associated with the accomplishment of cognition of all-knowingness, with solicitude for beings, any great friendliness and great compassion, and immeasurable and incalculable Buddha-qualities.

And one also considers the full enlightenment and its all encompassing residual happiness borne of contentment from right actions and contemplation, and perfection of sovereignty over all dharmas, and such an accomplishment of immeasurable and unconquered supreme wonderworking power which finally conquers all, and this power of the Tathagata's cognition of what is truly real, which is without a slightest of defiled covering, attachment or obstruction, unequalled, equal to unequalled, incomparable, without measure, and such power of Buddha-nature and cognition preeminent among these powers, the obtainment of such supreme ease which results from four grounds of self-confidence, and the obtainment of Dharma through realization of this ultimate reality of all dharmas.

One also considers the turning of the wheel of Dharma, the carrying of the torch of Dharma, the beating of the drum of Dharma, the filling up the conch shell of Dharma, the wielding of the sword of Dharma, the pouring down of the rain of Dharma, and the refreshment of all beings through the gift of Dharma, through its presentation to them. One further considers any store of merit of any and all who are educated and trained by demonstrations of Dharma, - whether these concern any dharmas of Buddhas, or any of Pratyekabuddhas, or of Disciples, - who believe in these, who are fixed on these, who are bound to end up in full enlightenment.

One also considers the store of merit, associated with these six perfections, of all Bodhisattvas of whom Buddhas and Lords have predicted full enlightenment. A Bodhisattva considers any store of merit of all persons who belong to the Pratyekabuddha vehicle, and of whom the enlightenment of said Pratyekabuddha is predicted. One considers the meritorious work founded on giving, morality and meditational development of the four assemblies of Buddhas and Lords, (i.e. of the monks and nuns, the laymen and laywomen). One considers the roots of good planted during all this time by Gods, Nagas,

Yakshas, Gandharvas, Asuras, Garudas, Kinnaras and Mahoragas, by beings and ghosts, and also by animals, at any such time as Buddhas and Lords demonstrate Dharma, and as these enter Parinirvana, and as these had entered Parinirvana - due to Buddhas and Lords, due to Dharma, due to Sangha, and due to persons of right mind-culture. In one's meditation the Bodhisattva piles up the roots of good of all these, all this quantity of merit without exception or remainder, rolls this into one lump, weighs this, and rejoices over this with the most excellent and sublime jubilation, the highest and utmost jubilation, with none above it and unequalled, equaling the unequalled. Having thus rejoiced, one utters the remark: "I turn over into full enlightenment this meritorious work founded on jubilation. May this feed full enlightenment of myself and of all beings!"

A Metaphysical Problem

Now, as concerns these foundations through which any person belonging to the Bodhisattva-vehicle rejoices, concerning these objective supports and points of view...does one apprehend in such a way as these objective supports and views are treated as signs?

Maitreya: No, these have not.

Subhuti: As one treats as an objective support or as a sign any foundation which does not in truth exist, or any objective support which does not in truth exist, does one at this point not have a perverted perception, perverted thought, perverted views? For in a greedy person also, as one discriminates a nonexisting entity [or foundation] and ponders on such - thinking permanence in impermanence, ease in suffering, any self in what is truly not any self, loveliness or not in what is thought either repulsive or not - here arises a perverted perception, perverted thought, perverted view. And as the foundation [or entity], the objective support, the point of view are non-existent, so is enlightenment, so is the thought of enlightenment and so all dharmas or points of view...what thought does one turn over into full enlightenment, or what meritorious work founded on jubilation does one turn over into what utmost, right and perfect enlightenment?

Maitreya: This is neither rightly intended nor understood to be taught or expounded in front of a Bodhisattva who has newly set out in the vehicle. For one may lose whatever little faith one may have gleaned, whatever little affection, serenity and respect which one may have gathered. Only in front of an irreversible Bodhisattva is this rightly intended, understood, taught and expounded. Alternatively, a Bodhisattva propped up by a good friend is hereby not cowed, nor becomes stolid, nor cast down, nor depressed, does not turn the mind away from this, nor has one's back broken, nor tremble, be frightened, be terrified. Thus does such a Bodhisattva turn over into all-knowledge the meritorious work founded on jubilation.

Subhuti: Thusly any thought by which one has rejoiced and turned over, or dedicated any wholesome root connected with jubilation, - any such thought of rejoicing is at the time of turning over extinct, stopped, departed, reversed. So here now, and in any time and way, what is any thought by which one turns over to full enlightenment? Or, what is any thought which turns over into full enlightenment (any) meritorious work founded on jubilation? Or, as no two thoughts can ever meet, how can anyone by one thought turn over, or dedicate, another thought? Neither is it possible to turn over nor overturn, nor transform any thought as far as its own being is concerned.

Sakra: The Bodhisattvas newly set out in the vehicle need to beware of being afraid upon hearing this exposition. How does a Bodhisattva turn any meritorious work founded on jubilation over into full enlightenment? And how does someone who takes hold of the meritorious work founded on jubilation succeed in taking hold of any thought connected with jubilation, and how does one who turns over this thought connected with jubilation succeed in turning it over?

Herein the Venerable Subhuti turned his mind to the Bodhisattva Maitreya, concentrated his mind on him, and spoke thus: Here the Bodhisattva considers any merit connected with these timeless Buddhas and Lords, in the way we described before. One piles up wholesome roots of all these, all of any quantity whatsoever of wholesome roots without exception and remainder, rolls such into one lump, weighs this, and rejoices over this. One thus thinks to turn this meritorious work founded on jubilation over to full enlightenment. How can the Bodhisattva when one thus turns over, be without perverted perception, perverted thought, perverted view?

How Perverted Views Can be Avoided

Maitreya: The Bodhisattva must not, as a result of any thought by which one is turning this over, become one perceiving any thought. It is thus meritorious work founded on jubilation becomes such as is turned into, or rather perhaps, revealed as full enlightenment.

Subhuti: If one does not perceive any thought, identifying it as 'this is that thought,' as such a Bodhisattva has no perverted perception, thought or view.

But if one perceives the thought by which one turns this over, identifying it as 'this is that thought,' as such one becomes one who perceives thought. As a result one has perverted perception, thought and view.

But any Bodhisattva turns over rightly, not wrongly, as one perceives and brings to mind any thought which turns over in such a way as one regards it as 'just extinct,' extinct as 'stopped, departed, reversed'; and as one reflects thusly, as what is extinct cannot be turned over; and as this extinctness as 'stopped, departed, reversed,' is the very dharmic nature also of any thought by which one turns over, and also of the dharmas through which one turns over, as well as of the dharmas to which one turns over, it is thus any Bodhisattva turn this over.

One considers any future Buddhas, present Buddhas, or past, future and present Buddhas in this same way in which one considers any past Buddhas.

So now, under which circumstances is one without perverted perception, thought or views? If, while one turns over, one brings to mind any dharmas as extinct, stopped, departed, reversed, and any dharma into which it is turned over as inextinguishable, this, [the wholesome root] becomes something which is turned over into full enlightenment. For one does not settle down in any process of dedication.

If further one considers no dharma can be turned over into a dharma, it becomes something which is turned over into full enlightenment. It is thus by which any Bodhisattva who turns over is without perverted perception, thought or view, for one does not settle down in any process of dedication. If further, one perceives any thought cannot cognize any thought, neither of itself nor another, nor can dharma cognize dharma, now too, this has become something which is turned over into full enlightenment. This is the supreme maturity of any Bodhisattva.

But if, on the other hand, a Bodhisattva perceives any accumulation of merit, one cannot turn it over into full enlightenment due to one settling down in some process of dedication.

If further one reflects this (any) accumulation of merit is isolated and quietly calm, and also any meritorious work founded on jubilation is isolated and quietly calm...one turns over into full enlightenment.

But, if in addition one does not even perceive any conditioned events are calmly quiet and isolated, such is perfection of wisdom of such a Bodhisattva. But one does not turn over into full enlightenment if one perceives this to be any wholesome root of Buddhas, the Lords having gone to Parinirvana; or as this wholesome root by which it is turned over is just as illusory and is of the same kind, has the same mark, belongs to the same class, has the same own-being. For Buddhas and Lords do not allow a dedication to take place through a sign.

One neither brings to mind nor turns over any wholesome root to full enlightenment if one brings about a sign by reflecting anything which is past is extinct, stopped, departed, reversed; what is future has not yet arrived; and of any present no stability is got at, and that this which is not got at has no sign or range.

On the other hand one also does not turn over to full enlightenment if one fails to bring about a sign or to bring to mind anything whatsoever as a result of sheer inattentiveness, or if one fails to attend as a result of lack of mindfulness, or of lack of understanding. But such and said wholesome root becomes something which is turned over into full enlightenment on condition of one bringing to mind such and said sign, but does not treat it as any sign. It is thus the Bodhisattva trains oneself herein. This is known as one's skill in means. When, through skill in means, one turns over any wholesome root, one is near to all-knowledge. The Bodhisattva wanting to train oneself in this skill in means, however, constantly commits to hearing just this perfection of wisdom, studying it and asking questions derived from it. For without the help of perfection of wisdom one untaught cannot enter on the work of dedication by means of perfection of wisdom. But one does not make a statement to any effect such as thanks to perfection of wisdom it is possible to transform any meritorious work into full enlightenment. For stopped are any such personal lives, stopped are any such karma-formations, calmly quiet, isolated, lacking in basis.

Moreover, as this person has brought about a sign, and made a discrimination, one perceives what is truly real in what is not truly real as it were truly real, and one would transform a basis into what is without basis. Buddhas, the Lords do not allow one's wholesome roots to become something which is in this way transformed into full enlightenment, for even these become to one so inclined a great basis. Even the Parinirvana of Buddhas and Lords, one so inclined treats as a sign and discriminates, thusly one believes oneself to get at Nirvana from a viewpoint, and this is not the dedication carried out by one who perceives any basis which the Tathagatas have called a source of great welfare. For this process of dedication is not without poison, not without torn.

It is just as with foods seeming excellent, but is really poisonous. Its color, smell, taste and touch seem desirable, but nevertheless, as poisonous it is best shunned and not eaten by circumspect people. Although food, stupid people might think it best to be eaten. The color, smell, taste and touch of this food promise happiness, but its transformation in any person eating it surely leads to a painful conclusion. As a result one incurrs death, or deadly pain.

Just so some perceivers of a basis who seize badly the meaning of what is well taught, badly distinguish it, badly master it, and misunderstand it, not understanding the meaning as it really is, these instruct and admonish others to consider the mass of merit of the past, future and present Buddhas and Lords, in the way described before, to rejoice at it, and to turn over into full enlightenment the meritorious work founded on jubilation. Thus this turning over, since it is being carried out by means of a sign, is turned into poisonousness. It is just like the poisonous food mentioned before. Here can be no turning over for someone who perceives a basis. For a basis is poisonous and has a range. Herein a person who belongs to the vehicle of Bodhisattvas does not train oneself thus. How now does one train oneself? How does one take hold of the wholesome root of the past, future and present Buddhas and Lords? And how does anything which is taken hold of become something which is successfully taken hold of? How does one turn over? And how does it become something which is successfully turned over into the supreme enlightenment?

Here the son or daughter of a good family who belongs to the vehicle of Bodhisattvas, and who does not want to calumniate Tathagatas, thus rejoices over all and any wholesome root, and turns it over thus: "I rejoice in this wholesome root which is considered in the way in which Tathagatas with their Buddha-cognition and their Buddha-eye know and see it, -its kind such as it is, its class such as it is, its quality such as it is, its own-being such as it is, its mark such as it is, and its mode of existence such as it is. And I thus turn this over in such a way as these Tathagatas can allow this wholesome root to be turned over into full enlightenment."

As one thus rejoices, thus turns over, a Bodhisattva becomes free from guilt. The righteousness of Buddhas, the Lords, is rejoiced in. This wholesome root becomes something which is turned over into full enlightenment. And one does not calumniate any Tathagatas. In this way one's turning over becomes a non-poisonous turning over, a great turning over, a turning over into the dharma-element; it becomes perfect, quite perfect, through this earnest intention and resolve of one thus turning over. Moreover, someone who belongs to the vehicle of Bodhisattvas turns this over with understanding all morality, concentration, wisdom, emancipation, vision and cognition of emancipation, are unincluded in any world of sense-desire, the world of form, the formless world, and as such these are neither past, future, nor present.

For everything that is in any three periods of time or in any triple world is un-included in ultimate reality. In consequence the turning over is also un-included, and so is the dharma [i.e. Buddhahood] into which this process of transformation is being turned, - if only one firmly believes this. As a Bodhisattva turns over in such a way, such ones as this one is can never again lose the turning over, and it becomes un-included, non-poisonous, a great turning over, a turning over of the dharma-element, perfect, quite perfect. But, on the other hand, as one settles down in what one may turn over, and treats it as a sign, one now turns it over wrongly. A Bodhisattva, however, turns over with the idea such as it is through this turning over into the dharma-element, as the Buddhas, the Lords know and permit it, this wholesome root becomes something which has been turned over into full enlightenment, successfully turned over. This is the right method of turning it over. And in this way it becomes something that has been turned over into supreme enlightenment, successfully turned over.

The Lord: Well said, Subhuti, well said. You perform the office of the Teacher as you demonstrate Dharma to the Bodhisattvas. For it is this turning over, which is the turning over of the dharma-element, which is the turning over of a Bodhisattva. He thinks: "As the Buddhas and Lords know and see this wholesome root in this dharmahood, -its kind such as it is, its class such as it is, its quality such as it is, its own-being such as it is, its mark such as it is, its mode of existence such as it is, -so I rejoice in it as these. And as these grant permission, so I turn it over."

Considerations of Merit

This heap of merit of a Bodhisattva, which is born from this turning over of any Dharma-element, is declared to be superior to the accumulation of merit on the part of someone instigating to, and establishing in the ten wholesome ways of action all beings in the great trichiliocosms which are countless as the sands of the Ganges. It remains superior also if these beings would gain the four trances, or the four Unlimited, or the four formless attainments, or the five superknowledges; or equally if these become Streamwinners, etc., to: Pratyekabuddhas. And yet this is not all. If all beings in all world systems set out for supreme enlightenment, and if, Subhuti, each single Bodhisattva were to furnish for aeons as countless as the sands of the Ganges all these beings in the various great trichiliocosms, countless as the sands of the Ganges, with all which may be needed...but give this gift while perceiving a basis...and now, proceeding in this manner, we imagine all these beings are a single one, and if each single Bodhisattva for aeons countless as the sands of Ganges did furnish all these Bodhisattvas with all these may ever need, and treat these with respect; if thus each single one of all these Bodhisattvas all together would give this gift, do not these Bodhisattvas on the strength of this beget a great deal of merit?

Subhuti: A great deal indeed, O Lord. This heap of merit defies calculation. Surely if it were a material thing, it could not find room in even the great trichiliocosms countless as the sands of the Ganges.

The Lord: So it is, Subhuti. And yet, this accumulation of merit, due to giving on the part of any Bodhisattvas perceiving a basis, is infinitesimal and even different, as concerns merit, when attempts are made to compare any such merit with anything whatsoever which may or even may not be begotten by someone belonging to the vehicle of Bodhisattvas, and who, as taken hold of by perfection of wisdom and by skill in means, affects this or any wholesome root so as to indicate to such it's turning over into full enlightenment by means of this turning over of the dharma-element. For although the basis-perceiving Bodhisattvas give a good many gifts, these also reckon these gifts up as 'good' and 'many.'

Now, upon this, twenty thousand Gods of the Four Great Kings, with folded hands paid homage to Lord, and said: "This transformation into all-knowledge of wholesome roots by any having been taken hold of by perfection of wisdom and by skill in means, is a great transformation of Bodhisattvas...for it surpasses any and all accumulation of merit, derived from giving, of any Bodhisattvas basing such giving on something, however great it may be."

So now, again upon this one hundred thousand Gods of the Thirty-three rain down on Lord heavenly flowers, incense, perfumes, wreaths, ointments, aromatic powders, jewels and garments. These worship the Lord with heavenly parasols, banners, bells, flags, and with rows of lamps all around, and with manifold kinds of worship. Playing on heavenly musical instruments [in honor of the Lord] these now say: "This transformation of dharma-element is surely a great transformation of any Bodhisattva, as it is in deed and view different than any and all heaps of accumulated merit resulting from gifts of Bodhisattvas having a basis in anything whatsoever, for this great transformation is taken hold of by perfection of wisdom and skill in means."

All the other classes of Gods appear on this scene, worshipping Lord, and now raise their voices saying: "It is wonderful, O Lord, to any such extent as this transformation of a wholesome root by these Bodhisattvas which, being taken hold of by perfection of wisdom and by skill in means, is different or other than any heap of merit of Bodhisattvas having a basis in something, even though it has accumulated for such a long time, and is procured by such manifold exertions."

Now the Lord speaks to these Gods, from the gods belonging to the Pure Abode downwards: "Let us leave the case of the accumulation of merit of all beings in countless world systems who are definitely set out for full enlightenment, and any giving gifts for the sake of gaining full enlightenment. Let us also, in the same manner, consider the case of all beings in countless world systems which, having made a vow to gain full enlightenment, and having raised thoughts to enlightenment, give gifts on the extensive scale described before. In this other hand we consider a Bodhisattva, taken hold of by perfection of wisdom and by skill in means, who takes hold of the wholesome roots of all the Buddhas, Bodhisattvas, Pratyekabuddhas and Disciples, and of all other beings also the wholesome roots which have been planted, will be planted, and are being planted, and who rejoices over these all in the way described above. Then infinitesimal and different is any accumulation of merit on the part of the former Bodhisattvas who give gifts while perceiving a basis - just because of this perceiving of any basis.

Subhuti: The Lord describes the jubilation over the wholesome roots of all beings as a most excellent jubilation. For what reason is this jubilation a most excellent one?

The Lord: If any person belonging to the vehicle of Bodhisattvas does not seize on this past, this future and present dharmas, does not mind these, does not get at these, does not construct, nor discriminate these, does not see nor review these, if one considers these with this conviction...'all dharmas are fabricated by thought construction, unborn, not come forth, not come, not gone,' and this, 'no dharma is ever produced or stopped in this past, this future or present'; if one considers any dharmas in such a way, herein one's jubilation is in accordance with the true nature of such dharmas, and so is one's transformation [of any merit] into full enlightenment. This is the first reason why the jubilation of the Bodhisattva is a most excellent one. The meritorious work founded on giving on the part of Bodhisattvas who perceive a basis, who have a basis in view, is infinitesimal and quite different when compared with the transformation of the wholesome root by any Bodhisattvas. Moreover, Subhuti, someone who belongs to the vehicle of the Bodhisattvas, wanting to rejoice in the wholesome roots of all Buddhas and Lords, rejoices in such a way: "As emancipation is unoriginated, [since the obstacles from defilements and from the recognizable have ceased], so the gift; so the morality, etc.; so the jubilation, so the meritorious work founded on jubilation; as emancipation, so transformation, so Buddhas and Lords, Pratyekabuddhas and Disciples who have entered Parinirvana; as emancipation, so transformation, so are any dharmas which are seen as past, or stopped; and likewise the dharmas which are seen as future, or not yet produced; and the dharmas which are seen as present, or proceeding just now; as emancipation so all seen as past, future and present Buddhas and Lords. Thus, I rejoice with the most excellent jubilation in the true nature of any dharmas, which are unbound, unfreed, unattached. So, now I turn this meritorious work founded on jubilation over into full enlightenment; but really no turning over takes place, as nothing is passed on, nothing destroyed. This is the second reason why the jubilation of the Bodhisattva is a most excellent one.

But to return to the question of merit. Let us now consider this case here as all these beings in countless world systems are definitely set out for full enlightenment, and so, in order to advance to full enlightenment, these, for countless aeons undertake the obligation of observing morality, i.e. good conduct of body, speech and mind, - but while perceiving a basis. Nevertheless their accumulation of merit is infinitesimal compared with this of a Bodhisattva's limitless equanimity derived from jubilation, - merely due to this simple fact in which these beings in countless world systems perceive a basis. And the same is true, if all these beings for countless aeons practice patience, although these were ever so much abused, struck and reviled; or if these practice vigour, and under no circumstances would be cast down, or conquered by sloth and torpor; or, finally, if these enter the trances. As long as any such as these carry out such practices while perceiving a basis, any merit is infinitesimal compared with this of any Bodhisattva who rejoices over the wholesome roots of all beings with the most excellent yet equanimous jubilation, and transforms this wholesome root into supreme enlightenment.

Chapter 7: HELL

Hymn to The Perfection of Wisdom

Sariputra: Perfection of wisdom, O Lord, is accomplishment of cognition of all-knowing. Perfection of wisdom is realized as all-knowledge.

The Lord: So it is, Sariputra, as you say.

Sariputra: Veneration towards perfection of wisdom polishes away obscurities, revealing light, O Lord. I pay homage to perfection of wisdom! She is worthy of homage. She is unstained, and thus entire worlds along with complete systems cannot stain her. Regardless whether viewed from, in or as absolute unification, beings come to reveal her as spontaneous source of light, having dispelled any limitations, and things of any triple worlds. Holding her in supreme reverence leads beings away from blinding darkness caused by defilements and wrong views. As this is her nature, we find shelter. Most excellent is her impartial abiding. Within us she is revealed as cause to seek the safety of wings of enlightenment. Realization of her brings light to the blind. Our being is permeated by her light so all fear and distress may be forsaken within her revelation. Veneration of her aquires the five eyes, and shows this path to all beings. She herself is an organ of vision. Her knowledge disperses the gloom and darkness of delusion. She does nothing about all dharmas. She becomes the path and guide any who have strayed on to an obscure road. She is identical with all-knowledge. She never produces any dharma because she cast off any residues relating to both kinds of coverings, these produced by defilements and these produced by any thing whatsoever. She does not stop any dharma, herself unstopped and unproduced...is this perfection of wisdom. She is mother of the Bodhisattvas, on account of emptiness of own mark. As the donor of the jewel of all Buddha-dharmas she brings about the ten powers (of a Buddha). She cannot be crushed. She protects the unprotected with the help of the four grounds of self-confidence. She is the antidote to birth-and-death. She reveals this clear knowingness of the true nature of any own-being of all dharmas, for she does not stray away from it. The perfection of wisdom of Buddhas, the Lords, sets in motion this wheel of Dharma.

Predominance of Perfect Wisdom Over Other Perfections

How does a Bodhisattva stand in perfection of wisdom, how attend and pay homage to it?

The Lord: In every way the perfection of wisdom is treated as our teacher.

Sakra now asks Sariputra: Wherefrom, and for what reason does this question of the holy Sariputra arise?

Sariputra: It arises as I hear it said, "a Bodhisattva being taken hold of by perfection of wisdom and skill in means transforms into all-knowledge any so-called meritorious work founded on jubilation. Ones such as these delve even beyond the entire meritorious works founded on giving, morality, patience, vigour, and trance of all Bodhisattvas observing any basis whatsoever." It is just perfection of wisdom which guides these five perfections in their intention and direction on this path toward all-knowledge. Just as, Kausika, people born blind, one hundred, or one thousand, or one hundred thousand of them, cannot, without a leader, go along a path and get to a village, town or city; - just so, Giving, Morality, Patience, Vigour and Trance cannot alone be called 'perfections,' for without perfection of wisdom these are as if born blind, here now without their leader and unable to traverse the path to all-knowledge, and still less can these reach all-knowledge. However, as Giving, Morality, Patience, Vigour and Trance are taken hold of by perfection of wisdom, now these are indeed and propriety termed 'perfections', for these five perfections acquire this organ of vision which enables these to evolve along this path to all-knowledge, and to reach all-knowledge.

Nothing Procured by Perfect Wisdom

Sariputra said to the Lord: How does any Bodhisattva consummate perfection of wisdom?

The Lord: By pure cognition and establishment in one's view of the non-consummation of form, feeling, perception, impulse, and consciousness. The non-consummation of the five skandhas, this is called 'consummation of perfection of wisdom'. In this way nothing is affected, so the consummation of the five skandhas is called consummation of perfection of wisdom.

Sariputra: When perfection of wisdom is consummated by such a consummation, what dharma, or what of any phenomena whatsoever does it procure?

The Lord: When consummated in such a way, perfection of wisdom does not procure any dharma, and in consequence of this fact she comes to be styled 'perfection of wisdom.'

Sakra: So, O Lord, perfection of wisdom does not even procure all-knowledge?

The Lord: Perfection of wisdom does not procure even this, as this is formed as, or from some basis, or some mental process, or some volitional act.

Sakra: So, how does perfection of wisdom procure?

The Lord: In so far as this does not procure, to this extent this procures.

Sakra: This is wonderful, O Lord, to see any extent to which perfection of wisdom neither produces nor stops any dharma. For the purpose of non-production and of non-stopping of all dharmas is perfection of wisdom set up, without, however, being really present.

Subhuti: If any Bodhisattva perceives this also, one might keep far away from perfection of wisdom, treating this as worthless and insignificant, and fail to act on it.

The Lord: This is quite true. For here perfection of wisdom is lit up, and here form does not become lit up, nor other skandhas, nor any fruits of this holy life, up to Buddhahood.

Subhuti: Perfection of wisdom is great perfection, O Lord!

Why the Perfection of Wisdom is Great

[Perfection of Wisdom is here stated as the Great Perfection. ...not bad for 1st Century.]

The Lord: Tell what you think, Subhuti, in what manner is perfection of wisdom a great perfection?

Subhuti: This neither makes form (solidity), feelings (sensations), perceptions (experiences) will (volition), and consciousnesses (states of mind) greater nor smaller, and does not assemble nor disperse form, etc. This also neither strengthens nor weakens the powers of Tathagata, nor does this assemble or disperse these. This does not even make all-knowledge greater or smaller, nor does this assemble or disperse it. For all-knowledge is unassembled [uncollected] and undispersed [undisturbed]. In the event any Bodhisattva perceives even this, one courses not in perfection of wisdom, so how much more so if one forms the notion: "Thus do I, endowed with cognition of all-knowing, demonstrate dharma to beings, thus do I lead these beings to final Nirvana." For this apprehension of these beings is a basis fact, for when one says, "I lead these beings to final Nirvana," this cannot be an outcome of perfection of wisdom. This indeed is a great basis of apprehension on one's part. For the absence of own-being in beings needs to be known as belonging to the very essence of perfection of wisdom. One needs know this perfection of wisdom is without own-being in the same way in which beings are without own-being; also, perfection of wisdom is unthinkable, because beings are naturally as well; also perfection of wisdom has an indestructible nature because beings do as well; and perfection of wisdom taken as it naturally is, does not undergo any process which leads to enlightenment as well...for beings, as these are naturally, do not undergo such a process ; also this way in which Tathagatas arrive at full possession of powers is understood as the way in which beings arrive thus at full possession of their power. It is in this manner which perfection of wisdom is the great perfection. [rdzogs chen]

Causes of Belief in Perfection of Wisdom

Sariputra: Bodhisattvas reborn here, resolutely believe or have direct knowing in deep perfection of wisdom without hesitation, doubt or stupefaction, here these decease and enduring beyond any duration do these practice. These ones following this doctrine of perfection of wisdom, understand its meaning, and instruct others in it both by any method which reveals the meaning and by any method which reveals the doctrine.

The Lord: Thus it is, Sariputra. One can know this as such Bodhisattvas are reborn here as decease in other world systems in which one honors and questions Buddhas, the Lords. Any such Bodhisattvas as decease in other world systems in which one honors and questions Buddhas, the Lords, are reborn here and upon hearing this deep perfection of wisdom being taught, identify perfection of wisdom as teacher, and are definitely convinced beyond even such questions one is face to face with ones teacher...such a one can know one sees the teacher. As perfection of wisdom is being taught, and as one listens attentively, pays respect to this even before one hears this, and does not cut this story short...such a Bodhisattva is known as one practicing for long, even beyond duration. And as well, one herein honors many

Buddhas.

Subhuti: Is it at all possible to hear perfection of wisdom, to distinguish and consider her, to make statements and to reflect about her? Can one explain or learn such as because of certain attributes, tokens or signs this is perfection of wisdom, or such as here this is perfection of wisdom, or over there...that is perfection of wisdom?

The Lord: No indeed, Subhuti. Perfection of wisdom cannot be expounded, learned, distinguished, considered, stated, or reflected upon by means of any or all skandhas, nor by means of any or all elements, nor means of any or all sense-fields. This is a consequence of fact. All dharmas are isolated, absolutely isolated without any basis, as said and known. Nor can perfection of wisdom be understood other than by the skandhas, elements or sensefields. For just the very skandhas, elements and sense-fields are empty, isolated and calmly quiet. [without basis] It is thus, Subhuti, as perfection of wisdom and skandhas, elements and sense-fields are neither many as more than one, nor even one, nor one divided. [again, without basis] As a result of emptiness, isolatedness and quietude these cannot be apprehended. The lack of a basis of, or for apprehension in any and all dharmas, this is called 'perfect wisdom.' Whatever, wherever, whenever, or however pure cognition reveals no perception, appellation, conception, contrivance or conventional expression, hereof one speaks 'perfection of wisdom.'

Subhuti: For how long is any Bodhisattva known as one who practices, who makes endeavours about this deep perfection of wisdom?

The Lord: One must make one's own distinction in this, owing to the unequal endowment of different Bodhisattvas.

Causes and Consequences of Disbelief

It is quite possible some Bodhisattvas, although perhaps seeing or having seen many hundreds, many thousands, many hundreds of thousands of Buddhas, and have led and continue to lead the holy life, in any present 'time' may nevertheless have no faith in perfection of wisdom. The reason is now as whenever, some have no respect for this profound perfection of wisdom as it is taught, even in the presence of Buddhas and Lords. Wherever might be a lack of respect for this is also in like measure a lack of desire to learn more about this, a lack of honor recognized in this, and thus a lack in faith and unwillingness to ask questions. Lacking in faith these hereupon walk out of assemblies. It is just because in any past these have produced, accumulated, piled up and collected karma conducive to the ruin of dharma that also at any present these walk out when this deep perfection of wisdom is being taught. From the lack of respect, without faith and firm belief in perfection of wisdom, these lack also in accord either in body or in thought. Lacking in accord these do not know, see, recognize or make known this perfection of wisdom. First any such as these do not believe, and so do not hear, so as to not see, and here these do not recognize this and thus produce, accumulate, pile up and collect karma conducive to the ruin of dharma within these lives, any and ultimately all. This in its turn will bring about karma conducive to weakness in wisdom. This in its turn will make such as these refuse, reject and revile this perfection of wisdom while it is being taught, and so rejecting this will walk out. But by rejecting this perfection of wisdom these reject the all-knowledge of Buddhas and Lords, past, future and present. Not content with having vitiated merely their own continuities, so too these as if all aflame, deter, dissuade, turn away others also, -beings of less intelligence, seemingly less wisdom, merit and wholesome roots, endowed with but a little faith, affection, serenity, and desire-to-do, beginners, essentially unqualified, -trying to take away even what little faith, affection, serenity and desire-to-do may be present. These bid one not to train in this, and finally declare this is not the Buddha's word. These first vitiate and estrange their own communities, and even those of 'others'. Hereby these calumniate perfection of wisdom. To calumniate perfection of wisdom means to calumniate all-knowledge, and hereof the past, future and present Buddhas. These cause themselves removal from the presence of the Buddhas and Lords, self-deprived of Dharma, self-expelled from Sangha. In each and every way these will be, of their own-self's shut out from Triple Jewel. Such activities cut down the welfare and happiness of all-beings, and these will collect karma conducive to the great hells. As these have raised such karma-formations, these will be reborn in great hells, for many hundreds of years, many thousands of years, indeed for many hundreds of thousands of niyutas of kotis of aeons. From one great hell these will pass on to another. After a long time this world of these is consumed by fire. Yet such as these are hurled into the great hells in another world system, and again these pass on from great hell to great hell. When also such as this world is consumed by fire, yet still these are hurled into the great hells in another world system, here still these pass on from great hell to great hell. When also this world is consumed by fire, this karma of ones such as these is still unexhausted, still has some residue of efficacy and, deceasing now here, these are still reborn in great hells and experience great sufferings in these, until the time when yet even this world is once more consumed by fire. These still as even unto our own-selves, as we see, experience a karma which involves many painful feelings. And why? Because their teachings are so misleading.

Sariputra: Does not even the effect of the five deadly sins bear no proportion to this misconduct of mind and speech?

The Lord: It does not. All these ones opposing perfection of wisdom and dissuading others from it are beings like unto ones by and to whom are not granted any vision. How can any become intimate with these, how can any gain wealth, honor, position? As a matter of fact, regard these as defamers of dharma, as mere rubbish, as pitchguards, as mere vipers. These are beings breeding misfortune, these ruin anyone listening. Regard these seeking to defame perfection of wisdom as beings which seek to defame Dharma.

Sariputra: The Lord has not told us about the length of time such a person must spend in the great hells.

The Lord: Leave that alone, Sariputra. If this were announced, anyone hearing it needs to beware lest hot blood spurt from their mouths, lest any incur death or deathly pain, lest harsh oppression weigh any down, lest the dart of grief enter their hearts, lest any drop down with a big fall, lest any shrivel up and wither away, lest any be overpowered by great fright. So...the Lord refused to answer the Venerable Sariputra's question. For a second time, for a third time the Venerable Sariputra spoke thus to the Lord: Tell me, O Lord, the length of such a person's sojourn in hell, as guidance for future generations.

The Lord: Because one has brought about, accumulated, piled up and collected this karma of mind and speech one must sojourn for a long while in the great hells. Just so much guidance will be given to future generations, so one will, in consequence of the unwholesome karma-formations of this misconduct of speech and mind, experience pain for just so long. The mere announcement of the measureless magnitude of one's pain will be a sufficient anxiety to virtuous sons and daughters of good family. The mere announcement will turn any of these away from activities conducive to the ruin of dharma, so even now these cause formations of merit, and these ones will not reject the good dharma, even to save their lives, for these do not wish to meet with such pains.

Subhuti: Such a person needs become well-restrained in the deeds of one's body, speech or mind. For so great a heap of demerit is begotten by such false teaching. Which, O Lord, is the deed, or are the deeds begeting so great a heap of demerit?

The Lord: Such false teachings do. Just here are deluded beings, persons who, having left the world for the well-taught Dharma-Vinaya, decide to defame, to reject, to oppose this perfection of wisdom. But to oppose the perfection of wisdom is to oppose the enlightenment of Buddhas and Lords. And this means one opposes such all-knowledge of Buddhas and Lords in this past, future and present. To oppose all-knowledge means to oppose Dharma. To oppose Dharma means to oppose the community of Disciples of Tathagatas. And as one opposes also the community of Disciples of Tathagatas, such a one is shut out in each and every way from the Triple

Jewel. One is acquiring an unwholesome karma-formation which cannot be equaled, for such is immeasurable and incalculable.

Subhuti: For what reason do these lack faith, and oppose this perfection of wisdom?

The Lord: Such as these are beset by Mara. One's karma is conducive to weakness in wisdom, and so one has no faith or serene confidence in profound Dharma. Endowed with those two evil dharmas one opposes this perfection of wisdom. Moreover, Subhuti, this person will be one who is in the hands of friends which are other than good; or may be one who has not yet practiced; or one who has settled down in the skandhas and determined a basis for things; or one who exalts oneself and deprecates others, looking out for faults. Endowed also with these four attributes is this person believing this perfection of wisdom needs opposition whenever and wherever this is being taught.

Chapter 8: PURITY

Depth and Purity of Perfect Wisdom

Subhuti: It is hard to gain confidence in perfection of wisdom if one is unpracticed, lacks in wholesome roots and is in the hands of any friend who may be other than good, this friend being any one possessed of less than right intent, speech, action, and concentration toward countless beings.

The Lord: So it is, Subhuti. It is hard to gain confidence in perfection of wisdom if one is unpracticed, has only diminutive wholesome roots, is dull-witted, does not care, learns little, displays inferior understanding of wisdom, relies on any friends who may be other than good, is not eager to learn, and who is unwilling to ask questions and who remains unpracticed in wholesome dharmas.

Subhuti: How deep indeed Lord, how profound is perfection of wisdom, as being so hard to gain confidence in?

The Lord: Form is neither bound nor freed, because form has no own-being as innate, inherent, or individualized in any true or absolute sense. Any material process is wont to be assumed if, or as any do not exist. Any starting point of any material process [or an equivalent to form] is neither bound nor freed within or beyond any perceptibility, because any starting point of any material process is without own-being. Any end of material process is likewise without own-being, because in this same way, any truly profound explicitness of being, be-ness, or presence, cannot exist as any part of a nonexistent own-being of some present form. Discursive facts within and of themselves are ephemeron, illusive, and transitory. And this same applies for any remaining skandhas, i.e., feeling, perception, impulse, and consciousness. In short...any 'thing' whatsoever.

Subhuti: It is hard, it is exceedingly hard Lord, to gain confidence in perfection of wisdom if one is unpracticed, has planted no wholesome roots, is in the hands of any friend who may be other than good, has come to be or is under what is descried to be the sway of Mara, is lazy or of small vigour, or is not attentive to mindfulness.

The Lord: So it is, Subhuti. Because purity of form is identical with purity of fruit, and purity of fruit is identical with purity of form. It is thus this purity of form and this purity of fruit can neither be multiplied nor counted as two, nor are these one divided. And Subhuti, not even can these be counted as one, as these have no basis, no ground from which to determine any singleness. Neither can these be broken, nor cut apart. It is thus, as this purity of form comes from purity of fruit, and purity of this fruit from this purity of form. And the same relevance exists between purity of form and purity of all-knowledge. The same applies to any other skandhas whatsoever.

Sariputra: Fathomless, O Lord, is perfection of wisdom!

The Lord: From purity is revealed dissolution of defilement and obscurity.

Sariputra: A source of illumination beyond any source is perfection of wisdom

The Lord: From purity.

Sariputra: A light is perfect wisdom.

The Lord: From purity.

Sariputra: Not subject to rebirth is perfect wisdom.

The Lord: From purity.

Sariputra: Free from defilement is perfect wisdom.

The Lord: From purity.

Sariputra: Here is neither attainment nor reunion as perfect wisdom.

The Lord: From purity.

Sariputra: Perfect wisdom does not reproduce any self.

The Lord: From purity.

Sariputra: Here is absolutely no rebirth of perfect wisdom, whether in any world of sense-desire, or in any world of form, or in any formless world.

The Lord: From purity.

Sariputra: Perfect wisdom neither knows or perceives.

The Lord: From purity.

Sariputra: What does perfect wisdom neither know nor perceive?

The Lord: Form, and the other skandhas. And why? From purity.

Sariputra: Perfect wisdom neither helps nor hinders all-knowledge.

The Lord: From purity.

Sariputra: Perfect wisdom neither gains nor abandons any dharma.

The Lord: From purity.

Subhuti: The purity of form, etc., is due to purity of self.

The Lord: Because such is absolutely pure.

Subhuti: The purity of fruit, and purity of all-knowledge, are due to purity of self.

The Lord: Because of such absolute purity.

Subhuti: The absence of attainment and reunion is due to purity of self.

The Lord: Because of such absolute purity.

Subhuti: The boundlessness of form, etc., is due to boundlessness of self.

The Lord: Because of such absolute purity.

Subhuti: Any Bodhisattva who understands such thus, is perfect wisdom.

The Lord: Because of such absolute purity.

Subhuti: Moreover, perfection of wisdom does not stand on any shore on this side, nor on any shore beyond, nor athwart the two.

The Lord: Because of such absolute purity.

Subhuti: A Bodhisattva treating even insight as any object of perception, hereby parts from perfection of wisdom, and gets far away from such.

Attachments

The Lord: Well said, Subhuti. For also names, as any things whatsoever are called and assumingly adjudicated as such, and signs, as any one thing or group of things owing or lending any more or less or even equal substantialness or reality to another, are sources of attachment.

Subhuti: It is wonderful, O Lord, to see any extent to which perfection of wisdom is well learned, well explained, well rounded off. The Lord even announces these sources of attachment.

Sariputra: Which, Subhuti, are these attachments?

Subhuti: It is an attachment if one perceives any skandhas are empty, or past dharmas are past dharmas, future dharmas are future dharmas, and present dharmas are present dharmas. Such are merely names. It is an attachment if one forms any notion such as "someone who belongs to the vehicle of the Bodhisattvas begets a great a heap of merit through one's first production of any thought of enlightenment." Such are merely signs.

Sakra: In which manner, Subhuti, is any thought of enlightenment a source of attachment?

Subhuti: One is attached as one perceives of any thought of enlightenment as "this is a [any] first thought of enlightenment," and one now thinks to convert such to full enlightenment while conscious one is doing so. For it is quite impossible to turn over essential original nature of thought, by thought. Any thought or thing neither is nor is not as truth and reality, as one is merely aware as such, and merely indicates in some way or fashion, such to such ('others') within Suchness.

To reveal or have such revealed in this way, one does not waste any self or thing away, and the manner which one rouses others to Suchness is the sanction of Buddhas. As such, one succeeds in abandoning any and all points of attachment.

The Lord: Well said, Subhuti, you make Bodhisattvas aware of these points of attachment. I now announce other, more subtle attachments. Listen to these well, and pay good attention as I teach these to you.

Say on, O Lord, and the Venerable Subhuti listened in silence.

The Lord: Here Subhuti, any son or daughter of good family, full of faith, attends to Tathagata through some sign. But, so many signs, so many attachments! Such as this is also, Subhuti, from signs comes attachment. It is in this way of being, as this one is conscious, that one rejoices in all dharmas with no outflows of Buddhas and Lords thought of as either past, or of some future or even this present. After such rejoicing one simply turns over into full enlightenment any wholesome root which is associated with one's act of jubilation. As a matter of difference however, this true nature of even these dharmas is neither past, nor future, nor present; for such lie quite outside any of these three periods called time. For this reason such cannot be converted, for as Suchness this quite simple truth is such as any dharmas whatsoever cannot be treated as any sign, nor as any objective support, and in absolute truth can neither be seen, nor heard, nor felt, nor known, for any and all of these involve one's illusive self in this much more complicated process of being as, perhaps, over and against this simple nature as such. (?)

Non-Attachment

Subhuti: Beyond any depth, beyond any presence, O Lord, is essential original nature of dharmas.

The Lord: Because such is isolated.

Subhuti: Unfathomable is essential nature of perfect wisdom.

The Lord: As any and all essential nature is pure and isolated, here is revealed perfection of wisdom as deepening toward essential nature, yet not as perfect wisdom.

Subhuti: Isolated is essential nature as perfect wisdom. I pay homage to perfection of wisdom.

The Lord: Also all dharmas are isolated as essential nature. And the isolatedness of essential nature to all dharmas is identical with perfection of wisdom. For Tathagatas fully know all dharmas as not made.

Subhuti: Here do all dharmas have the character of not being fully known by the Tathagatas?

The Lord: It is just through essential nature these dharmas are not some'thing'. Nature for such as these is no-nature, and no-nature are these as nature. All dharmas have one mark only, i.e. no mark. It is for such a reason all dharmas have a character of not being fully known by Tathagatas. Here are no two natures of dharma, but just one single one is nature of all dharmas. And nature of all dharmas is not nature, and no-nature is their nature. It is thus all these points of attachment are abandoned.

Subhuti: Deepening still, O Lord, is perfection of wisdom.

The Lord: Through depth such as this is like unto space.

Subhuti: Hard to understand, O Lord, is perfection of wisdom.

The Lord: Nothing is fully known by the enlightened.

Subhuti: Unthinkable, O Lord, is perfection of wisdom.

The Lord: Perfection of wisdom is neither some'thing' thought can know, nor which thought may even have any access to.

Subhuti: As such, not some'thing' made is perfection of wisdom, O Lord.

The Lord: As such, neither can maker be apprehended nor any'thing' be made.

Subhuti: How under these or any circumstances, does any Bodhisattva course as perfect wisdom?

The Lord: A Bodhisattva courses as perfect wisdom if, while coursing one does not course in skandhas; or if one does not course in any conviction such as skandhas are impermanent or are empty, or these are neither defective nor entire. And if one does not even course in any conviction such as form is neither any defectiveness nor entirety of itself as form, and the same for any 'other' skandhas, one courses as perfect wisdom, but only inasmuch as any perceptible manifestation to any of us may allow, or to such a greater or lesser degree as one may for one's self make perceptible. Whatsoever degree this may or may not come to be, to be sure perfect wisdom is beyond even such.

Subhuti: It is wonderful, O Lord, how well such reasons for attachment and non-attachment of Bodhisattvas is explained.

The Lord: One courses in perfect wisdom if one does not course in any idea such as form is with attachment, or without attachment. And as for form, so for any other skandhas, the sight organ, etc., to even such as feeling born from eye contact; so for any physical elements, the six perfections, the thirty-seven wings of enlightenment, the powers, any grounds of self-confidence, any analytical knowledge, the eighteen special Buddha-dharmas and fruits of holy life, from the fruit of a Streamwinner to all-knowledge. When one courses thus, a Bodhisattva does not generate attachment to anything, from form to all-knowledge. For all-knowledge is unattached, it is neither bound nor freed, and here is no-thing whatsoever which can rise above or beyond this, such as this is, even unto any self. It is thus, Subhuti, Bodhisattvas course in perfect wisdom through rising completely above any and all attachments. [196]

Like Space or an Echo

Subhuti: It is wonderful, O Lord, how deep is this Dharma, I mean perfection of wisdom. Demonstration neither diminishes nor increases this. Non-demonstration also neither diminishes nor increases this.

The Lord: Well said, Subhuti. It is just as if any Tathagatas, during one's entire life, speak in praise of space, without hereby increasing the volume of space; and space does not diminish either, while one is not speaking in praise for it. Or, it is as with an illusory man. Praise neither penetrates him nor wins him over. When here is no praise he is neither affected, nor frustrated. So, true nature of any or all dharmas is just so, whether such gets demonstrated or not.

Subhuti: A doer of what is hard is any Bodhisattva who, while coursing in perfection of wisdom, neither loses heart nor gets elated; who persists in making endeavours about this and does not turn back. Any development toward revealing perfect wisdom through dissolution of, or as any and all obscuration, is like some sort of development toward space. Homage is paid to any Bodhisattvas who are armed with this armor. For with space these want to be armed when, for the sake of beings these put on the armor. Armed with great armor is a Bodhisattva, a liberator is any Bodhisattva when one wants to be armed with an armor, and win full enlightenment for the sake of beings who are like space, who are like the realm of dharma. Such is one who wants to liberate like unto space, one who aspires even to get rid of space, one who has won this armor of this great perfection of vigor, this Bodhisattva who is armed with this armor for the sake of beings who are like unto space, who are like unto this realm of Dharma.

Hereupon a certain monk saluted the Lord with folded hands and said to the Lord: I pay homage, O Lord, to perfection of wisdom! For such neither produces nor stops any dharma whatsoever.

Sakra: If someone, holy Subhuti, makes efforts about this perfection of wisdom, what are these efforts about...or toward?

Subhuti: One makes efforts about or toward space. And one makes one's efforts about or toward a mere vacuity if one decides to train as perfect wisdom or to work toward such as perfection of wisdom.

Sakra: Please, O Lord, command me to shelter, defend and protect any son or daughter of good family who bears in mind this perfection of wisdom!

Subhuti: Sakra, can you see any dharma which you intend to shelter, defend and protect?

Sakra: Not so, holy Subhuti.

Subhuti: So when a Bodhisattva stands in perfection of wisdom as this is being expounded, just this is one's shelter, defense and protection. On the other hand, if and when one is lacking in view of perfect wisdom, beings and ghosts looking for entry will gain entrance into one such as this. One does, however, want to arrange shelter, defense and protection for a Bodhisattva coursing in view of perfect wisdom. What do you think, Kausika, are you able to arrange shelter, defense and protection for an echo?

Sakra: Not so, holy Subhuti.

Subhuti: Just so, any Bodhisattva coursing and dwelling in view of perfect wisdom, comprehends all dharmas are like an echo. One does not think about such, does not review, identify, or perceive such, and knows such dharmas do not exist, their reality does not appear, cannot be found, cannot be got at. If one dwells thus, one courses in view of perfect wisdom.

Conclusion

Hereupon and through the Buddha's might the four Great Kings in this great trichiliocosm, and all these Sakras, Chiefs of Gods, and all these great Brahma Gods, and Sahapati, the great Brahma -all came to this place the Lord is. Reverently these are saluting the Lord's feet with their heads and are walking three times round the Lord, and are now standing on one side. Through the Buddha's might and through his miraculous power their minds were impressed by sight of a thousand Buddhas.

In these very words, by these monks called Subhuti, etc., is this very perfection of wisdom being expounded, just this very chapter of perfection of wisdom. With reference to just this these Sakras, Chiefs of Gods, ask questions and counter-questions. At this very spot of earth is just this perfection of wisdom being taught. Maitreya also, the Bodhisattva, the great being will, as he wins the supreme enlightenment at this very spot of earth, teach this very same perfection of wisdom.

Chapter 9: PRAISE

Perfect Wisdom Perfectly Pure

Subhuti: To call this 'perfect wisdom,' O Lord, is merely giving this a name. And what this name corresponds to cannot be got at. One speaks of a 'name' with reference to any merely nominal entity. Even perfection of wisdom cannot be found or got at. In so far as this is a word, in so far is this perfect wisdom; in so far as this is perfect wisdom, in so far is this a word. No duality of dharmas between these two can either be found or got at. For what reason does Maitreya, the Bodhisattva, the great being, as he wins the supreme enlightenment, preach just this very same perfection of wisdom at this very spot of earth in just these same words?

The Lord: The reason is Maitreya will give cause to this fading away of any and all obscurations to his understanding, fully enlightened, the fact these skandhas are neither permanent nor impermanent, for such are neither bound nor freed, as these are absolutely pure.

Subhuti: Perfectly pure indeed is perfection of wisdom.

The Lord: Perfect wisdom is perfectly pure as any and all skandhas are pure, and so, do to non-production are perfectly pure, their non-stopping, their non-defilement and their non-purification. This is pure as space is pure and skandhas are stainless, and any defiling forces cannot in truth take hold of such as these. Perfect wisdom is perfectly pure for, like space or an echo, such is unutterable, incommunicable, and offers no basis for apprehension. Such is perfectly pure as being not covered by any dharma, either stained or stainless.

Effects of Perfect Wisdom

Subhuti: It is indeed a great gain to these sons and daughters of good family such as these even come to hear of such perfection of wisdom. How much greater the gain as these take up, bear in mind, recite, study, spread, teach, explain and master this. Their eyes, ears, nose, tongues and bodies come to be free from disease, and their minds free from stupefaction. These do not die any violent death. Many thousands of Gods follow closely behind. Whenever, on the eight, fourteenth and fifteenth day, one talks Dharma, any son or daughter of good family teaches perfection of wisdom, so here as well one begets a great deal of merit.

The Lord: So it is, Subhuti. Many thousands of Gods, Subhuti, follow closely behind this son or daughter of good family, and many thousands of Gods come to this place as perfect wisdom is being elucidated and revealed. Desirous of hearing Dharma, these, all of these, protect any preacher of Dharma who teaches perfection of wisdom to any with right intentions and the propensity to listen and learn. For perfect wisdom is most precious in the world with its Gods, beings and Asuras. This also is a reason why such a person begets a different type of merit than any which might be considered as great merit. On the other hand, here also are many obstacles to this deep perfection of wisdom being written, taken up, borne in mind, recited, studied, spread, developed, explained and repeated. For very precious things provoke much hostility. The more excellent such teachings are, the more violent the hostility. But this is most precious in entire world systems, this perfection of wisdom which is being undertaken for the benefit and happiness of these worlds by showing all dharmas as being neither produced nor destroyed, neither defiled nor purified. And perfect wisdom does not cling to any dharma, nor defile any dharma, nor take hold of any dharma. Any and all dharmas neither exist nor are any got at. As it is not apprehended perfection of wisdom is without any stain. 'To be free from stains,' is the same thing as perfect wisdom and it is the same thing such as skandhas are free from stains as perfect wisdom is without any stain. A Bodhisattva courses in perfect wisdom if one does not perceive even this, for beyond perception and concepts is perfect wisdom. Moreover, this perfection of wisdom neither enters nor places anything like 'itself' into any dharma, neither reveals nor defines any dharma, and neither brings in any dharma nor carries one away.

The Second Turning of the Wheel of Dharma

So, hereupon a great many thousands of Gods in this intermediate realm call out aloud with cries of joy, waving their garments, and saying: We now indeed see this second turning of the wheel of dharma taking place in Jambudvipa!

The Lord: This, Subhuti, is not the second turning of the wheel of dharma. No dharma can be turned forwards or backwards. Just this is a Bodhisattva's perfection of wisdom...just this approaches the pinnacle of perception and concept as this great perfection. This is beyond any such thing as turning.

Subhuti: This is a great perfection of any Bodhisattva who, unattached to all dharmas, wants to know full enlightenment, and who yet is not enlightened about any dharma, or who turns the wheel of dharma and yet does not show up any dharma. For no dharma is here got at, no dharma is indicated, and no dharma moves on any dharma. For absolutely, reproduction is alien to all dharmas. Nor does, nor can any dharma turn back any other dharma. From the beginningless beginning any and all dharmas are not being reproduced, since their essential nature is isolated.

The Lord: So it is, Subhuti. For emptiness does neither proceed nor recede, and such holds good also for the Signless and the Wishless. To demonstrate this is to demonstrate all dharmas. But no one has demonstrated this, no one has heard this, no one has received this, and no one realizes this, in this past, present or future. Nor by this demonstration of dharma does anyone ever go to Nirvana. Nor by this demonstration of dharma has anyone ever been made worthy of gifts.

Modes and Qualities of Perfect Wisdom

Subhuti: This is perfection of such as no-thing whatsoever is not, as space is not something which is. Perfection of wisdom equals any such as unequalled, dharmas are not apprehended. Perfection of wisdom is isolated, on account of absolute emptiness. Perfection of wisdom cannot be crushed, as dharmas are not apprehended. Perfection of wisdom is trackless, as both body and mind are absent. Perfection of wisdom has no own-being, neither comes nor goes. Perfection of wisdom is inexpressible, as any dharmas are not discriminated. Perfection of wisdom is nameless, as any skandhas whatsoever cannot be apprehended. Perfection of wisdom does not go away, as having not come hither, no dharma ever goes away. One cannot partake of this perfection of wisdom, as no dharma can be seized. Perfection of wisdom is inexhaustible, as indelible to inexhaustible dharma. Perfection of wisdom has no genesis, as no dharma ever really comes about. Perfection of wisdom does nothing, as no doer can be apprehended. Perfection of wisdom does not generate [cognize] anything, as any and all dharmas are without self. Perfection of wisdom does not pass on, as here is no genesis of decease or rebirth. Perfection of wisdom does not discipline, as this past, future and present periods are not apprehended. Perfection of wisdom is as a dream, an echo, a reflected image, a mirage, or an illusion, and is indicated as precision of non-production. Perfection of wisdom is free from defilement, as greed, hate, and delusion have no own-being. Perfection of wisdom knows no purification, as no possible receptacle [which might have to be purified] can be apprehended. Perfection of wisdom is spotless, as space is spotless. Perfection of wisdom is free from impediments, as spontaneously present throughout and beyond any and all mental attitudes to dharmas. Perfection of wisdom has no mental attitude, as it is imperturbable. Perfection of wisdom is unshakeable, as is stability of any realm of dharma. Perfection of wisdom knows no greed, as here is no falseness in dharmas. Perfection of wisdom does not rise up, as here is no discrimination in dharmas. Perfection of wisdom is quiet, as no sign is apprehended as all dharmas. Perfection of wisdom is faultless, as perfection of all virtues. Perfection of wisdom is undefiled, as imagination is something which is not. Neither living nor dying being is found as perfection of wisdom, as the reality-limit. Perfection of wisdom is unlimited, as the manifestation of all dharmas does not rise up. Perfection of wisdom does not follow after duality of opposites, as such does not settle down in any or all dharmas. Perfection of wisdom is undifferentiated, as all dharmas are still but speciously indicated. Perfection of wisdom is untarnished, as such is free from any longing for some jewel of Disciples and Pratyekabuddhas. Perfection of wisdom is undiscriminated, as this is basic identity to all which is discriminated. Perfection of wisdom is infinite, as any nature of dharma is unlimited. Perfection of wisdom is unattached, as this is non-attachment to all dharmas. Perfection of wisdom is unconditioned, as all dharmas are impermanent and merely an indication of such as this is. Perfection of wisdom is as space, as any nature of dharma is identical as impermanence. Perfection of wisdom is Empty, as any or all dharmas are not apprehended. Perfection of wisdom is not-self, as here is no settling down in any or all dharmas. Perfection of wisdom is markless, as here is no reproduction in dharmas.

Perfection of this is of total emptiness, as endless and boundless. Perfection of this is as the wings of enlightenment, such as is pillars of mindfulness, etc., as these cannot be apprehended. This is perfection of Emptiness, of the Signless, of the Wishless, as the three doors to deliverance cannot be apprehended. This is perfection of the eight deliverances, as these cannot be apprehended. This is perfection of the nine successive stations, as the first trance, etc., cannot be apprehended. This is perfection of the four Truths, as ill, old age and death cannot be apprehended. This is perfection of the ten perfections, as giving, etc., cannot be apprehended. This is perfection of the ten powers, as such cannot be crushed. This is perfection of the four grounds of self-confidence, as absolutely such cannot be cowed. This is perfection of the analytical knowledges, as such is unobstructed when unattached to all-knowledge. This is perfection of all the special Buddha-dharmas, as these transcend all counting. This is perfection of Suchness as Tathagatas, as here is no falseness in any and all dharmas. This is perfection of any as Self-existent, as all dharmas have not own-being. Perfection of wisdom is perfection of cognition of all-knowing, as such is aware within all of any modes of any own-being of all dharma.

Chapter 10: PROCLAMATION OF THE QUALITIES OF BEARING IN MIND

Past Deeds, and the Present Attitude to Perfect Wisdom

So now this thought is occurring to Sakra, Chief of Gods: These who come to hear of perfection of wisdom act in consideration and view of what is quite mundanely considered 'former' Jinas. These herein continue endlessly planting wholesome roots in view of countless Buddhas, take hold of, and are well taken hold of by good friends. Possessed of siddhis which are eventually realized as already in place beyond any common worldly determination as to why or how any dharma whatsoever comes to be, these who, taking up this perfection of wisdom bear in mind, study, spread and explain this, even now perform such acts.

In addition and also beyond any conscious or discursive efforts as such, these beings simultaneously train in Thusness and progress in Thusness, yet make no efforts whatsoever about Thusness. As thought, word, or concept, such is not inherent to anything from beyond any beginning yet effortlessly cognized as such, for as propensity and intent do come to allow, eventually is thus understood. These beings are endowed with more than trifling wholesome roots. These are beings honoring many Buddhas, and who again and again question these. It is just perfection of wisdom which these have heard in any past and yet still hear in this presence of manifest/unmanifest Tathagatas. These beings plant wholesome roots in view of all Buddhas. So, this is simply the way which these sons and daughters of good family are. As just this perfection of wisdom is being taught, these explain, understand and repeat this, do not become cowed nor stolid, do not become cast down nor depressed, do not turn their minds away from this nor have their backs broken, and as well, do not tremble, neither be frightened nor terrified.

Sariputra, now reading Sakra's thoughts says: As an irreversible Bodhisattva any person becomes and is so regarded who, when just this deep perfection of wisdom is being taught and explained, has faith in it, and, trusting, firmly believing, this one's heart full of serene faith, reveals to all sentient beings bodhicitta, a thought directed towards enlightenment, takes up, expounds, reveals, writes down, repeats, and/or develops this perfection of wisdom, trains in Thusness, progresses toward Thusness, and yet makes no effort about Thusness as basis or object. For this perfection of wisdom is exceedingly profound and herein someone with diminutive wholesome roots, who is unwilling to ask questions, learns nothing when face to face with any Buddhas and Lords in any time and who does not practice as yet in any time, cannot just here believe in this very profound perfection of wisdom. As to any who neither believe in this nor understand this, and who decide to reject this within these three times, these reject this deep perfection of wisdom as this is being taught, and this in consequence of inadequacy as regards their development of wholesome roots. For any who have not practiced do not now practice, and will not practice, such as these cannot believe in this perfection of wisdom. As these reject this now, these reject this equally in any past, for what's present is equally past as is likewise and at once this future. To see now, Sakra, is ever present in any mere thought of three times. For what seems passed only seems passed as any present thought could perceive, as well as any future which ever was to be. This is the reason why as this deep perfection of wisdom is being taught, in any time whatsoever these have no faith, or patience, or pleasure, or desire-to-do, no vigour, no vigilance or resolve. In any past as well, these presently, then, question neither Buddhas, the Lords, nor their disciples.

Sakra: Deep, indeed exceedingly profound, O holy Sariputra, is perfection of wisdom. So this is not at all astonishing, even as this is being taught that a Bodhisattva might not believe in this, if one did not practice in this past.

Sakra now said to the Lord: I pay homage, O Lord, to perfection of wisdom! One pays homage to cognition of all-knowing as one pays homage to perfection of wisdom.

The Lord: So it is. For from this comes forth all-knowledge of Buddhas, the Lords, and, conversely, perfection of wisdom is brought about as such which comes forth from cognition of all-knowing. This is why one aspires to course, stand, progress, and make efforts in perfection of wisdom.

Sakra: How does a Bodhisattva coursing in perfection of wisdom, become one who stands in perfect wisdom? How does one make efforts in regards to perfection of wisdom?

The Lord: Well said, well said, Kausika. Well said, again, well said, Kausika, since you have decided to question Tathagata about this matter, for in this questioning you have been inspired by Buddha's might. Here, Kausika, a Bodhisattva coursing in, or as perfect wisdom does not make any stand in form, feeling, perception, impulse or consciousness, does not develop as any basis any notion such as 'this is form, this is feeling, this is perception, this is impulse', or 'this is consciousness'...for this means one makes efforts about any or all of these as form, feeling, perception, impulse, or consciousness. One does not apply oneself to any notion such as this is form, this is feeling, etc. Insofar as one does not apply oneself to any notion such as 'this is form, this is feeling, etc.', one does not stand in any notion such as 'this is form, this is feeling, etc.' Thus, one is known as one standing in perfect wisdom, thusly one makes efforts in or as perfect wisdom.

Subhuti: Here a simile from a song of old presents to mind: A certain devata, in the far extreme of the night, her extreme radiance lighting up the entirety of Jeta's Grove, went to the Blessed One. On arrival, having bowed down to him, she stood to one side. As she was standing there, she said to him, "Tell me, dear sir, how you crossed over the flood."

"I crossed over the flood without pushing forward, without staying in place."

"But how, dear sir, did you cross over the flood without pushing forward, without staying in place?"

"When I pushed forward, I was whirled about. When I stayed in place, I sank. And so I crossed over the flood without pushing forward, without staying in place."

The devata: "At long last I see a brahman totally unbound, who without pushing forward, without staying in place, has crossed over the entanglements of the world." That is what the devata said.

The Teacher approved. Realizing that "The Teacher has approved of me," she bowed down to him, circumambulated him -- keeping him to her right -- and then vanished right there.

Sariputra: Deep, O Lord, is perfection of wisdom. Hard to fathom is perfection of wisdom. Hard to grasp is perfection of wisdom. Unlimited is perfection of wisdom.

The Lord: So it is, Sariputra. One does not stand in any notion such as "form, feeling, perception, impulse, or consciousness, is deep." Insofar as one does not stand in any such notion as, 'one makes efforts about form, etc.' one does not make efforts about any such notion as "form , etc., is deep." In so far as one makes no efforts about any such notion, one does not stand in any notion as "form, etc., is deep."

Qualifications of a Bodhisattva Who Obtains Perfect Wisdom

Sariputra: Only when presented to an irreversible Bodhisattva, to any Bodhisattva predestined to enlightenment, is deep perfection of wisdom understood, and only so may this herein be taught. For such do not hesitate, do not doubt, do not get stupefied, and not dispute this.

Sakra: What is the fault in teaching this perfection of wisdom in front of an unpredestined Bodhisattva?

Sariputra: If Kausika, unpredestined, a Bodhisattva obtains this perfection of wisdom, for vision, praise, worship and hearing, and if one remains unafraid as one hears this, one can be sure this one comes from afar, is set out for long in this vehicle, and this one's wholesome roots are well matured. It is not long from now onwards until this one receives the prediction to supreme enlightenment. One can be sure this prediction is near, and comes to one before one passes by one, two or three Tathagatas. And, of course, one pleases the Tathagatas whom one passes by, pleases these permanently, and so one sees to it the vision of these Tathagatas bears the fruit of the prediction, so it leads one to the prediction to supreme enlightenment [itself]. Once come from afar, O Lord, set out for long in this great vehicle, with wholesome roots well matured is this Bodhisattva obtaining this perfection of wisdom for vision, praise, worship, hearing and understanding. How much more so if one not only hears this, but also takes this up, bears this in mind, preaches, studies, spreads, explains and repeats such as this.

The Lord: So it is, Sariputra, as you have said.

Five Similes to Illustrate Nearness to Full Enlightenment

Sariputra: A simile or example flashes into my mind, O Lord. Just as we are sure a person belonging to this vehicle of Bodhisattvas, when one dreams that one sits on the terrace of enlightenment, is actually near to supreme enlightenment...just so, we can be sure a person who fulfils these conditions just outlined has come from afar, and is set out for long in the vehicle of the Bodhisattvas, and is near this prediction to enlightenment. We can be sure Buddhas, the Lords, will predict this Bodhisattva to win full enlightenment. For a Bodhisattva is set out for long in this vehicle, and one's wholesome roots are mature, if one gets to this deep perfection of wisdom, even if one gets no further than hearing this. How much more so if one would also bear it in mind, etc., to: repeat it. For the thoughts of beings not without an abundance of accumulations of karma conducive to the ruin of dharma become adverse to this deep perfection of wisdom, do sway away from this. Through the abundance of such karma, beings who do not collect wholesome roots find neither satisfaction nor faith in this reality-limit. But any such beings who do find satisfaction and faith in this are people who collected wholesome roots, well collected these.

A person coming out of a huge wild forest, one hundred miles big, up to a thousand miles big, might see certain signs which indicate a town, or other inhabited place, -such as cowherds, or cattle keepers, or boundary lines, or gardens, or groves. From these signs one infers the nearness of an inhabited place. One feels happier, and robbers no longer worry this one. Just so a Bodhisattva for whom this deep perfection turns up can know one is quite near to supreme enlightenment, and before long one will receive the prediction to such. One also no longer need be afraid of the level of the Disciples and Pratyekabuddhas. For this sign has appeared to this one, i.e., one has received this deep perfection of wisdom for vision, praise, worship, hearing, and/or understanding.

The Lord: So it is, Sariputra. May you make clear also this section. For what you say, and what you will say, is due to the Buddha's might.

Sariputra: A person, desirous of seeing the great ocean, might travel to it. As long as on one's travels one sees a tree, or the sign of a tree, a mountain, or the sign of a mountain, one knows the great ocean is still far away. But when one no longer sees either tree or mountain, one knows the great ocean is quite near to here. For this great ocean gradually slopes away, and within it there is neither tree nor mountain. So, although one may not yet see the great ocean directly before one's eyes, one nevertheless can be quite certain the ocean is quite near, not much farther away from here. Similar is the case of any Bodhisattva hearing this deep perfection of wisdom. One can know this...even although perhaps one has not yet been face to face with these Tathagatas, and predicted to supreme enlightenment, nevertheless one is quite near this prediction. For one has received this deep perfection of wisdom for vision, praise, worship, hearing, and/or understanding.

Likewise, in this spring, O Lord, as last year's leaves are withered away, one can see sproutings on many trees. The people of Jambudvipa are glad, because as these see these symptoms in the woods, these ones know soon also flowers and fruits come out. For they see such signs in the trees. Just so, O Lord, one can be sure that a Bodhisattva, when one receives this deep perfection of wisdom, as this even turns up for one, such a one has become matured in one's wholesome roots for a long time. It is just because of the existence of these wholesome roots in such a one, this deep perfection of wisdom has bent over to whoever this is. Then any divinities who see the Buddhas of any past are delighted, overjoyed and enchanted, as these feel surely it is not long until this Bodhisattva receives this prediction to full enlightenment, since also with any Bodhisattvas of any past these are the symptoms of their coming prediction to full enlightenment.

Likewise O Lord, a woman pregnant with a heavy womb, is twisted and all weary, she does not walk about a great deal, takes little food, finds little rest, speaks little, has little strength but many pains, often cries out aloud and abstains from habitual cohabitation. She realizes she experiences all these unpleasant feelings in her body as a result of indulging in unwise attention in the past, practicing it, developing it, making much of it. As these symptoms are being seen in her, one can be sure before long she will give birth to a child. Just so, when for a Bodhisattva this deep perfection of wisdom turns up for the sake of vision, praise, worship, hearing, and/or understanding, and if, as one hears this, one's thought delights in this, and one develops aspirations toward this, so one can be sure before long one will receive prediction to full enlightenment.

Why Bodhisattvas are Well-Favored by the Buddhas

Subhuti: It is wonderful to see this extent to which the Tathagata well takes hold of Bodhisattvas, well encompasses and favors such as these.

The Lord: This is because these Bodhisattvas practice for the weal and happiness of the many, out of compassion for the world. Out of compassion for Gods and men, for the benefit, the weal and happiness of a great mass of people do these want to win supreme enlightenment, and hereafter to demonstrate supreme Dharma.

The Right Attitude to Perfect Wisdom

Subhuti: How does a Bodhisattva which courses toward perfect wisdom, become increasingly perfect?

The Lord: A Bodhisattva courses toward perfect wisdom as this coursing itself being neither any growth nor any diminution of form, feeling, perception, impulse, and/or consciousness, and is reviewed as one reviews neither dharma nor no-dharma. This is how, and thus one's coursing toward perfect wisdom is realized as increasingly perfect.

Subhuti: This is surely unthinkable.

The Lord: Ultimately, form is as unthinkable as any skandhas, or, things being thought of as going together to make-up other things. As ultimately one perceives neither any nor all of form, feeling, perception, impulse, and/or consciousness as unthinkable, one courses in perfect wisdom.

Sariputra: Who or what with zeal, complete dedication, and earnest devotion is merely aware, even unto emptiness?

The Lord: Any Bodhisattva practicing with zeal, complete dedication, and earnest devotion, in verity even unto emptiness as perfect wisdom, is merely aware, even unto emptiness.

Sariputra: What is Bodhisattva practice, and what is the meaning of the word 'practice'?

The Lord: A Bodhisattva neither constructs power nor ground such as self-confidence nor Buddha-dharmas, nor even all-knowledge...for power or ground as self-confidence, Buddha-dharmas, or even all-knowledge is as unthinkable as any and all dharmas. Thus as practice, a Bodhisattva courses neither within nor without perfect wisdom. For no true reason is one called Bodhisattva, as such is the meaning of the word 'practice'.

Obstacles to Perfect Wisdom

Subhuti: Deep, O Lord, is one's learning, realizing and understanding as perfection of wisdom is indicated as such. Such is a heap of treasure. Such is a pure heap, as pure as space. It is not surprising many obstacles arise to any reciting, reading, writing, studying, contemplating and/or understanding perfection of wisdom as such.

The Lord: Many obstacles to one's reciting, reading, etc., this perfection of wisdom are always present. For Mara, the Evil One, is seen as making many difficulties, as even here for one of these, one hurries with one's task of copying this out. If one has one month to do it in, or two months, or three months, one need merely carry on with this writing. If one has a year or more, even so one need just carry on with writing perfection of wisdom [since after, or even during this time, one may be slowed or even prevented by any kind of interruptions]. It is a fact, such as in respect of precious things, difficulties are wont to arise.

Subhuti: Here, O Lord, when perfection of wisdom is being studied, Mara, the Evil One, is seen in ways to show zeal, and exert himself to cause difficulties.

The Lord: In spite of this he is powerless to cause really effective obstacles to any Bodhisattva which gives undivided attention to any task.

The Bodhisattva Sustained by the Buddhas

Sariputra: O Lord...as Mara the Evil One is seen as any presenting preventative obstacles to this studying perfection of wisdom, how can any beings actually study this, and through whose might can these progress?

The Lord: Through might of Buddhas, Lords, and Tathagatas these study, these progress and train in or as Thusness. This same nature of Buddhas and Lords which stands, holds and maintains immeasurable and incalculable world-systems, brings to mind and upholds anyone learning and studying perfection of wisdom. Buddhas bring to mind and assist any such as these. It is impossible to cause any obstacle to any beings brought to mind and upheld by Buddhas.

Sariputra: Is this Buddha's might, sustaining power and grace which Bodhisattvas deeply study as perfection of wisdom, and progressively train in or as Thusness?

The Lord: So it is, Sariputra. As such, these are known to Tathagatas, these are sustained and seen by Tathagatas, and the Tathagatas behold these with this Buddha eye. And these Bodhisattvas which study perfection of wisdom progressively train in or as Thusness, stand as such with no true ground in any decision to enlightenment. Just to study perfection of wisdom without progressively training in or as Thusness, these do not stand poised in Suchness but nevertheless are known to Tathagatas, sustained and seen by Tathagatas, and the Tathagatas behold these with this Buddha eye. With continual study of perfection of wisdom, the mental excitation is greatly profitable to these, a great advantage, fruit and reward. For, as aiming at ultimate reality, perfection of wisdom is set up for penetration by all beings into this nature of what dharmas truly are.

Prediction about the Spread of Perfect Wisdom

Moreover, these Sutras in accord with six perfections continue as such after the parinirvāna of Tathagata, appearing in this South. As in this South these spread to this East, and as well this North and West -- at any time this Dharma Vinaya is as freshly made cream, and as good law, dissolves as Dharma-Body (dharmakaya). In equal taste with, as, and by these which put forth right effort, and study, devote, dedicate, and preserve perfection of wisdom, are with, as, and by Tathagatas. Tathagatas accord with, sustain and see such as these, and behold these with this Buddha eye.

Sariputra: Will perfection of wisdom at the last of time, in the last period, be deeply widespread in this northern direction, in this northern part of the world?

The Lord: Even in this North, any which make right efforts deep in perfection of wisdom, even as these simply hear this, make this widespread. As set out for long in this vehicle the Bodhisattvas who know study this perfection of wisdom and beyond even this.

Description of Bodhisattvas Who Will Study Perfect Wisdom

Sariputra: Bodhisattvas in this North which deeply study perfection of wisdom, are these many or few?

The Lord: These are many, a good many Bodhisattvas in this North. But only a few are among these which deeply study perfection of wisdom, and which as this is being taught, are not demoralized by it. As set out for long in this vehicle are known already beings such as these which pursue, question, and worship Tathagatas - one's thus gone as one's thus come. These are as perfect, enhancing as well as benefiting all beings. As such these are, as is all. Mere awareness and bare realization are these as spontaneously self-existent, primordial and beyond even purity itself. As, for, and to these do Tathagatas speak as, for, and to all-knowledge. Even as these pass beyond present births, any thoughts, even unto all-knowledge and perfection of wisdom, persist by force of habit [karma]. And this very discoursing these both discuss and are contented within concerning the ultimate enlightenment. Such as these are perfection of wisdom and all-knowledge as related to this. These are neither obstructed nor diverted even by Mara, much less other beings, whether such use will, power, or mantras. As diamond resolve (avidriya samadana) and irresistibly these approach full enlightenment. From hearing perfection of wisdom these daughters and sons of good family gain an uncommon degree of zest, confidence and unshakable faith. For all beings these plant wholesome roots. Face to face with Tathagatas, these utter a vow: "Coursing in practice of Bodhisattvas, we are this we indicate, the way to full enlightenment of many hundreds of living beings, yea, many naiyutas of kotis of living beings. We indicate perfect enlightenment to these, instigate and empower, help such to come forth, help these to establish such, help these to irreversible right effort and action." And as these are thought as my thought, these daughters and sons of good family belong to the vehicle of Bodhisattvas who make this vow. As these are confirmed in their faith these attain to rebirth yet in many Buddha-fields, and even here come face to face with Tathagatas, which indicate Dharma and as such these hear in deep detail perfection of wisdom. In many Buddha-fields these indicate this view for all beings as dissolving obstacles to full realization, and help these beings as this quest for full enlightenment of all.

Sariputra: It is wonderful to think this past and future, as present dharma is no-thing. Tathagatas do not experience such as unaware...no dharma is not cognized, yet beyond even purity...aware as space. Neither is conduct as anything, anywhere, nor any being unaware. Such as these cognize even conduct of Bodhisattvas who are zealous for enlightenment, yet even of the slightest earnest intent, for these too exert vigour, if even of slight. And yet O Lord, among these born of good family who at any time deeply study this perfection of wisdom, and exert themselves on behalf of these six perfections and of the benefit of all beings, and seek, search and strive deeply to obtain perfection of wisdom, some still do not obtain this, while others obtain this without striving to get this. What, O Lord, is the reason for this?

The Lord: So it is, Sariputra. In this past and future, or as present, dharma is nothing. Tathagatas do not see, hear and feel such as unaware. It is further true at these times in these periods, some Bodhisattva who hunt and search for perfection of wisdom do not get this. Others do get this without hunting and searching. These are Bodhisattvas which in this past persistently hunted and searched for this perfection of wisdom. It is of such impetus of this former wholesome root these realize perfection of wisdom, in spite of the fact these do not now hunt and search for this. And also Sutras different from this, which welcome perfection of wisdom, of their own accord come to these. It is a principle Sariputra, a Bodhisattva which persistently hunts and searches for perfection of wisdom, after one or two births, realize this, also the other Sutras in accord with perfect wisdom come to one on their own.

Sariputra: Will only these Sutras in accord with six perfections come to this one, and no others?

The Lord: Here also other profound Sutras come to this son or daughter of good family of their own accord. It is as a rule Sariputra, that, Bodhisattvas which indicate this teaching for others on their way to full enlightenment, helping these in their quest for such, help them to irreversibility, and these who also train in this, after these pass through this present birth, on their own these deep Sutras come to these, Sutras which are in accord with non-apprehension of a basis, and which accord with emptiness, and also accord with the six perfections.

Chapter 11: MARA'S DEEDS

Various Deeds of Mara

Subhuti: The Lord proclaims virtues of sons and daughters of good family. Are any obstacles here which arise in such ones?

The Lord: Many obstacles are here, and are seen and thought of as the deeds of Mara.

Subhuti: What kind of obstacles are these?

The Lord: The Bodhisattvas discoursing this perfection of wisdom, either understand this after a long time, or, as understanding is generated, it immediately becomes disturbed. Or some write yawning, laughing and sneering, or study this with thoughts disturbed. Or write with minds on other things, not gaining in mindfulness. These may write as deriding or sneering at one another, or with distracted eyes. This writing is in mutual discord. "We gain no firm footing in it, we derive no enjoyment from it"...with such words these take their leave. As such thoughts derive from a source seemingly devoid of serene faith these think "I am not predestined for perfection of wisdom,"...and get up and leave. Or, as these merely see and think this book does not name the place they're born, does not mention their own name and clan, nor of their mother and father, nor of their family, these may decide to not listen to perfection of wisdom, and take their leave. Each time these take their leave, again and again these take to birth-and-death for as many aeons as they have productions of thought, and still even now, at some point during these aeons these ones may make new efforts. All this, and for what reason? Bodhisattvas refusing to listen deeply to perfection of wisdom cannot go forth to spiritual dharmas, be these worldly or supramundane.

The Perfection of Wisdom and the Sutras of the Disciples

In addition, some of us may or may not recognize whether or not we belong to this vehicle of the Bodhisattvas, and some give up and think to abandon perfection of wisdom...this understanding beyond knowledge which nourishes this cognition of all-knowing. We might decide to look for other Sutras, the understanding of which may or may not come to reveal this uniform awareness for our nourishment, this pure cognition common to beings beyond number, yet exceedingly rare to be found and understood. Indeed, as rare as a turtle which happens upon a single life preserving float amidst an infinite ocean, which ferries it upon it's natural currents to a shore of rest and nourishment. Indeed, Subhuti, exceedingly rare is this.

Many of us do not learn and understand perfection of wisdom, and thus presently do not want to train in both worldly and universal spiritual dharmas, nor do we avail ourselves of these. As we do not learn and understand perfection of wisdom, we cannot avail ourselves of worldly or universal spiritual dharmas.

Though all possess this identical potential, some get rid of and abandon perfection of wisdom, which is the root of the comprehension of worldly and universal spiritual dharmas as these are, and instead decide to look for support in what are different branches. As a dog spurns a morsel of food offered by it's master, and takes a mouthful of water from a servant instead, just so, beings recognized as implicitly related to this vehicle of Bodhisattvas spurn perfection of wisdom which is the taproot revealing cognizance of all-knowing, yet decide to look for the core, for growth, for Buddhahood, in vehicles of Disciples as Sravakas and Pratyekabuddhas, which corresponds to branches, leaves and foliage. This also may be seen as done to them by Mara.

Again, all beings have equal potential yet do not equally recognize concentrated right effort and mindfulness towards perfection of wisdom and apply this, hereby nourishing cognition of all-knowing.Still most of us at one time or another get rid of, abandon, spurn, or even simply forget perfection of wisdom, and decide to study, as if superior to this, Sutras by which we welcome the level of a Disciple or Pratyekabuddha which are compared to branches, leaves and foliage. A Bodhisattva does not train in the same way in which a being recognized as belonging to the vehicle of a Disciple or Pratyekabuddha is trained.

How does a Disciple and Pratyekabuddha train? Well, I make up my mind thus, following this teacher over here and the knowledge I derive hereof, I in my turn teach others what I come to understand, and so one single self I have tamed, one single self I pacify, one single self I lead to final Nirvana. Thus I undertake exercises and practices which are intended to bring about wholesome roots for the sake of taming myself, pacifying myself, leading myself to Nirvana.

Bodhisattvas train ourselves differently. On the contrary, we train ourselves thus: "To benefit infinite sentient beings equally as one, in coming to realize Suchness as such and indicating such to sentient beings beyond number. This process of perfection of wisdom as well as this Bodhisattva vehicle is being so indicated, shown, and proven as available to all, hereby clears the path for liberation from samsara of infinite sentients and revelation of Nirvana. Also, propensities allowing, karma neutralized...the eventual clearing of obstructions to the reality-limit, any may become revealed to full enlightenment and advancement to parinirvana...the whole immeasurable universe of beings. With this right intention a Bodhisattva engages all the exercises which bring about the wholesome root. But one boasts not regarding this...For imagine a being which, unable to see an elephant, would try to determine its color and shape. In the darkness this one would touch and examine the foot of the elephant, and decide that the color and shape of the elephant should be inferred from his foot. Is this an intelligent thing to do?

Subhuti: No, Lord!

The Lord: The same is true of any persons who belong to the vehicle of the Bodhisattvas, who do not understand this perfection of wisdom and ask no questions.

Yet, while desirous of full enlightenment, these spurn this and prefer to look to the Sutras which welcome the level of Sravakas or Pratyekabuddhas. Also this is -seen- as being done -to- any one of these by Mara. If a person who desires jewels would not look for them in the great ocean, but in a puddle in a cows footprint, and would thus in effect equate the great ocean with the water in a cow's footprint, would this one be using one's potential for intelligence wisely?

Subhuti: No, Lord!

The Lord: Well and now, the same applies to any beings which vow to this vehicle of Bodhisattvas which...though we make ourselves available to perfection of wisdom, we nevertheless cut ourselves off from continuous exposure and reference to this, without plunging or probing at all times, in all times exceedingly deeper as a means of perfection to endless, placeless, timeless wisdom.

Yet...we may still prefer the Sutras which welcome any level of Sravakas or Pratyekabuddhas through advocating dwelling in concentrated but unconcerned inactivity, and which do not recommend the vehicle of the Bodhisattvas, but only the taming, appeasing, Nirvana of one single self. The decision to seclusion, to the fruits of a holy life, from the fruit of a Streamwinner to Pratyekabuddhahood, to enter Parinirvana after one has in this very life freed thought from the outflows without further clinging, -that means to be in accord with the level of a Sravaka as Disciple or

Pratyekabuddha.

Bodhisattvas do not focus thought only to such as this. For as we have set out in this great vehicle Bodhisattvas don a great armour. Our thoughts are not singularly focused to any unconcernedness whatsoever. For we are concentrated as diamonds, guides of the world, promoters of the world's weal. Here, we continuously and always train in and as these six perfections. But as beings which vow to the vehicle of the Bodhisattvas, and without knowing and understanding Sutras which accord with the six perfections spurn perfection of wisdom, and prefer these Sutras which welcome this level of Sravakas as Disciples, or Pratyekabuddha, -our wholesome root is yet immature, our intelligence still obscured and yet lacking in profound qualities, our resoluteness still weak. We may reflect as a mason, or mason's apprentice, who wants to build a palace of the size of the Vaijayanta palace, and who takes its measure from measuring the car of sun or moon. A similar procedure is adopted by us if we are to reject perfection of wisdom and in earnest try to find all-knowledge through Sutras in accord with this level of Sravakas as Disciples, and Pratyekabuddhas, Sutras which recommend the taming, appeasing, and Nirvana of nothing more than one individual being as self only. If we would look for such Sutras and train with these intentions, would these Bodhisattvas, this type which we turn to be, be using much of our intelligence?

Subhuti: No, Lord!

The Lord: This also is -seen as being- done to such by Mara. In truth and ultimately undeniable my friend, such is done unto ourselves by this turn within and pandering to what is wantonly believed to be the sole needs and comforts of singularity and individual appeasement, and, while yet donning a cloak of austerity, hereby yielding still only a mask of humility...and misleading and contrived wisdom.

So, suppose a person who first sees a universal monarch, and makes determinations from the signs of what is seen in his complexion, shape, beauty and majesty. Then, this person does the same with the commander of a fort. If the person were unable to make a distinction, and then this one were to say to the commander of a fort, just like this is the universal monarch in complexion, shape, beauty and majesty, if this one were to, in other words, equate universal monarch with the commander of a fort, would this be an intelligent thing to do?

Subhuti: No, Lord!

The Lord: The same applies to persons who avow themselves to this Bodhisattva-vehicle and who in some future reject this perfection of wisdom, and seek for all-knowledge through sutras associated with level of Sravaka as

Disciple, or Pratyekabuddha. This also is -seen as- done to these ones by Mara. On the contrary, I certainly do not say, "Bodhisattvas, seek for all-knowledge through the Sutras associated with the level of Sravaka as Disciple or Pratyekabuddha." Bodhisattvas certainly do not go forth to reveal supreme enlightenment unless trained in what Tathagatas have announced in the perfection of wisdom as the skill in means of these Bodhisattvas. For the full knowledge of a Bodhisattva is unknown in other Sutras.

Here now, Subhuti, Tathagatas seeing this advantage in perfection of wisdom, by manifold methods show this to Bodhisattvas, instigate and introduce these ones to this, fills these with enthusiasm about this, make these rejoice at this, entrusts these with this, in the knowledge herein that any Bodhisattva may become irreversible to full enlightenment. Subhuti, do these Bodhisattvas appear to be very intelligent who, having obtained and met with the irreversible, the great vehicle, and then again abandon this, turn away from this, and prefer an inferior vehicle?

Subhuti: No, Lord!

The Lord: If a starving man refuses superior and excellent food, and prefers to eat inferior and stale food, is he using the full potential of his intelligence?

Subhuti: No, Lord!

The Lord: Just so, Subhuti, in the future some Bodhisattvas still refuse this perfection of wisdom, and prefer the Sutras associated with the level of Sravaka, the Disciple or Pratyekabuddha, and still seek all-knowledge through Sutras which welcome the level of Disciple or Pratyekabuddha. Do these Bodhisattvas use the full potential of their intelligence?

Subhuti: No, Lord!

The Lord: Also, this is -seen as- being done to these ones by Mara. A man who had got a priceless gem and who considered it equal to a gem of inferior value and quality, is he using the full potential of his intelligence?

Subhuti: No, Lord!

The Lord: So, here too, in this future some persons belonging to the vehicle of the Bodhisattvas who, though these have got this deep and brightly shining gem of perfect wisdom, nevertheless think this should be considered equal with the vehicle of Sravakas, these Disciples and Pratyekabuddhas, and decide to seek all-knowledge and skill in means on the level of Disciple or Pratyekabuddha. Are these using the full potential of intelligence?

Subhuti: No, Lord!

The Lord: This also is -seen as- being done to such as these by Mara.

Various Deeds of Mara (2)

Moreover Subhuti, as perfection of wisdom is being indicated, demonstrated, explained, learned, recited, repeated, or even merely written down, many flashes of insight come up in bewildering multitudes, and these make for confusion of thought. This also -is seen as having been- done to us by Mara.

Subhuti: Is it at all possible to write down perfection of wisdom?

The Lord: No, Subhuti. It is also -seen as- a deed of Mara as one writes down perfection of wisdom, this one either thinks this is perfection of wisdom which is written down, or is not perfection of wisdom which is written down, or one adheres to perfection of wisdom either in the letters, or as something not in the letters.

Moreover Subhuti, while these write down perfection of wisdom, our minds are on all sorts of things: places, villages, towns, cities, country districts, nations, royal cities, pleasure groves, preceptors, tales, robbers, bathing places, streets, palanquins, occasions for happiness, occasions for fear, women, men, neuters, unsuitable situations, mother and father, brothers and sisters, friends, maternal relatives, kinsmen, chief wives, sons and daughters, houses, food and drink, clothes, beds, seats, livelihood, obligations, occasions of greed, hate and delusion, on right times, lucky times, unlucky times, on songs, music, dances, poems, plays, treatise, business, jokes, musical shows, sorrows, troubles, and...ourselves.

These and other acts of attention Mara, the Evil One, -is seen to- arrange as perfection of wisdom is being indicated, studied, or merely written down, and thus he -is seen to cause- obstacles and confusion of thought to Bodhisattvas. Bodhisattvas recognize this as being -merely seen as a deed of- Mara, and avoid it, mostly by avoiding seeing it as such. [!] In addition, our thoughts may also be on kings, royal princes, elephants, horses, chariots and troops of soldiers. Also this is -seen as having been- done to us by Mara. In addition, our thoughts may be on fire, temptations, money, corn and affluence. This also Mara is -seen as- doing to him.

Moreover, difficulties arise about gain, honor, robes, alms-bowl, lodging, and medicinal appliances for use in sickness, or alternatively, thoughts relishing gain...honor and fame torment Bodhisattvas which indicate, explain, repeat or merely write perfection of wisdom. This also is -seen as- Mara doing this to us. We recognize and avoid -seeing these as- "deeds of Mara".

Furthermore, Mara, the Evil One, comes while Bodhisattvas indicate, expound, write, etc., perfection of wisdom, and he brings along those very deep Sutras which are in accord with the limits of Sravakas as Disciples and Pratyekabuddhas. He advises us to...train in these, write, expound, and repeat these, for from this all-knowledge is created. But, Bodhisattvas skilled in means are not long for these Sutras. For although these indicate Emptiness, the Signless and Wishless, still any skill in means of Bodhisattvas are neither announced nor alluded to. A Bodhisattva which remains without this more refined knowledge of distinction of the cognition of cognition of skill in means, deeply spurns this true perfection of wisdom, and seeks instead skill in means in the Sutras which accord with the limitations of Sravakas as Disciples and Pratyekabuddhas. This also is -seen as- Mara's deed being done to this Bodhisattva.

Sources of Discord between Guide and Pupil

As well, here are deeds which are seen to be of Mara and have the potential to ruin any or all chances of cooperation between any guide and pupil. First of all, perhaps the pupil is enthusiastic, and aspires to engage perfection of wisdom, but the guide is indolent, and does not aspire to demonstrate Dharma.

Or, the guide is untiring, and inspired to indicate perfection of wisdom, while the pupil is tired or too busy. Secondly, it may be that the pupil is quite diligent, and aspires to engage, to bear in mind, indicate, study, spread, or merely to write about this process of perfection of wisdom, is clever, intelligent and blest with good memory; but the one who may guide moves into a different district, or is unacquainted with main points, unacquainted with details, and without higher knowledge.

Or, this guide may be untiring, in possession of the higher knowledge, inspired to indicate perfection of wisdom; but the pupil set out for another district, or is unacquainted with main points, unacquainted with details, without higher knowledge. Further, the guru may be a person who attaches weight to fleshly things, to gain, honor and robes, while the pupil is a person of few wishes, easily contented, and quite detached.

Or one or the other or both may be persons unwilling to give away anything of value. This also causes discord, when it is a question of training toward perfect wisdom, or of copying this, such as this is. On the other hand, a pupil may be full of faith, inspired by merely hearing of the process of perfection of wisdom and of understanding the meaning of this, liberal and generous; but the lama has no faith, is too easily satisfied, and does not aspire to expound regarding perfection of wisdom.

Or, the pupil may be full of faith, and aspire to hear and to understand the meaning; but it may be that the guru, because some obstacle hinders access to Dharma, does not have these Sutras, or cannot fathom them; a pupil would obviously be out of touch with a guide who has not obtained these.

Or again, a guide may aspire to point out, while a pupil is not single-minded and aspiring at least to hear this. Further, it may be that the pupil does not want to listen because hindered by sloth, weighed down by bodily fatigue, but the Rinpoche is willing to point out; conversely, any guide may, although the pupil wants to listen, not want to teach because hindered by sloth or physical fatigue. This discord also makes writing, speaking and study difficult.

Misdirection of Aim

Moreover, while beings write, or indicate perfection of wisdom, or train in the process, someone comes along and belittles life in the hells, in the animal world, among the Pretas and Asuras, saying "so ill are all these forms of life, so ill are all conditioned things; do make an end to just this length of cloth, and leave these beings to their fate." This also is -seen as- a work of Mara.

Or again, some being comes along and praises life among the Gods: "So happy are the Gods, so happy is life in the heavens. One will do well here to end sense-desires in the world of sense-desires, enter into the well-known trances in the world of form, and enter into the well-known attainments in the formless world."

Considered in a view with wisdom, all this is nothing but rebirth in suffering. The Lord has said: "I do not praise any kind of rebirth in becoming, because this lasts no longer than a finger-snap. For everything conditioned is impermanent.

"Anything causing fear is ill. All in the triple world is empty. All dharmas are without self. As any of these wise may come to understand all is thus devoid of eternity, is impermanent and ill, doomed to reversal, now these may just here attain to the fruits of holy life, from the fruit of a Streamwinner to Arhatship.

"However, let us now beware of meeting any further with such attainments, which are really failures, and which abound in suffering. But nevertheless, to some Bodhisattvas this is a source of anxiety [because these come to feel deterred from the quest for full enlightenment in favor of aspiring to rebirth among the Gods.] This also is -seen as- Mara doing this." (!)

More Discord between Lama and Pupil

Furthermore, the Lama may be a monk who is fond of solitude while the pupils prefer a communal life. He tells them he will give this perfection of wisdom to any coming to where he is, but not to any who do not. In their desire and zeal for dharma which these value they go to where the lama is, and still he gives these no opportunity to learn anything. He is one eager for trifling bits of fleshy things, but these do not want to give him anything that he values. Wherever he goes he is short of food, surrounded by troubles, and in danger of his life. And his pupils hear from others that that place is short of food, full of troubles and dangers to life. And that lama will say to these children of good family: This place is short of food. Of course, all you of good family, you may come here if you wish. But I am afraid that you will regret having come. This is a subtle device by which he outwardly rejects them. In disgust they will interpret these remarks as signs of refusal, not as signs of a desire to give. Convinced he does not want to give, they do not go to where he is.

Moreover, this lama may have set out for a spot where there is danger from vermin, from beasts of prey, from ghosts. And he yet still moves from there to a wilder place with beasts of prey, snakes and robbers, marked by drought and famine. To these prospective pupils he says: "You are aware, I suppose, in this spot for which we have set out are many dangers, from vermin, beasts of prey, flesh-eating ghosts, and it is swarming with snakes and robbers, it has neither food nor water. So you must be able to experience a great deal of suffering." Thus he outwardly rejects these with a subtle device. Disgusted, they do not go with him, and turn back.

Finally, the teacher may be one of the monks who attaches weight to relations with the friendly families who feed them. All the time he goes to see them, he is kept very busy that way, and refuses those prospective pupils on the ground that, first of all, there is someone I must go and see. This also is a source of discord when this perfection of wisdom is being written and studied. This also is -seen as- Mara's work. In such ways Mara appears to bestir himself to prevent people from learning, studying, teaching and writing this perfection of wisdom. Here then, Subhuti, all these factors which prevent cooperation between guide and pupil needs be only recognized as Mara's deeds, and being so seen, one is admonished to try to avoid them.

Mara seen as Dissuading from Perfect Wisdom

Subhuti: What, O Lord, is the reason why Mara is seen to make such great efforts and bestir himself to prevent, by this or that device, people from learning and studying this process of perfection of wisdom?

The Lord: Perfection of wisdom is a beginningless and thus endless source of all-knowledge of Buddhas, the Lords, which in its turn is the source of endless devotion of Tathagatas, which leads immeasurable and incalculable beings to dissolve their defilements and obscurations by this simple revelation. So, to any, having dissolved their defilements, Mara is seen as not being able to gain entry, and this gives him cause for distress and being dispirited, and the dart of sorrow is realized as having vexed him. In consequence, as the process of this perfection of wisdom is being written and studied, he is seen as making in his great tribulation a tremendous effort, bestirring himself, and with this or that device, to attempt to prevent the study of this perfection of wisdom. Mara, the Evil One, is seen moreover, as coming along in a guise of a Sramana, a religious mendicant, and attempting to cause dissent.

In order to dissuade the ones born of good family who have but recently set out in the vehicle he will say: "This is not the great perfection of wisdom which your Honors listen to. As it has been handed down in my Sutras, as it is included in my Sutras, such is the perfection of wisdom. Thus it is seen as some 'him', or an 'other', attempting to sow doubts in the minds of the Bodhisattvas having but recently set out in the vehicle, whose intelligence is usually not too expansive, but rather sluggish and limited, who are usually lacking in vision, and whose enlightenment in any future is not as yet predicted. Seized by doubt these will not learn, study or write this perfection of wisdom. This also is seen as Mara doing this to them. Moreover, Mara may be seen as coming along in guise of a Buddha, with magically created monks around him, and maintain that some Bodhisattva coursing in profound Dharmas is one who realizes the reality-limit, and should be happy to become a Disciple and NOT a Bodhisattva, as this
Bodhisattva certainly has. This also is seen as one of Mara's deeds. Subhuti, when this perfection of wisdom is being written and studied, Mara, the Evil One, produces these deeds which I mention, as well as many others. These all may come to be seen, recognized by a Bodhisattva, and avoided, not cultivated. The Bodhisattva may come to reply to these with vigour, mindfulness and self-possession.

Antagonism between Mara and Buddha

Subhuti: So it is, O Lord. Whatever is very precious, this provokes much hostility. Because it is so superior, being hard to get, and of great value. One can herein expect as a rule many obstacles will arise to this perfection of wisdom. When, overawed by these obstacles, someone becomes lazy, one can come to know that those people who decide not to learn, study and write this perfection of wisdom are people who are seen as beset by Mara have but recently set out in the vehicle, their intelligence is small, sluggish, limited and perverted, [251] and their thought refuses to function in these very sublime dharmas.

The Lord: So it is, Subhuti. And while it is true that these deeds of Mara which we see as such are bound to arise, a great many agencies will arise in their turn which oppose the faults of Mara. Those who decide to learn, study and write this perfection of wisdom are swayed by Buddha's might, by his sustaining power, by his grace. [252] For whereas Mara, the Evil One, will be seen to make great efforts to cause obstacles, the Tathagatas in turn send help.

Chapter 12: SHOWING THE WORLD

Perfect Wisdom the Mother of All Buddhas

The Lord: It is as with a mother who has many children, - five, or ten, or twenty, or thirty, or forty, or fifty, or one hundred or one thousand. As she falls ill, we each do whatever is possible to prevent this mother from dying, to keep her alive as long as possible, to keep any unpleasantness away from her body. As we are aware of the fact to her we owe our existence, as in her own great pain she brings us into this world, as she instructs us in the way of this world.

We now look directly to her, give her anything to ease her discomfort and suffering, protect her well, make much of her, and we hope she is free from pain- derived from contact with eyes, ear, nose, tongue, body or mind, or coming from wind, bile, phlegm, or a disorder of the humours, or from stinging insects, mosquitoes, or crawling animals, from beings or from ghosts, from anything falling upon her, or tearing her asunder, or from a disastrous crash.

In this way we honor our mother by giving her all this which may ease her suffering, allow for her to know how dear she is, cherish and protect her, as we are aware she is our mother and begetter, who, in her own great pain, brings us into this world and instructs us always in the way of this world.

In just this same way Tathagatas bring this perfection of wisdom to mind, and it is through their might, sustaining power and grace we write, learn, study, spread and repeat this. And these Tathagatas, which also dwell in other world systems just now, -for the weal and happiness of all, with great compassion for all and for the weal and happiness of this great body of beings, with compassion as this absolute sameness of all beings- these bring this perfection of wisdom to mind, and are of great zeal, as this perfection of wisdom is lasting, as it is not destroyed, as what's seen as Mara and his host cannot prevent this perfection of wisdom from being taught, written, and practiced.

So fond are Tathagatas of this perfection of wisdom, as much do these cherish and protect its process of perfection. Wisdom is mother and begetter, her process of perfection indicates and reveals to us all-knowledge, her perfection instructs us as the way of the world. As her perfection do Tathagatas appear.

As her perfection begets, indicates and realizes pure cognition as all-knowing, this perfection indicates to us and as us this world as it is. This all-knowledge of Tathagatas appears as her most profound perfection.

Tathagatas of three times as well as beyond are enlightened perfection of wisdom. It is as this perfection of wisdom these Tathagatas are instructed and generated...and instruct and generate us in this world, so we may be instructed and generated...and instruct and generate as well. Thus we come, thus we go.

Flashes of enlightening and pure undifferentiated awareness, identical with absolute emptiness, this dark as pitch notion, infinite as space.

How Tathagatas Know the World

Subhuti: How does perfection of wisdom instruct Tathagatas in this world, and what is this the Tathagatas call 'world'?

The Lord: The five skandhas are by the Tathagatas declared as 'world' [loka]. Which five? Form, feeling, perception, impulse, and consciousness.

Subhuti: How do five skandhas come to be shown up by perfection of wisdom of Tathagatas, or what is shown up by her?

The Lord: Skandhas are shown and realized by this perfection of wisdom of Tathagatas as 'this world' [loka], as these do not crumble, nor crumble away [lujyante, pralujyante]. These five skandhas are emptiness as to any own-being and devoid of any own-being and sameness, inasmuch as can be said with any meaning whatsoever of emptiness, so, can neither crumble nor crumble away. As this sense, this perfect wisdom instructs these Tathagatas in this world. As emptiness can neither crumble nor crumble away, so the Signless, the Wishless, the Uneffected, the Unproduced, Non-existent, and all-completeness of any Realm of Dharma.

How Tathagatas Know Thoughts of All Beings

Moreover Subhuti, due to this perfection of wisdom, Tathagatas quite naturally know immeasurable and incalculable beings as these really are. This comes about through the inevitable dissolution of obscurations. For, herein is simultaneously revealed an increase toward, or away from pure cognition, depending on one's perspective and relationship to these six perfections and Noble Eightfold Path, primarily right intention and right action. Eventually this 'pinnacle' awareness comes about as all-knowledge. This is, however, completely different and other than bits and pieces of knowing formulated of some discursive thought process. This naked realization is of an objectless and purely undifferentiated experience of this uniform non-existence of any individualized or collective own-being within any sentience whatsoever.

Again, Tathagatas are naturally aware of thoughts and actions of immeasurable and incalculable beings, since 'here' or anywhere, in anytime, or in any way for any beings is no real existence. This indication only of some thing called existence, exists neither as separate individualities as many 'ones', nor any totality of individualities, neither any singular one, nor any grouping of two or more, and not even simply as one divided into many...because ultimately and this means even now, any beings and things are incalculable and immeasurable. And even still, Tathagatas, again due to this perfection of wisdom, are naturally aware of the collected thoughts of countless beings as only 'collected thoughts'. And how do Tathagatas come to be cognizant of this?

This is naturally cognized, for as pure awareness, this "collectedness of thought" is realized as equivalent to extinct [for, any thing called singular, lone or individual thought, etc., speaking also in terms which are 'thought of' as having an existential basis and from some 'point of view' in existence, does not exist, and is purely cognized as not-other than already as infinitely absolute by Tathagatas. But, this doesn't materialize or manifest as having been thought of. - What does matter in truth is...what is such as eventually becomes thought as any relative result of it's 'original' pristine continuum of absolution? or even, What is any thought at any 'time' or 'place' a result of, in spite or regardless of what we may think?]

This extinction is just non-extinction, as this which is realized as extinct, 'is' no-thing to be extinct and as such is merely non-extinct. Furthermore, Tathagatas are naturally cognizant of distracted thoughts of beings as such, as these Tathagatas realize 're'-occupation with any thought as mere distraction, for just as objects of this world, even thought is known as external, and a grave distraction from this sourceless-source of which these are spontaneously manifest with neither time nor limitation. Not even mindfulness can be effortlessly directed as such toward this realm of Dharma. For even as in this consideration of 'the one divided into many', ...in truth, what is this dreamed of 'one anything' other than, as a basis (?), from which to determine its singularity? As here is no-thing other than this 'one', this 'one' has no-thing or support upon which to lean to determine either itself, or any phenomena whatsoever as this or these dharmas. So as even one cannot be determined as such, how much more so hundreds of ones? How much more so hundreds of thousands of ones? How much more so hundreds of thousands of niyutas of kotis of ones? Such is what is meant as immeasurable and incalculable. Such, in this true aspect is infinite. This 'one', all 'ones', are exactly identical as being only an instantaneous reflection of an inexplicable and spontaneous interdependence merely seeming to be individuated by habits coming to be established from beyond any thought or knowledge of this process of reification, hereby 'creating', first of all, this duality called thought itself, (ignorance) so as to attempt to determine some separateness of an illusion of even this non-existent oneness...an appearing of some thing, from the essentially pure infinite space/awareness as ground of any and all being. Suchness is a wholeness at once of space and primordial awareness. Here is neither one nor parts of one, neither many individual ones nor none. As Suchness is beyond thought and measurement, Such is as Suchness is.

On another hand, Tathagatas realize these thoughts as ultimate reality, and as such are without marks, cannot extinguish, just as any true continuity is not interrupted, not distracted. These cannot, as emptiness, be directed on external objects. Tathagatas are cognizant of and realize the infinite and inexhaustible mind of being, of be-ness. Tathagatas are aware, as compassion. All beings are understood, for as cognizant mind these buddhas naturally realize immeasurable non-extinction of space as immeasurable non-extinction of mind. Buddha-Mind as this infinite continuum is neither produced nor sustained in any time, cognizes neither production nor cessation, neither gives nor requires any support. As infinity cannot be measured, as inexhaustible is Dharma. Tathagatas realize obscured minds and the cause of obscuration. Such as Tathagatas realize these minds of people are not actually obscured by perverted views, which, as nothing other than wrong ideas, are also not sustained. Tathagatas realize unobscure thoughts. Tathagatas see these minds being transparently luminous as essential original nature. Tathagatas realize slack thoughts as well as the reasoning by which they occur. Tathagatas realize these thoughts are unable to slouch on any resting place. Tathagatas cognize tensely active thoughts as these are. A Tathagata realizes these thoughts are exerted so as to win dispassion, and these can no longer be exerted when nothing is left which can be seized upon.

Tathagatas realize thoughts as outflows. As such one realizes even these thoughts as without own- being, as false representations of no-thing. Tathagatas realize thought as this is merely as this might seem. Anyone merely aware comes to realize, as an outflow any thought is non-existent. As continuity is pure, no-thing neither is nor is not directed, or not. Tathagatas realize any thoughts such as these merely seem to be, yet are not as these are.

Tathagatas realize a greedy mind is not mind as empty awareness, as mind is not a greedy mind. Tathagatas realize 'any' mind as free from greed. Such as these realize any mind as with thoughts of greed is not a greedy mind, as thought of greed and even mind non-exist as 'true reality', as mind which forsakes greed is not greed, nor even mind as detached from greed. Tathagatas naturally realize minds as greedy and as free from greed. These realize in the same manner, minds as hateful and as free of hate, as deluded, as well as without delusion. Tathagatas as awareness realize any thoughts of beings. Tathagatas realize thoughts as not joined to this world of appearance, as these do not appear as the world of appearance. Tathagatas realize extensive or abundant thoughts. Tathagatas realize thoughts neither diminish nor increase; as thoughts cannot depart. For thought cannot do so as thoughts cannot be other than this realm of Dharma, thus is here no-where here and nothing outside this to even consider, inasmuch as thought merely could. Tathagatas realize thoughts as neither great, as this which these may be, nor lacking as this which these may not. These Tathagatas realize these thoughts neither come hither nor go away, as any reality such as thought, is not included in the present as such.

Tathagatas realize thoughts which are thought of as great, merely appear different, as any and all are the same, for such neither appears as sameness, yet neither are these different, nor do these exist in any form of own-being whatsoever. For here, any thought which is thought of as 'here' is no thought nor other, nor even awareness as present. Tathagatas realize thought without limitation, as such lean on nothing. Tathagatas realize thought with perceiving attributes perceive thought as own-being, for as no thought exists without perceptible attributes, still any and all thought is without marks, these are neither isolated nor not isolated as any object, nor as imperceptible, neither within nor without any range of the three or five kinds of vision. As primordial emptiness/awareness, Tathagatas realize reacting thoughts as emptiness, and as devoid of objective support as these are of subjective sustanence. Tathagatas realize non-reacting thoughts without 're'-occupation as non-dual, as neither having any own-self nor other against which to react. Tathagatas realize lower [energy] thoughts as no self-conceited imagining. Tathagatas realize supreme [infinitely energetic] thoughts as unimpeded, just as the least thought is neither apprehended nor ignored.

Tathagatas realize unconcentrated thoughts as attached to differences; [directed as faulty representations of this world as separate things, such thoughts are distracted], for any such thoughts cannot achieve synthesis, due to these being unconcentrated. Tathagatas realize concentrated thoughts as neither same nor different from dharma, for distractions dissolve, revealing synthesis, and increasingly concentrated and rarified thoughts are like unto space. Tathagatas realize this which appears as unemancipated thought is already now emancipated, as these are non-existent as 'own-being'. Tathagatas realize emancipated thoughts, as these cannot grasp any thought of any past, nor of any future, or even any present, as thought is not even present. Tathagatas realize imperceptible thoughts as neither here nor perceived as reality, as such cannot be discerned; for even as such, thought being discerned falls short of perfect reality, and such cannot be grasped, - not by the eye of wisdom, not by the heavenly eye, how much less by the fleshly eye, since it does not come within the range of any of these eyes.

Furthermore, Tathagatas naturally realize tendencies of countless beings to make positive and negative statements about objects. [269] These ideas arise in dependence on form and other skandhas. How do any beings discern dependence on these skandhas of these positive and negative statements? If we take such statements as, "Tathagatas continue to exist after death", and "Tathagatas do not continue to exist after death", and "Tathagatas do and do not continue to exist after death", and "Tathagatas neither do nor do not continue to exist after death", these statements refer to these skandhas known as 'Tathagatas' only and these statements have no basis in the true reality of Tathagatas. This holds good of similar statements, i.e. when one says: "Eternal are self and the world, -just that is the truth, everything else is delusion." And so if one maintains either self and the world are non-eternal, are both eternal and non-eternal, neither eternal nor non-eternal, such statements still refer merely to these skandhas. [270] Or, similarly, if one maintains that self and the world are finite, or not finite, or both finite and not finite, or neither finite nor not finite. Or, finally, if one says "that which is the soul, that is the body," or "one thing is the soul, another the body," all these statements refer only to skandhas. It is a result of perfection of wisdom [in verse and application] these Tathagatas realize these positive and negative statements for what these are. [271] Tathagatas cognize even skandhas as identical with Suchness.

This is how and why as a result of perfection of wisdom [in verse and application], these positive and negative statements are realized as these are. It is thus Tathagatas reveal to realization Suchness of Tathagatas, as of skandhas, as Suchness of positive and negative statements. And just as this is Suchness of skandhas, as well is this Suchness of worlds. As this is said by Tathagatas..."these five skandhas are reckoned as world(s)." So here, Subhuti, as such is Suchness of skandhas, such is Suchness of these worlds; as such is Suchness of this world, such is Suchness of all dharmas; as such is Suchness of all dharmas, such is Suchness as fruit of a Streamwinner, so on up to: as such is Suchness of Pratyekabuddhahood, such is Suchness of Tathagatas. As a result, Suchness, -Suchness of Tathagatas, of skandhas, of dharmas, of holy Disciples and Pratyekabuddhas- is just Suchness without a trace of variety such as positivity and negativity, as nothing beyond even one, non-different, non-extinguishable, unaffected, non-dual, nor with even a question of duality. [272] In humbleness and compassion of perfection of wisdom, Suchness as Tathagatas is neither realized nor not realized, as Such is as Suchness. Thus Tathagatas reveals this world to this infatuated world [as such is also] preoccupied as unreasoned passion(s). Thusly this vision of worlds takes place. Thus...perfect wisdom is mother of Tathagatas, as such spontaneously appear, neither as her result nor not. Thus...Tathagatas, neither realizing nor not realizing Suchness, cognize Suchness of worlds, as Non-falseness, as unaltered Suchness. Thus, as these neither do nor do not 'realize' Suchness [tathata] Tathagatas are called, 'Tathagata'.

Subhuti: Suchness is beyond fathom and unfathomable, O Lord. Enlightenment of Buddhas and Lords is neither brought about nor revealed through nor by Suchness, yet merely as Suchness...neither within nor without any times, any place, neither as direction nor directionless. Whoever else neither realizes nor does not realize Suchness? Any irreversible Bodhisattvas, or Arhats whose right intentions are fulfilled, or persons whom achieve as right views these fathomless stations described by Tathagatas as Suchness, as Tathagata are enlightened as these.

The Lord: So it is, Subhuti. Suchness, as Tathagatas fully neither do nor do not 'realize', is inexhaustible, as Tathagatas are purely aware [beyond thought and word...as space] of Suchness as such, and can describe Suchness as inexhaustible...for Suchness, neither fully 'realized' nor not...is infinitely pure awareness [as space...dharmakaya].

Fathomless Marks and How They are Fastened

So now, headed by Sakra, Chief of Gods, the Gods of the realm of sense-desire and of the realm of form and twenty thousand of the Gods of the realm of Brahma have come to see the Lord, salute his feet with their heads, and standing to one side, these ask: As fathomless dharmas are revealed, how, O Lord, are the marks fixed onto these? [273]

The Lord: Marks are fixed on to the fact these fathomless dharmas are empty, signless, wishless [the three doors to deliverance], not brought together, not produced, not stopped, not defiled, not purified, so, as such these non-exist, beyond even samsara and nirvana, as does also this realm of Dharma, and Suchness. As these marks are not supported by anything such are like unto space. These marks are not fixed on by Tathagatas, as these cannot be reckoned among skandhas. As these are not dependent on skandhas, such are not fixed on by Gods, Nagas nor any beings, and these cannot be shaken off by the world with its Gods, beings and Asuras. For even this world with its Gods, beings and Asuras has just this mark. No hand has fixed on these marks. Would this be correct to say space is fixed on something?

The Gods: No, Lord, as it would have to be conditioned.

The Lord: Well said, and this is true, O Gods. Regardless of whether Tathagatas are produced or not, [274] these marks stand out just as such. In accordance with what stands out, just as such Tathagatas describe this reality, as such Tathagatas fully realize it. As such are Tathagatas called 'Tathagata'.

Subhuti: Fathomless, O Lord, are these marks as Tathagatas fully realize perfection of wisdom as unattached cognition/awareness of Tathagatas. This field in this unattached cognition is perfection of wisdom, this range of Tathagatas.

The World Shown as Empty

The Lord: So it is, Subhuti. With this process of perfection of wisdom are Tathagatas instructed within worlds. As Tathagatas are spontaneously interdependent with dharma, as also with this perfection of wisdom, to this extent are these dharmas which stand without support fully realized by Tathagatas, as these take their stand nowhere. As such, these dwell interdependently as just Dharma. Tathagatas treat Dharma with respect, revere, worship and adore this, as these realize this essential nature of dharma is just perfection of wisdom. Just as all-knowledge of Tathagatas is realized as perfection of wisdom, Tathagatas are grateful and thankful for her. With justice can Tathagatas be called "grateful and thankful" [kritajna kritavedin]. With gratitude and thankfulness Tathagatas [275] favor and cherish this vehicle for such is this path by which these realize full enlightenment. One knows this gratitude and thankfulness of Tathagatas. In addition, Tathagatas fully know all dharmas as neither made [akrita] nor unmade, as not brought together. This also, one knows as gratitude and thankfulness of Tathagatas. It is as gratitude to perfection of wisdom this cognition of Tathagatas thus proceeds in all dharmas. This is another aspect of the fact this perfection of wisdom simultaneously instructs Tathagatas in this world.

Subhuti: But how can perfect wisdom instruct Tathagatas in this world if all dharmas are unknowable and imperceptible?

The Lord: It is good, Subhuti, as you question Tathagata about this matter. All dharmas are indeed unknowable and imperceptible as these are empty, and cannot lean on anything. It is thus all these dharmas are, as perfect wisdom, fully known by Tathagatas. Another reason also perfection of wisdom can be regarded as the instructress of Tathagatas in this world is that none of the skandhas is viewed.

Subhuti: How can here be a non-viewing of form, feeling, perception, impulse, or consciousness?

The Lord: As in this continuum arises merely an apparent act of consciousness which has no skandhas as objective support, here this non-viewing of form, etc., takes place. But, just this non-viewing of the skandhas is viewing of the world. This is the way in which this world is viewed by Tathagatas. Thus perfection of wisdom acts as instructress in these worlds to Tathagatas. And how does perfection of wisdom show up this world for what it is? She shows this world as empty, unthinkable, calmly quiet. As purified of itself she shows up the world, she makes it known, she indicates it, yet does nothing.

Chapter 13: UNTHINKABLE

Five Attributes of Perfect Wisdom

Subhuti: Unfathomable, O Lord, is perfect wisdom. As a great enterprise this perfection of wisdom becomes of itself when illucidated and revealed through any exceedingly refined vortex of cognition and awareness. Such comes to be simply revealed as unthinkable, incomparable, immeasurable, incalculable, ...as an enterprise equaling the unequalled.

The Lord: So it is, Subhuti. How and why does this come to be an unthinkable enterprise? Unthinkable is Tathagatahood, Buddhahood, [our] spontaneous self-existence which is at all times empty of any self or notions whatsoever, truly as this state of all-knowledge, yet still comes to be revealed as such. On such as this one cannot reflect with one's thought, since this can be neither any object as thought, nor of volition, nor of any dharmas which constitute thought. Why is it this incomparable enterprise? One cannot reflect on Tathagatahood, etc., nor compare these as such. Why is it immeasurable? Tathagatahood, etc., is immeasurable. Why is it incalculable? Tathagatahood, etc., is incalculable. Why is any enterprise equal to such as this unequalled? Nothing can equal Tathagatas, as fully Enlightened Ones, as Self-existent, as All-knowing, can anything be superior to such as these as totally equanimous?

Subhuti: Do these five attributes apply only to Tathagatahood, etc., or also to the skandhas, and to all dharmas?

The Lord: These attributes apply to skandhas as well as all dharmas also. Also the skandhas, and also all dharmas are unthinkable. As skandhas (i.e., form, feeling, perceptions, impulses, and/or consciousness) regard or 'show up' as in relation to true essential nature, here is neither thought nor volition, nor any of these dharmas which constitute thought, nor any comparing. For and as this reason, skandhas and all dharmas are also unthinkable and uncomparable. These are also immeasurable, as one cannot conceive of a measure of any nor all skandhas, since such a measure cannot itself exist as a consequence of infinitude [and as all dharmas relate to such]. These are also incalculable, as these are beyond any possibility of counting. These are also equal to the unequalled, as all dharmas are space. So do you think, Subhuti, here even exists (as related to space)...any sameness, or counting, or measure, or comparison, or thought, or any dharma which might even constitute thought?

Subhuti: No, Lord.

The Lord: In like manner Dharma is unthinkable, incomparable, immeasurable, incalculable, equal to no-thing even such as no equal...as Tathagata-dharma. Tathagata-dharma is unthinkable as all thought is as naught, is incomparable as such is beyond all comparison. Words such as 'unthinkable' and 'incomparable' denote any and all objects as consciousness as do 'immeasurable', 'incalculable' and 'equal to the unequalled'. Any measure, calculation and sameness is as naught, as Tathagata-dharma is immeasurable, incalculable, equal to no-thing as such has no equal. This is immeasurable, incalculable, equal to no-thing as this immeasurableness and incalculability is as space. Dharma is incomparable as any sense, as space is incomparable. Dharma cannot be placed side by side, as such cannot be compared. Dharma is unthinkable, incomparable, immeasurable, incalculable, equal to no-thing as such in this same sense, as space is this attribute.

Spiritual Rebirth Resulting from This Knowledge

As any doctrine of unthinkability, etc., is being taught, the minds of hundreds of monks who are ripened are freed from the outflows, without further clinging, and so are the minds of two thousand nuns in similar ripeness. [i.e., Four outflows; 1) sense-desire, 2) becoming 3) ignorance 4) false views. The extinction of these four outflows constituted arhatship.] Six thousand lay brethren and three thousand lay sisters obtain the pure, dispassionate, unstained eye of Dharma. Twenty thousand Bodhisattvas secure the patient acceptance of dharmas which fail to be produced. The Lords have predicted these to secure enlightenment in this very Bhadrakalpa [an auspicious aeon in which one thousand Buddhas are to appear]. And as to these lay brethren and lay sisters, whose dharma-eye is purified, these also are predestined by the Lords, and these also are free, without further clinging, from any outflows.

Nothing To Take Hold Of

Subhuti: Unfathomable, O Lord, is perfect wisdom. Certainly as a great venture this is set upon.

The Lord: So it is, Subhuti. All-knowledge is entrusted to perfection of wisdom, and so is these levels of a Pratyekabuddha and the level of all the Disciples. An anointed king, a Kshatriya, who feels strong and secure in his kingdom, entrusts all his business concerning his kingly office, and the city and the kingdom to his minister, and he himself has few cares and his burden is light. Just so, whatever dharmas of Buddhas, Pratyekabuddhas, or Disciples may be possible are all entrusted to the perfection of wisdom. It is the perfection of wisdom which in these does the work. It is in this manner that perfect wisdom is set upon for a great venture, i.e. so one cannot take hold of form, feeling, perception, impulse, or consciousness, nor settle down in it and so also for skandhas, so also for the fruits of this holy life, from the fruit of a Streamwinner to this state of all-knowledge.

Subhuti: In what way is perfection of wisdom set upon so one cannot take hold of this state of all-knowledge, nor settle down in this?

The Lord: Do we view Arhatship as any real dharma which we could take hold of, or settle down in?

Subhuti: No, Lord!

The Lord: So it is, Subhuti. I also do not view Tathagatahood as real, and here I do not take hold of it, do not settle down in this. For this reason all-knowledge also is a state in which one neither takes hold of anything, nor settles down in anything.

Subhuti: Bodhisattvas who have but newly set out in the vehicle, and whose wholesome roots are but small, must beware not to tremble when hearing this exposition. On the other hand, Bodhisattvas do, on hearing this unfathomable perfection of wisdom, firmly believe this as these may have become suitable for Buddhahood, have fulfilled their duties in view of the Jinas of any time, and have planted wholesome roots continuously.

The Lord: So it is, Subhuti.

Reaction of the Gods

So now...the Gods of the realm of sense-desire and of the realm of form said to the Lord: Unfathomable, O Lord, is this perfection of wisdom, hard to see, hard to understand. Bodhisattvas who resolutely believe in this unfathomable perfection of wisdom fulfill their duties in accord with Jinas of any time, must have planted wholesome roots continuously. If, O Lord, all the beings in this great trichiliocosm, for an aeon or the remainder of an aeon, course as any stage of a Faith-follower; on the other hand someone for one day only is finding pleasure in patient acceptance of this unfathomable perfection of wisdom, and as one searches this, as one reflects on this, weighs this up, investigates this and is meditating on this, this latter being unveils realization of view and knowledge as all these things.

The Lord: As someone hears, O Gods, this unfathomable perfection of wisdom, meditation, joyful effort, patience, self-discipline, generosity... then one can rightly expect one's realization to take place more quickly than realizations of those who course on any stage of a faith-follower for an aeon, or for the remainder of an aeon.

The Gods: A great perfection is this perfection of wisdom! With these words, they saluted the Lord's feet with their heads, thrice walked round the Lord, decided to go away from this presence of the Lord, took friendly leave of him, and moved away. Before these had not gone far, yet these disappeared from sight, and these Gods of the realm of sense-desire departed for the world of sense-desire, and these Gods of the realm of form departed for the Brahma-world.

Chapter 14: SIMILIES

Future and Past Rebirths

Subhuti: As a Bodhisattva, on merely hearing this, immediately believes in this unfathomable perfection of wisdom, does not become cowed, stolid, paralysed, or stupefied, does not doubt or hesitate, but delights to perfect wisdom, -where does one decease, where is one reborn?

The Lord: As a Bodhisattva reacts in such a way to perfection of wisdom, delights in seeing and hearing this, bears this in mind and develops this, keeps one's attention fixed on this without diverting it elsewhere, feels an urge to take this up, bears this in mind, speaks this, studys and spreads this, as, once one hears perfect wisdom, one follows and pursues the reciters of dharma and does not let these go, until one realizes this perfection of wisdom in one's heart or has it in the form of a book, just as a cow does not abandon her young calf, -this Bodhisattva deceases among the most superior people.

Subhuti: Is a Bodhisattva, which is endowed with just these qualities crossed in other Buddha-fields just as being reborn here?

The Lord: It is possible any Bodhisattva which is endowed with these qualities, is, just as being reborn here, crossed in other Buddha-fields, as such honors and questions Buddhas and Lords. One may also cross among Tushita Gods. This may be, as such honors Maitreya, the Bodhisattva, and persistently questions him concerning this perfection of wisdom.

Past Deeds of a Bodhisattva Who Fails in Perfect Wisdom

On another hand, as any Bodhisattva past or present hears this unfathomable perfection of wisdom and yet asks no questions, or so doing listens not to any reply, this one may be reborn among people and hear this unfathomable perfection of wisdom being taught, hesitates and is stupefied and cowed, this is one of these who are unwilling to ask questions and listen. Any Bodhisattva, again, may have had or does have a right attitude to this unfathomable perfection of wisdom, for one, two, three, four or five days, and for a certain time has faith in this, but again is withdrawn and no longer feels like asking questions about nor listening to this. It is a fact such a Bodhisattva has not or does not all the time ask questions about nor listen to and pursue this unfathomable perfection of wisdom and as such, one may at one time feel urged to pursue and hear this fathomless perfection of wisdom, but not so at other times urged to pursue and listen; such a one again falls from faith and is disheartened, as intelligence is unsteady like cotton wool. Such a Bodhisattva has but lately set out in the vehicle. Having come but lately to this vehicle, one loses faith, serene confidence and one's urge to this. In other words one no longer takes up this perfection of wisdom nor pursues it. Such a one moves on either of two levels, on the level of a Disciple, or on the level of a Pratyekabuddha.

Four Similes

As a ship is wrecked in the middle of the ocean, people die in the water without getting to shore, unless these find support on a log, or plank, or any floating object. These who manage to gain such support do not die in the water; this being so, safely and unhindered these cross over to a shore beyond, and stand, unhurt and uninjured, on firm ground. In this same way, any Bodhisattva which is endowed with but little faith, just little serene confidence, little affection, little aspiration, and which does not gain support of perfection of wisdom, incurrs a fall in the middle of a bad road, and, without having attained to the state of all-knowledge, stands in Discipleship or Pratyekabuddhahood. Different is this case for any Bodhisattva of full faith, which accepts this patiently, develops a taste for this, as full aspiration, vigour, vigilance, resolve, earnest intention, renunciation, a title which is respected, joyous zest, elation, serene confidence, affection in this, and persistence to realize full enlightenment, which gains support as perfection of wisdom; in realizing this perfection of wisdom, one stands in all-knowledge. As one uses a badly baked jar to carry water in, this jar does not last long, and actually quickly falls to pieces and melts away. In its unbaked condition this jar actually soon comes to an end on the ground. Likewise, although any Bodhisattva obtains all these qualities enumerated above, from faith to a persistent aspiration for enlightenment, as one does not take hold of perfection of wisdom and skill in means, one is bound to come to a bad fall in the middle of a bad road, in other words, one falls on this level of a Disciple or Pratyekabuddha. But, as one which carries water, from a river, or lake, or pond, or well, or any water-bearing place in a well-baked jar, a jar such as this, with the water, gets safely and uninjured to the house, simply due to the well-baked condition of this jar. Just so, any Bodhisattva, which develops not only these qualities enumerated above, but which in addition takes hold of perfection of wisdom and skill in means, does not in the middle of a bad road incur a fall, and, unhurt and uninjured, stands in all-knowledge.

A person who is exercising little intelligence launches into the water a seafaring vessel which was not caulked or repaired, and had been tied to its moorings for a long time, overloads it with goods, and climbs on board, and sets out on it. This ship is doomed to collapse before it has conveyed the goods across the water. When this ship bursts asunder, this merchant, exercising little intelligence, who is unskilled in means, loses a huge fortune, a great source of wealth. Just so a Bodhisattva with all the qualities enumerated above, but lacks perfection of wisdom and skill in means, without realizing the wealth of all-knowledge collapses midway, incurrs a fall; this Bodhisattva loses a great deal of wealth, and has also lost a great deal of wealth for others, having lost all-knowledge, which is a huge fortune and a great source of wealth; not to mention the collapse in the middle of the bad road, resulting in realization unto the level of Disciple or Pratyekabuddha. An intelligent merchant, on the other hand, constructs a solid ship and launches it with proper care into the water, loads it with goods and distributes these evenly, and with a favourable wind this vessel gradually sails to the country which is the goal of this voyage. This ship does not collapse in the water, it goes to as it is meant to go, and the merchant will win great wealth in the shape of world-like jewels. Likewise, as any Bodhisattva of peerless faith, and these other qualities enumerated above, in addition is taken hold of by perfect wisdom through her perfection and does not lack skill in means, one such as this does not collapse in the middle of a bad road, does not incur a fall, and stands fully enlightened like unto Suchness. It is a fact as a Bodhisattva with peerless faith, and the other qualities enumerated above, in addition, develops these dharmas as is taken hold of by perfect wisdom through her perfection, and does not lack skill in means, these do not hasten obscurred thought realizing the level of a Disciple or Pratyekabuddha. On the contrary these dharmas face all-knowledge, as such these set out for this, as these dissolve any obscurations to realization of full enlightenment.

As any person is aged, even advanced in years, physically weakened, say one hundred and twenty years old, and as one falls ill in one's body, could one rise from one's bed without being taken hold of by others?

Subhuti: No, Lord!

The Lord: And as one such as this does rise from one's bed, this one has not the strength to walk even for half a mile. Wasted away by both old age and illness this one does not walk about for any length of time, even as this one may be able to rise from this bed. Likewise, as any Bodhisattva as having developed all these qualities enumerated above, does not oneself come to be magnetized by perfect wisdom through her perfection, and lacks skill in means, although set out for full enlightenment, one such as this nevertheless collapses in the middle of a road, and incurrs a fall, as this one produces subtle obscurities and now realizes the level of Disciple or Pratyekabuddha. This is an unavoidable consequence of the fact of not bringing oneself to a point of being magnetized by perfect wisdom through her perfection, and is lacking skill in means. So...here now, as two strong beings take hold of this old and sick being, and carefully lift this one up, and promise this one may go wherever this one wishes, and as far as this one wishes, as these are assisting this one, and one does not fall along this way to the place one is headed to. In this same way, a Bodhisattva of peerless faith, etc., and which is assisted by perfect wisdom and her perfection, and endowed with skill in means, does not collapse in the middle of a road, does not incur a fall, and is able to reach this station, i.e. the station of full enlightenment.

Chapter 15: GODS

The Beginner's Task

Subhuti: How does a Bodhisattva which is just beginning stand in perfect wisdom... how train oneself?

The Lord: Such a Bodhisattva tends to, loves and honors good friends. Any good friends are such as instruct and admonish this Bodhisattva in perfection of wisdom, and such as expound its meaning. These expound this perfection as follows: "Come here, you born of good family, make endeavours in these six perfections. Achieve generosity, guard morality, perfect patience and exert with vigour, enter into concentration [293] or mastery of perfection in wisdom, - all this turn over for no reason. Such is nature as Suchness...unthinkable, intangible, full enlightenment. Do not misconstrue full enlightenment as form, or any skandhas. Intangible also is all-knowledge. Neither long for nor settle in any levels, as for instance, of Sravaka as Disciple or Pratyekabuddha."

It is thus Subhuti, a Bodhisattva beginning gradually through these good friends enters into the perfecting of wisdom, by, through, and from her unlimited and all permeating perfectness.

How a Bodhisattva Helps Beings

Subhuti: Doers of what is difficult are these Bodhisattvas which set out to realize fully benevolent enlightenment. Due to this practice of these six perfections as herein described, these do not wish to realize some private Nirvana of some own-being. Bodhisattvas survey these highly painful worlds of beings. These aspire to realize full enlightenment, and still these do not tremble at birth-and-death.

The Lord: So it is. Doers of what is difficult are these Bodhisattvas which set out for the benefit and happiness of worlds, out of compassion. - "We are a shelter for worlds, a refuge, a place of rest, a complete relief, islands, lights, and leaders of worlds. We equanimously reveal full enlightenment and resort to these worlds," - with these words these ones make diligent efforts to realize such full enlightenment. [294]

1. How is any Bodhisattva awakened to full enlightenment and come to be the shelter of worlds?These bring to light the nature of suffering and even by doing this, so offer protection from sufferings which belong to these deep skandhas of birth-and-death. Also these struggle and make efforts to rid the worlds of any and all sufferings, whether a hurt by some slight of heart, a bruised knee or deep and severe as causing the pains of both birth and death.

2. How are these the worlds refuge?

These reveal as free from birth, decay, illness, death, sorrow, lamentation, pain, sadness and despair any beings who are doomed to undergo these by bringing understanding of the true and complete nature of these conditions, to any beings who desire to know and are willing to listen.

3. How are these the worlds resting place?

Tathagatas demonstrate Dharma to beings so they may learn to not embrace anything whatsoever.

Subhuti: How does this non-embracing come about?

The Lord: Non-embracing comes about, or more accurately, is realized regarding form, feeling, perception, impulse, and consciousness, and is the same as in any skandhas (dharmas or phenomena). What comes to be revealed is an inherent non-arising and uniform non-sustainability, from which is non-production, and so non-stopping. [295] As no thing whatsoever CAN BE revealed in, or, of any beginning, how could any such thing stop? This is revealed and eventually realized as true of any and all skandhas -which would have been- seen, or thought of, or experienced as either thoughts, words and writings, or even actions, as these merely indicate notions only of form, feeling, perception, impulse, or consciousness of anything whatsoever as already being non-embraced. What does not exist, in truth cannot BE embraced. One thus learns not to even think to embrace anything as a result of this cognition and vision. Non-embracing is "already established" as of itself and timelessly self-existent. Once revealed, what comes about is our realization of Such. All dharmas are non-embracing for such cannot be embraced, and these are also non-arising as lacking attributes such as, coming into being (to begin with!), and consequently dwelling in time, duration and place, and ceasing to exist.

4. How are these the complete relief of worlds?

Any state of form is not form, but formless; and so beyond form, and this same fact applies to any state of feeling, perception, impulse and consciousness, and all dharmas.

Subhuti: If form, etc., and all dharmas (as any phenomena) are beyond mere appearance, as such these Bodhisattvas fully know and realize all dharmas, as here is no discrimination between them. [the gradual dawning of the realization of all-knowledge.]

The Lord: So it is. Beyond these mere appearances, here is no discrimination. Through this non-discrimination are all dharmas fully known to Bodhisattvas. This also is most difficult yet effortless, as Bodhisattvas meditate on all dharmas (at once), and neither realize [296], nor are cowed, and these meditate thus: "In this way are all dharmas fully known...and thus awakened as full enlightenment, we demonstrate and reveal these dharmas."
5. How are these the islands of worlds?

'Islands' are pieces of land limited by water, as rivers or great lakes. Just so form, etc., is only limited at its perceived beginning and end, and so are all dharmas. This limitation of all dharmas is the same as this Calm Quiet, this Sublime, as Nirvana, as this which is Really Existing, the Unperverted or Undifferentiated.
6. How are these the lights of worlds?

Here these Bodhisattvas, once having come to realize full enlightenment, cannot help but to reveal it's light and subsequent knowledge to help dispel this dark obscurity and defiled gloom of non-cognizance from beings who for long are enveloped as the membrane of this eggshell of ignorance, and overcome by darkness, so these illuminate these beings through wisdom. [297]
7. How are these leaders of worlds?

As these are enlightened, Bodhisattvas demonstrate Dharma in order to reveal this absence of production and stopping as but one attribute of infinite quintessential nature of skandhas, and also as these very same dharmas which constitute and distinguish ordinary people, Sravakas as Disciples, Pratyekabuddhas, Bodhisattvas and Buddhas, indeed all dharmas which are no dharma, yet uniform in essence and no thing in general.
8. How are these the resort of worlds?

As these are enlightened, Bodhisattvas demonstrate Dharma by teaching these skandhas are situated as one and the same as this space of worlds. All dharmas exist in equal balance and exchange, as and with space. This does not come, this does not go, this is the same as space. Space neither comes nor goes, is neither made nor unmade, nor affected; space neither stands up to, nor as such does space last, nor endure; such is neither produced nor stopped. The same is true of all dharmas which are, as this fashion of space, indiscriminate. [298] Only within mind's less refined activity as consciousness is thought lent of itself to discriminate...and such fathers this great delusion, mothers this great illusion, and begets this great suffering. Only within mind's exceedingly refined activity toward cognizance of pure spacelike awareness is thought lent of itself to reveal it's nature from beyond even uniform stillness and emptiness. As such is realized as naught, and devoid of any possible notion evolved of subjective states or objective perusal, is begotten of nothing and purely spontaneous. To even say borne of the stuff of stars, does Suchness no justice, yet provides a general directive. As this emptiness of skandhas neither comes nor goes, neither does this emptiness of dharmas, for dharmas are situated as emptiness, and situated as such these dharmas do not depart. These are situated as signless, wishless, ineffective; as non-production, no-birth, non-arising as absence of relativity and polarity, as dream and self, as this boundless, as this calm quiet, as Nirvana, as this Unrecoverable; these neither come, nor go, and are situated as immobility; these are situated as form, etc., [299] and also as full enlightenment of Arhats and Pratyekabuddhas.

Description of Perfect Wisdom

Subhuti: Who can understand this perfection of wisdom?

The Lord: Bodhisattvas which course under Tathagatas, and which mature these wholesome roots.

Subhuti: What is own-being to such as these?

The Lord: To these, own-being is isolated from any need for discipline.

Subhuti: Bodhisattvas so situated as these fully know this resort, these demonstrate and show this as available to all beings? Is it in this sense these resort to all beings? [300]

The Lord: So it is, Subhuti. It is in this sense a Bodhisattva, as one knowing full enlightenment, resorts to countless beings.

Subhuti: A doer of what is difficult is any Bodhisattva which arms oneself with this armor: "To immeasurable and incalculable beings I indicate Nirvana."

The Lord: This armor of such a Bodhisattva is, however, not connected with skandhas, nor is it put on for any sake of form, feeling, perceptions, impulses, or consciousness. It is not connected with any level of Sravakas as Disciples, or Pratyekabuddhas, or any Buddha, nor put on for any own-self nature. Truly unconnected with any and all dharma is this armor of any Bodhisattva which is armed with this great armour.

Subhuti: Three standpoints one does not aspire to as a Bodhisattva which is armed with this great armor and which courses thus in unfathomable wisdom. Which three? The level of a Sravaka, or, Disciple, or of a Pratyekabuddha, or of a Buddha. [301]

The Lord: For what reason do you say this? This is, of course, impossible, here cannot be any Bodhisattva belonging to either vehicle of the Sravakas as Disciples or Pratyekabuddhas. But, since ones such as these put on this armor to benefit all beings, these truly aspire to become Buddhas.

Subhuti: Fathomless, O Lord, is perfect wisdom as such is perfection. This cannot be developed by anything, nor by anyone, nor is anything or anyone to be developed. As perfect wisdom nothing whatsoever has been brought to perfection. The development of perfect wisdom is like development of space, or all dharmas, or non-attachment, the infinite, what is non-arising, or has no-taking-hold-of.

The Lord: So it is as you say, any Bodhisattva making adjustments toward unfathomable and perfect wisdom is regarded as irreversible unto realization. Now, as such a Bodhisattva does not and cannot settle down within unfathomable and perfect wisdom, nor in the declarations or counsels of others; one does not merely go by 'someone else' whom one puts one's trust in. As fathomless perfection of wisdom is taught, one is not cowed, or stolid, nor does one turn one's back; one does not tremble, nor manifest fright or terror; one does not hesitate nor doubt, nor get stupefied, but one is immersed in and fully saturated, is resolutely intent, and delights in being totally permeated in and by this vision and hearing. One knows in a former life already one explores perfection of wisdom. As now, as unfathomable perfect wisdom is taught as her perfection, one does not tremble, is not frightened, nor terrified.

Subhuti: By means of what mode does any Bodhisattva which does not tremble as this unfathomable perfection of wisdom is taught apperceive perfect wisdom?

The Lord: A Bodhisattva apperceives perfect wisdom through a series [of thoughts] which are inclined toward all-knowledge. Such is this process of perfection of wisdom.

Subhuti: How does one apperceive such a series of thoughts? [303]

The Lord: As a series of thoughts which indicate space, are prone to space, steadily yield non-substance as space. This apperception is realized as a series of thoughts which indicate full awareness. And why? Full awareness is immeasurable and unlimited. What is immeasurable and unlimited...this is not form, nor any skandha. This is not attainment, nor reunion, nor getting anywhere; not any path nor its fruit; not cognition, nor consciousness; no genesis, nor destruction, nor production, or passing away, or stopping, neither development, nor annihilation. Such is not made by anything, nor does this come from anywhere, such does not go to anywhere, as such does not stand in any place or spot. On the contrary, such can merely be indicated as "immeasurable, unlimited." As immeasurable infinite space is immeasurable full, or infinite awareness. This is immeasurableness as such does not, nay cannot lend itself to being fully known by anything, be it form, or any skandha, or any of these six perfections. Form is all-knowledge, and so are the skandhas, and even these six perfections.

Here now, Sakra approached [304] and said: Unfathomable, O Lord, is perfect wisdom. It is impossible to fully fathom, impossible to fully see, impossible to fully cognize or understand. This thought of Tathagatas which considers this depth of dharma, and who, seated on this terrace of enlightenment, has just realized full enlightenment, is inclined to carefree non-action, and not to demonstration of dharma.

The Lord: So it is. Deep certainly is this dharma I fully know. Nothing has been, or will be, or is fully known, and such is this unfathomable depth of this dharma. This dharma which I fully know is unfathomable as the depth of space, beyond the depth of the self, the depth not-coming of all dharmas, and of their not going. [305]

Sakra: It is wonderful, O Lord, it is astonishing, O Well-Gone! As contrary to the ways of the whole world is this dharma demonstrated, - it teaches one not to seize upon dharmas, yet this world is wont to grasp at anything.

Chapter 16: SUCHNESS

Tathagata-Suchness

Subhuti: As non-observation of all dharmas, to be sure, is this dharma set forth. Nowhere is this dharma obstructed. Identical with space this dharma is, beyond even ultimacy marked with non-obstruction, as no trace can be purely cognized of such prior to, during, or after, any dharma which is indicated only by, what's best described as objective observation and appearance. When purely cognized unconditionally, dharma (as all phenomena whatsoever) comes to be revealed as some 'thing' which can only seem to be what it is, yet neither is nor can be what it seems. No-dharma exists as such yet all dharmas are. At what seems the very least, perception will vouch for such. Yet, perception 'itself' is identical with this mysterious dharma. These are 'all' identical. So now, any dharmas -as- such, cognized -in- such cannot be purely cognized as other -than- such. So, here is no counterpart, as pure emptiness without any second, nor even a first from which a second might be determined Such is incalculable, beyond number, immeasureable, truly infinite...purely no-thing whatsoever. Here is no opponent, as such is beyond all opposites. Such as this is appears without a trace. Here can be no cause, indeed, here is no cause to become as such. This is non-produced (as, by some other acting as producer, or doing something to produce), as here is no occasion such as rebirth from some thing other than what this simply is. Here can be no path, as in truth no path exists which can be cognized.

Sakra and the Gods: Born as this image of the Lord is Disciple holy Subhuti, this Elder. Whichever dharma Subhuti demonstrates is merely indicated, truly an emanation of emptiness. [307]

Subhuti: As he is not born is Subhuti the Elder born as this image of Tathagata. He is born as this reflection of Tathagatas Suchness. As neither coming nor going, so Subhuti, of Suchness neither comes nor goes. With nothing whatsoever to establish any beginning, Subhuti the Elder simply is this Tathagatas Suchness. Suchness as Tathagata and Suchness as all dharmas is this same thing...these are 'both' Suchness and same as Subhuti this Elder. This image as Subhuti the Elder is Suchness; hence this same manner of Tathagatas.

Yet, Suchness is also empty of anything as Suchness, so as this non-image of

Suchness Subhuti emanates. It is in this sense Elder Subhuti is emanated as this image of Tathagatas as a result of the non-establishable order of Suchness of Tathagata. Subhuti's Suchness is immutable and unchangeable, undiscriminated and undifferentiated Suchness of Tathagatas. Thusly Subhuti this Elder, immutable, unchangeable, undiscriminated, undifferentiated, through this Suchness, is this very image of any and all Tathagata.

So again, just as this Suchness of Tathagatas, immutable and undifferentiated, is nowhere obstructed, so also Suchness of all dharmas is immutable and undifferentiated. Suchness of Tathagatas, and this Suchness of all dharmas, are infinite and unlimited Suchness, neither two, nor any division of any one is possible. A non-dual Suchness, however, is nowhere, is 'from' nowhere, 'belongs to' nowhere. It is as it is Suchness belonging nowhere it is non-dual. Here through non-producible Suchness this Elder Subhuti is emanated even as non-image of all Tathagatas. Non-producible Suchness, however, is no time not Suchness [308] and non-dual. It is in this non-sense [be careful with this!] Elder Subhuti emanates as any and all imagery of 'the race' of Tathagatas beyond any and all phenomena. As Suchness of Tathagata is undiscriminated and undifferentiated, at all times and in all dharmas, so Suchness of the Eminent Subhuti.

For this reason, although this seems a duality in which Subhuti has been conjured up from Suchness of Tathagatas, nevertheless nothing is lopped off 'from' any Suchness, which as unbound infinity devoid even of any center or direction, remains perfect and unbroken, as one cannot apprehend any real OR imagined outside agent which could break such apart. In this sense is the Eminent Subhuti the Elder [as other than Eminent] emanated as this image of any Tathagata.

As Suchness of Tathagata cannot be other than, or outside Suchness of any and all dharmas, so also Suchness of Subhuti. So also, whatever is, or appears as outside Suchness of dharmas, this is nothing which is not also Suchness. Suchness of Subhuti is here just the same as Suchness of all dharmas, Suchness of all Tathagatas. Subhuti the Elder undergoes this experience of Suchness of all dharmas. As such an emanated image of Suchness is Subhuti called "emanated such as Tathagatas." It is also by and as Suchness of Tathagatas [and not only his own] he conforms to Suchness. It is just through Suchness of Tathagatas he conforms to any 'past' Suchness, as it is also through any 'past' Suchness he conforms to Suchness of Tathagatas. Likewise with future and present dharmas as Suchness. It is through Suchness of Tathagatas he conforms to any such 'thing' as past, future and present Suchness, and it is through any past, future and present Suchness he conforms to Suchness of Tathagatas. In this sameness of elucidation, Suchness of Subhuti, and any past, future and present Suchness, and Suchness of the Tathagatas, are not two, nor any division such as any past, future, or present. Suchness of any and all dharmas and Suchness of Subhuti are anywhere or as anyway not two, nor any division. [309] And also, Suchness of the Lord as he is a Bodhisattva is Suchness of the Lord as he realizes full enlightenment. And this is same Suchness through which any Bodhisattva, as one definitely realizes full enlightenment, comes to be called a 'Tathagata'.

The Earth Shakes and Many Are Saved

As this disquisition of Suchness of the Tathagatas takes place, the great earth shakes in six ways, stirs, quakes, is agitating, resounding and tumbling, as Tathagata remove any obstruction to full enlightenment.

Subhuti: It is thus, O Gods, Subhuti the Elder is emanates as this formless form of Tathagata. But he is not emanated as an image of form, nor any fruits of a holy life, from the fruit of a Streamwinner to Buddhahood. As any dharmas which may appear to be born after the image of anything, or in any image of which these may appear to be born, do not exist, still are these not got at, thusly Subhuti the Elder emanates in the image of Tathagata.

Sariputra: Suchness, O Lord, courses beyond even depth!

The Lord: So it is, Sariputra.

Yet as this disquisition of Suchness is expounded, the minds of three hundred monks are freed from the outflows, without any further clinging. Five hundred nuns obtain the pure, dispassionate and unstained dharma-eye. [310] Five thousand Gods, who in the past had made the necessary preparations, acquire this patient acceptance of dharmas which fail to be produced. And the minds of six thousand Bodhisattvas are freed from the outflows, without any further clinging.

Perfect Wisdom and Skill in Means

Sariputra knows the thoughts of these Bodhisattvas are free from the outflows, without any further clinging, and asks the Lord for the reason, or cause, of such.

The Lord: These Bodhisattvas honor five hundred Buddhas, and during all this time are generous, disciplined, perfecting patience, exercise diligence, and concentration. But these are not upheld by perfect wisdom and lack in skill in means. And so, although these gain this path of emptiness, course in Signlessness, put their minds to work on Wishlessness, yet still wanting skill in means these realize the reality limit, and come forth on the level of Sravaka Disciple or Pratyekabuddha, still not coming forth toward the level of a Buddha. Suppose here is a very huge bird, one hundred, or up to five hundred miles large, but without any wings, or with crippled or damaged wings. This bird now wants to fly down to Jambudvipa from the Heaven of the Gods of Thirty-three. In intermediate space, the middle of its journey [311] to Jambudvipa, it wants to return to the Gods of Thirty-three, is it able to do so? Sariputra: No, Lord.

The Lord: And can it hope to come down on Jambudvipa without damage or injury?

Sariputra: No, Lord. It is bound to get damaged and injured, and as it drops down on Jambudvipa it incurrs death or deadly pain. Just the fact that, whereas its body is huge, the strength of its wings is insufficient, so it just drops down from above.

The Lord: So it is, Sariputra. Even as a Bodhisattva, after one raises one's mind to full enlightenment, for countless aeons, gives gifts, shows discipline, perfects patience, exercises diligence, and has excellent concentration, how ever great this setting forth and this thought raised to full enlightenment, -as one is not upheld by perfect wisdom and lacks skill in means, one is bound to fall on the level of Sravaka Disciple or Pratyekabuddha. Furthermore, Sariputra, it may be as this Bodhisattva brings to mind, and retains in one's mind, [312] of the Buddhas and Lords, past, future and present, the self-discipline, the concentration, the wisdom, the emancipation, the vision and cognition of emancipation, -but all this after the manner of a sign, this sign being an object of attention, a basis of recognition, or some such occasion for entrancement. This one now neither knows nor sees self-discipline of Tathagatas, nor their concentration, or wisdom, or emancipation, nor their vision and cognition of emancipation. Ignorant of these, blind to these, one hears this word 'emptiness', treats this as a sign, and wishes to covert [this (imagined) mass of merit] over into full enlightenment [which one regards as emptiness]. As consequence such a one as this remains on the level of a Sravaka Disciple or Pratyekabuddha, -as the fact is, this one is not upheld by perfect wisdom, and as well does this one lack in skill in means, both more silent than a whisper, and a gentle wind from space providing innate guidance.

Sariputra: As I understand the meaning of the Lord's teaching, although a Bodhisattva is joined to a huge carriage of merit, as long as this one is not upheld by perfect wisdom and is without skill in means, such a one lacks the good friend, and this one's attainment of full enlightenment is uncertain. A Bodhisattva aspiring to reveal full enlightenment for others and self, in this develops this perfection of wisdom, even as skillful means.

The Lord: So it is, Sariputra.

Sakra and the Gods: Unfathomable, O Lord, is perfect wisdom! Difficult to win, exceedingly hard to win is full enlightenment!

The Lord: So it is, O Gods. Deep is this perfection of wisdom. Difficult to win, exceedingly hard to win is full enlightenment, as one is weak in wisdom, below the mark in diligence and resolve, unskilled in means, and as one serves friends who have less than good intent and action.

Enlightenment and Emptiness

Subhuti: How is it the Lord says full enlightenment is difficult to know , exceedingly difficult to acknowledge, as here is no one who can get at enlightenment? As emanations of emptiness are all dharmas, no dharma exists which is able to win enlightenment. All dharmas are empty. This dharma for the forsaking of which dharma is demonstrated, this dharma does not exist. As well is this dharma which [314] might have been enlightened in full enlightenment, and this which could have been enlightened, and this which might have cognized [the enlightenment], and this which could have cognized such, -all these dharmas are empty. In this manner I am inclined to think that full enlightenment is easy to win, not hard to win.

The Lord: As this cannot possibly come about is full enlightenment difficult to obtain, attain, or get at, as in reality this enlightenment is not here, for this can neither be discriminated nor figured as any base or ultimacy whatsoever, as this is not fabricated [in either reality or false appearances].

Sariputra: As this is empty is this hard to win, O Subhuti. Such does not occur to space as winning full enlightenment. As such...for instance, as without own-being...any and all dharmas are [already] known in enlightenment. All dharmas are space. And, Subhuti, if full enlightenment were easy to win, then countless Bodhisattvas would not turn away from this. As countless Bodhisattvas do turn away from this, here one can discern [315] full enlightenment is hard to win, exceedingly hard to win.

Subhuti: But, Sariputra, does form, feeling, perception, impulse, or consciousness, turn away from full enlightenment?

Sariputra: No, Subhuti.

Subhuti: Is this dharma which turns away from full enlightenment other than form, etc.?

Sariputra: No, Subhuti.

Subhuti: Does Suchness of form, etc., turn away?

Sariputra: No, Subhuti. [316]

Subhuti: Is this dharma which turns away from full enlightenment other than the Suchness of form, etc.?

Sariputra: No, Subhuti.

Subhuti: Does form, etc., know full enlightenment?

Sariputra: No, Subhuti.

Subhuti: Is the dharma which knows full enlightenment other than form, etc.?

Sariputra: No, Subhuti.

Subhuti: Does Suchness of form, etc., know full enlightenment?

Sariputra: No, Subhuti. [317]

Subhuti: Is the dharma which knows full enlightenment other than the Suchness of form, etc.?

Sariputra: No, Subhuti.

Subhuti: Should form, etc., be known in full enlightenment, or any dharma other than form, etc. [318] or the Suchness of form, etc., or a dharma other than the Suchness of form, etc.?

Sariputra: No, Subhuti.

Subhuti: Does Suchness turn away from full enlightenment?

Sariputra: No, Subhuti.

Subhuti: Is some dharma which turns away from full enlightenment in Suchness?

Sariputra: No, Subhuti. [319]

Subhuti: What, Sariputra, is this dharma which turns away from full enlightenment, as we consider this as standing in this nature of dharmas, which is just emptiness, as so to is this manner of taking no stand in any dharma? Or what dharma is this Suchness? Is it perhaps Suchness is turned away?

Sariputra: No, Subhuti.

Subhuti: As thus in ultimate truth and as things stand, no dharma is apprehended as real, what is this dharma which is turned away from full enlightenment?

Sariputra: As one adopts this method of considering dharmas as ultimate reality, which Subhuti the Elder uses in this exposition, indeed here is no dharma which turns away from full enlightenment. But now, Venerable Subhuti, here is no longer any ground for the distinction of these who set their hearts on enlightenment into three kinds of persons, who differ with respect to the vehicle which these have chosen, as described by the Tathagata. According to this exposition of the Venerable Subhuti, here is only one vehicle [for those whose hearts are set on enlightenment], this being the Buddha-vehicle, the Bodhisattva-vehicle, the great vehicle.

Purna: First of all the Venerable Sariputra must ask the Venerable Subhuti the Elder whether he admits even one single kind of being whose heart is set on enlightenment, and who uses either the vehicle of the Sravaka Disciples, or that of the Pratyekabuddhas, or the great vehicle.

Sariputra: Subhuti, do you admit even one single kind of being whose heart is set on enlightenment, and who uses either the vehicle of the Disciples, or that of the Bodhisattvas, or the great vehicle? [320]

Subhuti: Sariputra, do you see as Suchness of Suchness even one single being whose heart is set on enlightenment [i.e. as a real entity], be this one who uses the vehicle of the Sravaka Disciples, or that of the Pratyekabuddhas, or the great vehicle?

Sariputra: No so, Subhuti. Suchness, first of all, is not apprehended as of three kinds, how much less any being whose heart is set on enlightenment.

Subhuti: Is now Suchness apprehended as of one kind even?

Sariputra: Not so, Subhuti.

Subhuti: Do you now perhaps see in Suchness even one single dharma which would constitute a being whose heart is set on enlightenment?

Sariputra: Not so, Subhuti.

Subhuti: Thus in ultimate truth and as things stand, such a dharma which constitutes any being whose heart is set on enlightenment cannot be apprehended, where do you get the idea "this one belongs to the vehicle of the Disciples, that one to the vehicle of the Pratyekabuddhas, that one to the great vehicle?" Any Bodhisattva which hears this absence of difference, distinction or differentiation between the three kinds of persons who set their hearts on enlightenment, in so far as we are each and all 'encompassed' as Suchness, and do not become cowed or stolid in mind, do not turn back, now any of these one's know such as these go forth to enlightenment. [321]

The Lord: Well said, Subhuti. Through this might and sustaining power of Tathagata you are inspired to say this.

Sariputra: To which enlightenment, O Lord, will these Bodhisattvas go forth?

The Lord: To this full and supreme enlightenment, so difficult to win.

Requisites of Going Forth To Enlightenment

Subhuti: How does a Bodhisattva behave, how does one train, as one wants to go forth in realization to this full enlightenment?

The Lord: The Bodhisattva adopts the same attitude towards all beings, one's mind is even, equanimous towards all beings, one does not handle others with an uneven mind, but with a mind which is friendly, well disposed, helpful, free from aversion, avoiding harm and hurt, and handles others as if these were one's mother, father, son or daughter. [322] As a refuge and one able to benefit any and all beings does any Bodhisattva behave towards all beings, does one train oneself, as one wants to know full enlightenment. A Bodhisattva stands in abstention from all evil, as also one gives gifts, guards discipline, perfects patience, exerts diligence, enters into mental stabilization, achieves mastery through perfection of wisdom, surveys conditioned co-production, both in direct and in reverse order; and also one instigates, incites and encourages others to do the same. One takes the same stance in everything from the meditation on these truths, to such a stage as one reaches certainty. As a Bodhisattva this one is liberated from defilements and samsaric bondage, and as one matures any and all beings, instigates these to do the same, and incites and encourages these. As one longs eagerly for all this and trains oneself in it, so everything is uncovered to ones such as these, from form to the established order of dharma.

Chapter 17: ATTRIBUTES, SIGNS, AND TOKENS OF IRREVERSIBILITY

Various Tokens of Irreversibility

Subhuti: What, O Lord, are any attributes, tokens and signs of an irreversible Bodhisattva, and how do we know any Bodhisattva is irreversible?

The Lord: This level of 'we common people', this level of 'we Disciples', this level of 'we Pratyekabuddhas', this level of 'we Buddhas' -- these levels and we are all called the 'Level of Suchness'. Thought as well, all these are Suchness, not two, nor any one divided, neither discriminated amongst, nor undiscriminated between, a Bodhisattva is revealed as within Suchness and not other than this nature of dharma. Realizing one's firm stance as Suchness, one neither imagines nor discriminates in this. With this sense awakened is one revealed thus. Once this is realized, even if one goes away from this assembly, because one's hearing is also Suchness, one does not and cannot in any circumstance hesitate, does not and cannot become perplexed, does not and cannot doubt, and one is not stupefied by thought [concerning any or all of form, feeling, perceptions, impulses, or consciousness] as 'it is not thus'. On the contrary, one is firmly aware as 'it is just thus, just Suchness', and with this, one realizes one's being as such. Just so, one does not prattle away about everything which comes into one's head. Such a one only speaks if this is considered beneficial for another, and not if this may not. One does not look in final judgement on what others do or don't do. Endowed with such attributes, tokens and indications of Suchness, a Bodhisattva may be borne in mind as irreversible from full enlightenment.

An irreversible Bodhisattva cannot pander to Shramanas and Brahmins of 'other schools', telling these what anyone knows is worth knowing, or what anyone sees is worth seeing. [324]

A Bodhisattva pays no homage to strange Gods, offers these no flowers, incenses, etc., and cannot put one's trusts in these. A Bodhisattva is no more reborn in places of woe, nor does one ever again become a different sex. As well, Subhuti, an irreversible Bodhisattva undertakes to observe the ten avenues [ways] of wholesome action. One observes, as one instigates others to observe, abstention from taking life, abstention from taking what is not given, abstention from wrong conduct as regards sensuous pleasures, abstention from intoxicants as tending to cloud the mind, abstention from lying speech, abstention from malicious speech, abstention from harsh speech, abstention from indistinct prattling, abstention from covetousness, abstention from ill will, abstention from wrong views. [325]

It is true an irreversible Bodhisattva observes these ten ways of wholesome action, and instigates any others to observe these, incites and encourages these to do so, establishes and confirms others in these. Even in Bodhisattva dreams one never commits offenses against these ten precepts, and one does not build on such offenses in one's mind. Even in one's dreams an irreversible Bodhisattva keeps the ten wholesome paths of action present in mind. Also, as an irreversible Bodhisattva masters a text of dharma, and offers this to others, in mind one builds upon the welfare and happiness of all beings as such, and one offers this gift of dharma in common to all beings, with no distinction. [326]

What's more, as deep dharmas are taught, a Bodhisattva is not hesitant, is not perplexed, is not doubtful, is not stupefied. One only says what is beneficial, speaks gently and in moderation. One exhibits little sloth and torpor, and loses all latent biases to evil. Whether one goes out or comes back, this mind does not wander, but one's mindfulness is fixed. As one steps on this ground one knows what one does, and as one lifts up and puts down one's feet one neither loiters nor hurries but remains at ease. A Bodhisattvas robe is free from lice, one's habits are clean, one is rarely ill, and afflictions are few. In one's body these eighty thousand families of worms which are present in the bodies of other beings cannot at all develop, as these wholesome roots insure one's place within this whole world. And as these wholesome roots such as these go on increasing, in due course one gains perfect purity of body, speech and thought. [327]

Subhuti: What is known as perfect purity of thought on the part of a Bodhisattva?

The Lord: As these wholesome roots go on increasing, in due course one gains a state of mind in which one develops few cares, and is free from treachery, deceit, crookedness and craftiness. In addition this perfect purity of thought also consists in transcending through and beyond levels of Sravaka Disciples and Pratyekabuddhas, while yet facing these, and being in perfect accord with any such ways, still just as intent on mutuality and benevolence. And what's more, an irreversible Bodhisattva is not one to attach exclusivity to gain, honor, or fame, or to robes, alms bowl, lodging or medicinal appliances for use in sickness. This is not one who is full of envy and meanness. And, as profound dharmas are revealed, one does not lose heart; but intelligence grows steady, and, one's intelligence runs deep. With respect one hears Dharma from others, ever with a view to learn. All these dharmas one hears from others are united as perfection of wisdom, and also all worldly arts and professions one unites, thanks to this perfection of wisdom, as this very nature of dharma. Here is no dharma which one does not see as yoked to the nature of dharmas, and each dharma one sees is simply engaged in this effort.

Mara's Deeds

So now, Mara, the Evil One, is (only thought of as being) the one conjuring up visions of the eight great hells, with many hundreds, many thousands, many hundreds of thousands of Bodhisattvas in these, and he says to an irreversible Bodhisattva: "These Bodhisattvas, described by the Tathagata as irreversible, are reborn in these great hells. Just so you also, since you are described as irreversible, fall into these great hells. Confess this, this thought of enlightenment is an error! What is Buddhahood to you? Abandon it! In this way you avoid rebirth in the hells. As you act thus you are one who goes to heaven." As the mind of the Bodhisattva does not waver, is not put out, is certain in one's knowledge an irreversible Bodhisattva cannot possibly be reborn against one's will in the hells, this is another token of his irreversibility.

Even so, Mara, the Evil One, is seen as coming along possibly in the guise of a Shramana, and saying: "Give up what you hear up to now, abandon what you gain so far! As you follow this advice, we again and again approach you, and say to you: 'What you hear just now is not the word of Buddha. It is poetry, the work of poets. But what I here teach to you, this is the teaching of Buddha, this is the word of the Buddha.'" Upon hearing this, as any Bodhisattva wavers and is put out, one can know, such is not predicted by the Tathagata, this one is not fixed on full enlightenment, [329] as this one does not stand firmly in this element of irreversibility. But again, even as one hears these words of Mara, one does not waver, but remains as this nature of dharma, to Non-production, to Non-stopping, to the Unaffected, this is not one of these who put their trust in others.

An Arhat, a monk who has outflows dried up, does not go by what is said by merely someone else whom one trusts in, but has placed the nature of dharma directly before one's own eyes...before, or beyond, anyone or anything whatsoever...and Mara is seen as having no access to one such as this.

Just so, any irreversible Bodhisattva can neither be crushed nor inflated by beings belonging to the vehicle of Sravaka Disciples and Pratyekabuddha, and one cannot, by this very nature, backslide into the level of Disciples or Pratyekabuddhas, as any such as this are fixed on all-knowledge, and end up in perfect enlightenment. It is quite certain any Bodhisattva who stands firmly in the element of irreversibility cannot possibly be led astray by others.

So, someone may come to the irreversible Bodhisattva and say: "A journey in birth-and-death is this coursing in perfection of wisdom, and not a journey of someone who is in quest of enlightenment. If you put an end to all suffering in this very life you no longer experience all the sufferings and disappointments which are bound up with this plane of birth-and-death. Aye surely, in this very life already this personality of yours is finished, so why do you think of taking upon yourself another one [for the benefit of other beings]?" Even now the Bodhisattva neither wavers nor is put out, even as Mara himself appears to say to this one: "Just look at these Bodhisattvas which for countless aeons present the necessities of life [330] to Buddhas and Lords, which lead holy lives in the presence of countless Buddhas, which honor countless Buddhas and Lords, and question these about just this vehicle of the Bodhisattvas, asks these how a Bodhisattva should stand, hear the answer of the Tathagatas, and act on it!

"In spite of the fact these stand, course and exert as they do, this very day these do not yet know full enlightenment! These stand firm in instruction, train themselves like this, -but do not reach all-knowledge! How do you reach full enlightenment ever?" Even as one does not waver and is not put out, then Mara, the Evil One, seems to conjure up some monks in this place, and say: "These monks are Arhats, with outflows dried up. These who set out for enlightenment, in the meantime have reached Arhatship, and are established in it. How do you ever reach full enlightenment?" It is quite certain any Bodhisattva must be irreversible from full enlightenment for, as this is being said and expounded, one's mind does not waver and is not put out.

As this mind of a Bodhisattva which hears from a stranger these discouraging remarks still does not become excluded from the true nature of dharma, and one does not go back on it, as one does not change one's mind, as one recognizes these deeds of Mara as appearing for exactly what these are, it is quite impossible for one which courses correctly in these perfections not to reach all-knowledge.

Mara, the Evil One, cannot possibly gain entry to a Bodhisattva which not only courses but also trains oneself correctly, which does not lack in these practices described by Tathagatas, which is completely adjusted to this mental activity which is associated with these perfections. [331] As any Bodhisattva recognizes these deeds of Mara, as one hears discouraging remarks from strangers, one does not desist, nor slide back, nor change one's mind, and one perceives these deeds of Mara for exactly what these are, this is another token of irreversibility.

So now, an irreversible Bodhisattva does not piece together a perception of skandhas, (i.e. form, feeling, perception, impulses, or consciousness), nor produce one. As the irreversible Bodhisattva which through dharmas empty of their own marks definitely entered on this certainty of salvation, as a Bodhisattva does not apprehend even this dharma we now behold (in any moments)...so this one cannot piece it together, or produce it. One says here, "a Bodhisattva is irreversible as one patiently accepts the cognition of non-production." This is another token of irreversibility.

What's more, Mara, the Evil One, comes along in the guise of a monk and tries to deter the Bodhisattva with the words: "The same as space is this all knowledge. It is a dharma which is not, it is non-existent. Who can anoint oneself with such as this, who fully know it? Here is no one who goes forth to such, here is no one who can fully know such, nothing can be fully known, here is no one who understands, here is nothing which can be understood. Due to this fact that at all times these dharmas are the same as space, it is useless to resist, revealed and seen as a deed of Mara is this doctrine which 'one knows full enlightenment,' is not a Buddha's teaching." A son or daughter of good family now cognizes, realizes and knows this [332] kind of critical examination is seen as just a deed of Mara. After one makes this reflection, one makes one's mind firm, unshakeable, irrestible. This is another token of irreversibility.

More Tokens of Irreversibility

So now, an irreversible Bodhisattva is one inquiring even beyond, and transcending any level of Disciples and Pratyekabuddhas, and proceeding in a direction toward all-knowledge. According to plan one comes to first, second, third and fourth trance stages, and dwells within absorbtion in these four trances. One realizes complete mastery over these trances, meaning one enters into trances, but a future rebirth is not determined by their influence. It is on dharmas of the sphere of sense-desire one bases one's rebirth. This also is known as a mark of irreversibility in irreversible Bodhisattvas.

Also an irreversible Bodhisattva does not attach weight to any name, nor to renown, title or fame. One does not get attached to any [particular] name [which in any case is absent in emptiness]. One's mind remains undismayed, and interested only in the welfare of all beings. Whether one goes out or comes back, one's mind does not wander, and one remains ever mindful.

When one lives the life of a householder, one has no great love for pleasant things, and one does not want these too much. For, it is realized that it's with fear and disgust one possesses all pleasant things. [fear of the possessed item's loss, and disgust at their decrepitude or lacking being better than what it is]. Situated in a wilderness infested with robbers one would eat one's meals in fear, and with the constant thought [333] of getting away, of getting out of this wilderness, and not with repose.

Just so an irreversible Bodhisattva living the life of a householder, possesses pleasant things simply without caring for too much for them, without eagerness, without attachment. One is not one of these people who care for dear and pleasant forms. These who live the lives of householders and who are involved in the five kinds of sensuous pleasures do not earn their living in an irregular way, but in the right way. Neither do these incur death in a state of sin, nor do these inflict injuries on others. These incite all beings to realize this supreme happiness, -these worthy beings, these great beings, superbeings, excellent beings, splendid beings, powerful of beings, sublime beings, valiant beings, heroes of beings, leaders of beings, waterlilies of beings, lotuses of beings, thoroughbred beings, Nagas of beings, lions of beings, trainers of beings! It is in this spirit which Bodhisattvas live the life of householders, in as much as these are impregnated with the power of perfection of wisdom, and this is another token of their irreversibility.

So now, Vajrapani, the great Yaksha, constantly follows behind the irreversible Bodhisattva. Unassailable, the Bodhisattva cannot be defeated by either men or ghosts. All beings find it hard to conquer one, and one's mind is not disturbed [by their attacks]. One's faculties are all complete, and one is not deficient in any of these. One possesses the organs of a virile being, [334] not those of an impotent being. One does not in any way embark on these spells, mutterings, herbs, magical formulae, medical incantations, etc., which are the work of beings. One earns one's livelihood in a clean way, not in a wrong way. One's character is neither quarrelsome nor disputatious. One's views are upright, one does not exalt oneself nor deprecate others. With these and other similar qualities this one is endowed. Such as these do not predict to women or men these will have a son or daughter. Such faulty ways of making oneself acceptable will not be this one's. All this is another token of irreversibility.

So now, Subhuti, I'll indicate the attributes, tokens and signs of an irreversible Bodhisattva. Endowed with these one is known as irreversible from full enlightenment. Again, which are these? The following: One does not give oneself over to occupation and preoccupation with the skandhas, the sense-fields, the elements, and with conditioned coproduction. One is not preoccupied with the kind of talk a person is fond of in society, with talk about kings, and robbers, about armies and battles; about villages, [335] cities, market towns, countries, kingdoms, and capitals; about oneself, about ministers and prime ministers; about women, men and neuters; about journeys, parks, monasteries, palaces, pools, lakes, ponds, lotus ponds, woods, gardens and mountains; about Yakshas, Rakshasas, Pretas, Pishacas, Kataputana-demons and Kumbhanda-demons; about food, drink, dresses, ornaments, perfumes, garlands and ointments; about roads, crossroads, streets, markets, palanquins and people; about songs, dances, tales, actors, dancers, and wandering singers; about the ocean, about rivers, about islands.

These do not devote themselves to talk which obstructs dharma, to the kind of talk which delights the common people, but to talk on perfection of wisdom, and these are people who do not lack in mental activities which are associated with all-knowledge. But talk about fightings and strife, about quarrels and disputes these avoid. These are willing for what is right, and not willing for what is wrong. These praise without causing dissension, and not in order to cause dissension. These want friendship, and not its opposite. These speak dharma, and not its opposite. These plan to gain a vision of Tathagatas which dwell in other world systems, and thus these increasingly produce thoughts which lead to their presence. According to plan these are come near them, and so these do not lack in the vision of Tathagatas, [336] nor in opportunities for honoring and serving them. Furthermore, as an irreversible Bodhisattva definitely terminated one's existence among the Gods, -whether these belong to the sphere of sense-desire, or the sphere of form, or the formless sphere, -one is turned over to just this middle region, in Jambudvipa. For in the border countries are only a few beings with a good knowledge of the arts, of poetry, of mantras, of secret lore, of the standard treatises, of portents and of the meaning of religion, but in the middle region these are turned to abundance. But any who are turned over to the border regions these are at least revealed again in the big towns. This is another mark of irreversibility.

Furthermore, to an irreversible Bodhisattva it does not occur to ask oneself whether one is irreversible or not. No question about it arises, as one is not uncertain about the stage one made, and one does not sink down below such. Just as a Streamwinner has no hesitations or doubts about the fruit of a Streamwinner, if that is the stage which is this one's right, just so an irreversible Bodhisattva neither questions nor doubts about being on this stage of a Bodhisattva, as this stage is one's right stage, here is no uncertainties about this stage which is right, nor does one sink below such. And one quickly sees through any deed appearing as Mara's that may arise, and does not come under his sway. [337] A person who commits one of the deadly sins never again, until one's death, loses this thought of this action, one cannot get rid of it or remove it, but it follows after one until the time of one's death. Just so this irreversible mind of an irreversible Bodhisattva learns to stand firm on this irreversible stage which is one's right, and even this whole world, with its Gods, beings and Asuras, cannot deflect, divert or diverge such a one from this. One recognizes any deeds as being -only seen to be- of Mara which may arise, as these do, and does not come under their sway.

One such as this is free from hesitations and doubts about this stage which any can realize, even after one passes through this present life the thoughts which are characteristics of Disciples and Pratyekabuddhas do not arise in beings such as this. As one passes through this present life one thinks: "Here is not a case in which any shall not realize full enlightenment. Anyone is sure to realize full enlightenment, I stand firm on this stage which also I realize as such."

One can no longer be led astray by others, and on the stage which is anyone's by nature, one can neither be crushed nor inflated, if one in one's nature adheres to the principle of Suchness in and as all, and beyond even such, as such is. For, as one stands firm on this, one's mind is insuperable, one's cognition is insuperable. Suppose Mara, the Evil One, in the guise of Buddha himself were to come to this one, and say: "Realize Arhatship in this very life! You are not predestined to full enlightenment. You have not the attributes, tokens and signs with which a Bodhisattva must be endowed in order to realize full enlightenment. Why now do you course in this?"

If the Bodhisattva now experiences a change of heart, one can know one is not predicted to full enlightenment by the Tathagatas of the past. [338] On the other hand, as one considers, "I see this, surely, as Mara, the Evil One, who comes along after he by magical means, adopts the disguise of the Buddha, as all are beset by Mara, this is but one of Mara's magical creations, but certainly not Tathagata. A Tathagata speaks to the effect as one not realizing only Arhatship, and not otherwise," as one sees and understands "I see this, surely, is as Mara, the Evil One, who is manufacturing a magical double of the appearance of the Buddha, and who wants to estrange any and all beings from supreme enlightenment," and now at this Mara turns back...this Bodhisattva certainly in the past is predicted to full enlightenment by the Tathagatas, and stands firmly in this irreversible Bodhisattva stage. Where these attributes, tokens, and signs are found as a Bodhisattva, here one can be certain, beyond any shadow or doubt of this: -as one exudes these qualities, so this one is predicted by Tathagatas in the past, and stands firm on this irreversible Bodhisattva-stage and as one exudes such attributes, tokens and signs of an irreversible Bodhisattva this is another token of irreversibility. In addition to this...an irreversible Bodhisattva gains this good dharma even as this costs one one's life and any belongings. Here one makes a supreme effort to gain this good dharma, through affection and respect for Buddhas and Lords, past, future and present. In one's firm conviction- "the Dharma-bodies are Buddhas and Lords"...one realizes this good dharma not only of the past Buddhas and Lords, but also of the present and future Buddhas and Lords. One is convinced as one also is within the ranks of these which are reckoned as future Buddhas and Lords, ...as one also is predicted to this supreme enlightenment, also one is known as already having gained this good dharma. So, these considerations one bears in mind as, in one's efforts to gain this good dharma, one renounces even one's life and one's belongings, as one does not lose heart, nor become indolent. This is another token of irreversibility. Moreover, as Tathagata demonstrates dharma, an irreversible neither hesitates nor doubts.

Subhuti: Does one also neither hesitate nor doubt when a Disciple demonstrates dharma?

The Lord: No, such a one does not. For a Bodhisattva which acquires this patient acceptance of dharmas which fail to produce, or be productive or produced, neither hesitates nor doubts as one hears about this unobstructed true nature of all dharmas. Endowed with these virtues a Bodhisattva is irreversible. These also are known as the exudation of attributes, tokens and signs of a Bodhisattva which is irreversible from full enlightenment.

Chapter 18: ~EMPTINESS ~

Unfathomable Stations

Subhuti: This is wonderful, O Lord, how great and with what unlimited and measureless qualities a Bodhisattva is endowed!

The Lord: So it is, Subhuti. Irreversible Bodhisattvas come to reveal TO self and others pure, undifferentiated cognition as non-produced, innate and simply beyond any conceptual fixations AS 'self and others', and still just beyond any notions born OF these [skandhas]. Suchness comes to be realized as it's truth of center-lessness, boundary-lessness, beginning- and thus end-lessness, and to which Sravaka Disciples and Pratyekabuddhas as yet have no claim.

Subhuti: Truly beyond any convention or standard whatsoever the Lord can and does expound how an irreversible Bodhisattva represents and emanates these attributes, tokens and signs. So now might the Lord indicate these unfathomable positions of Bodhisattvas as are connected through inconceivable perfect wisdom?

The Lord: Well said Subhuti. Surely, you bring up unfathomable positions as you want to hear discoursing on this subject as well. "Unfathomable", Subhuti, is Emptiness which is a synonym of Signlessness, Wishlessness, Uneffectedness. Such is Unproduced, as in...No-birth, Non-existent, Dispassioned of Cessation, Nirvana and Departing. [342]

Subhuti: Is this a synonym only of these, or of all dharmas?

The Lord: Indeed Subhuti, such is a synonym of all dharmas, as form, feeling, impulses, perception and consciousness, is unfathomable. Choose any dharma or dharmas whatsoever, and 'unfathomable', among all such and unlimited is synonymous with and as such. How are any and all skandhas unfathomable? Just as unfathomable as Suchness, so unfathomable is any and all skandhas. As unfathomable Suchness is any and all skandhas, etc., to include nothing throughout, even as no skandha...so completely unfathomable is form, feeling, perception, impulse and consciousness. Even as here is no form, etc., this is the fathomlessness of form, etc.

Subhuti: Such is wonderful, O Lord, how subtle a device is -such- as allows for this relativity of form, etc., and indicates Unfathomable Nirvana at this same time.

How to Attend to Perfect Wisdom

The Lord: As a Bodhisattva reflects, ponders and meditates on these unfathomable positions which are connected through inconceivable perfect wisdom, and strives to stand, train and progress as is ordained, described and explained in this perfection of wisdom, [343] now, as one may do so for, say, one day only, how great the deed is which one does during this one day! As a person, moved by considerations of greed, had made a date with a handsome, attractive, and good-looking other person, and as now this other person is held back by yet something or other and could not leave one's house, what do you think, Subhuti, with what would this other person's preoccupations be connected?

Subhuti: With this other person, of course. One thinks about this other one coming, about things these do together, and about joy, fun and delight one has with the other.

The Lord: Does this person entertain many such ideas in the course of this day?

Subhuti: Many indeed, O Lord.

The Lord: As many such ideas as this person entertains in the course of this day, so for each vibration comprising each of the thoughts from each idea, hundreds, thousands, hundreds of thousands of kotis of aeons for each of these vibrations, a Bodhisattva spurns birth-and-death, turns one's back on it, and has resolve enough to end this.

Merit

As one stands, trains, progresses, meditates and strives as is ordained, described and explained in this perfection of wisdom, one's faults and obscuring defilements dissolve which are a turning away from full enlightenment. [344] As one Bodhisattva gives one's self up to devotion to perfect wisdom, and does deeds for one day only while dwelling completely in mental activities connected with perfect wisdom; and yet another Bodhisattva lacks connections with perfect wisdom, but gives gifts for countless aeons...more discretely refined attributes has the Bodhisattva which, for one day only, makes endeavours connected with perfect wisdom. A Bodhisattva which for one day only makes endeavours connected with perfect wisdom, begets merit other than the greatest merit of another Bodhisattva which for countless aeons gives and bestows gifts on all classes of holy persons, -from Streamwinners to Tathagatas - but lacks this discretion regarding perfect wisdom. And, as the other Bodhisattva not only bestows gifts as indicated, but in addition observes these moral precepts, but still lacks in connecting these with perfect wisdom, this Bodhisattva which dwells in connection with perfect wisdom, begets other merit, as this one emerges from this mental work on perfect wisdom, and demonstrates dharma. And this remains true [345] even as the other Bodhisattva in addition were endowed with patience. Even as in addition the other Bodhisattva exerts vigour, and makes endeavours about the trances and wings of enlightenment, but is still lacking connections in perfect wisdom...a Bodhisattva which, as one gives this gift of dharma, as said before, turns this over to full enlightenment, one such as this begets a different type of merit all together which benefits all sentient beings, than the Bodhisattva which yet does not make such connections in perfect wisdom. The merit of a Bodhisattva which not only gives this gift of dharma, not only turns this over to full enlightenment, but employs the kind of turning over which is being taught in this perfection of wisdom begets another type of merit indeed...beyond any reckonings whatsoever, of 'greater or lesser'. So, as a Bodhisattva which does all this, makes no further efforts than these visible and more tangible ones about it in meditative seclusion, [346] this one's merit is very great perhaps, yet still, different than this merit of one which also makes effort about this in meditative seclusion and which in addition, is taken hold of by perfect wisdom as coursing in her perfection, and now is open in this meditative seclusion, and is not devoid of perfect wisdom. The latter begets yet other merit.

Immeasurable, Empty and Talk

Subhuti: How can one say that one begets the greater merit since the Lord has described all accumulations as the result of false discrimination?

The Lord: In this case also the accumulation of merit on the part of any Bodhisattva who courses in perfect wisdom must be described as just empty, worthless, insignificant and unsubstantial. To the extent any Bodhisattva goes on contemplating all dharmas in this manner, to this extent this is one which does not lack affinities with perfect wisdom. And to the extent one does not lack affinities with perfect wisdom, to this extent one begets immeasurable and incalculable merit, beyond any tabulation of such as would result in some accumulation deemed as worth or of some value.

Subhuti: Is any distinction made or difference noticed between immeasurable and incalculable?

The Lord: Such is "immeasurable" as in such, even measurement cannot exist nor take place. Such is "incalculable" as even any sense or effort to count such is exhausted and even numbers to count such as one or many, or even as one divided into many cannot take place.

Subhuti: Is here any reason to assume skandhas (form, feeling, perception, impulse, consciousness) are immeasurable?

The Lord: Yes. [347]

Subhuti: Of what is this term "immeasurable" a synonym?

The Lord: Are not all dharmas described as "empty"?

Subhuti: Yes, and simply so, as quite empty Tathagata describes all dharmas.

The Lord: And being empty, such are also inexhaustible of emptiness. And what is emptiness is also immeasurableness. So here and now, according to ultimate reality, neither distinction nor difference is apprehended between dharmas, nor can any 'between' dharmas even begin to be assumed. As talk these are described by Tathagata. One merely talks as one speaks of "immeasurable", or "incalculable", or "inexhaustible", or of "empty", or "signless", or "wishless", or 'this Unaffected", or "Non-production", "no-birth", "non-existence", "dispassion", "cessation", "Nirvana". This exposition is being described by Tathagata as the consummation of demonstrations. [348]

Subhuti: It is wonderful to see such an extent to which Tathagata demonstrates true nature of dharmas, and yet one cannot properly talk about true nature of dharmas, [in any sense of even predicating distinctive attributes to truly non-existent separate real entities around and through us]. As I humbly understand this meaning of Tathagatas teaching, neither any nor all dharmas can be talked about, in any proper sense.

The Lord: So it is, for none can properly express emptiness of dharmas in words, and ever and always can such, be merely indicated.

Neither Growth nor Diminution

Subhuti: Can something truly have growth, or diminution, as it is beyond all distinctive words, and even characteristics?

The Lord: No Subhuti.

Subhuti: But, as no growth or diminution occurs of any entity or dharma which is beyond all distinctive words and even characteristics, so also can neither growth nor diminution of these six perfections occur. And now, how does a Bodhisattva realize full enlightenment through the force of these six perfections, as these do not grow, and how does one even come close to full enlightenment, since without fulfilling these perfections, one cannot come close to full enlightenment? [349]

The Lord: So it is, Subhuti. Here is certainly neither growth nor diminution of a perfection-entity. A Bodhisattva coursing in perfection of wisdom who develops affinities toward perfect wisdom, and comes to be skilled in means, does obviously not think, "this perfection of giving grows, this perfection of giving diminishes". Rather, such a one knows, "this perfection of giving is a mere word and a characteristic". As one gives a gift one IS turning any and all 'merit' over thus: in totally equanimous reflection for any accountability whatsoever, one comes to reveal that such as 'merits' cannot be had outside of or in addition to the infinite fullness of emptiness, for such IS "always" already had...merely in the simple realization that even the mental activities, the production of thought, the roots of good which are involved in the act of giving...IS to and for the total benefit of countless sentient beings. However, IN such a revelation one turns these over in such an 'automatic' way as one respects this actual reality of full enlightenment. One proceeds in this way as one takes upon oneself these moral obligations, as one perfects oneself in patience, [350] as one exerts diligence, enters into the trances, courses in perfection of wisdom, AS one develops and maintains affinities to perfect wisdom. See?

Subhuti: So now, what is this supreme enlightenment? [351]

The Lord: It is Suchness Subhuti. However, Suchness neither grows nor diminishes. A Bodhisattva which repeatedly and often dwells in mental activities connected with Suchness dwells near supreme enlightenment, and any such as these do not lose these mental activities. This is certain as here can be neither growth nor diminution of any entity or dharma as such is beyond any and all words and even characteristics, and here neither the perfections, nor any dharmas, can grow or diminish. So, it is thus as dwelling in mental activities of this kind a Bodhisattva is one ever nearing perfect enlightenment, yet in Suchness also are neither considerations of distance as, near or far, nor of time as, sooner or later. For now Subhuti, this is all.

Chapter 19: ~THE GODDESS OF THE GANGES ~

Conditioned Co-production

Subhuti: As a Bodhisattva realizes full enlightenment, is this due to production of the first thought of enlightenment, or due to the last thought of enlightenment? These two acts of thought are nowhere synthesized [and here these cannot cooperate in producing a result]. How can any accumulation of a Bodhisattva's wholesome root take place?

The Lord: What do you think, Subhuti, is this wick of this burning oil lamp burned up at the first incidence of the flame, or at the last incidence of the flame?

Subhuti: Not so, O Lord! It is not burned up at the first incidence of this flame, nor independent of it, and is also not burned up at the last incidence of this flame, nor independent of it.

The Lord: Is now this wick being definitely burned up?

Subhuti: Yes, Lord.

The Lord: In this way is it neither through this first nor through this last thought of enlightenment, nor independent of these [353] that a Bodhisattva realizes full enlightenment. One does not come to realize this through any of these productions of thought, nor other than through them. And yet one does realize full enlightenment.

No Development

Subhuti: Unfathomable is this conditioned coproduction!

The Lord: Subhuti, does even the slighest portion of this first thought...whether just at this outset of this thought, or during this thought, or more towards the end of this thought...which seems to have stopped after its momentary appearance...does this get produced again at the time of the second thought? Consider also Subhuti, what of the outset of the outset, and during the duringness, etc., etc., do even these get produced again?

Subhuti: No Lord.

The Lord: Also once this thought thus produced is now past, (!) is this due to its very nature doomed to stop?

Subhuti: Yes it is, O Lord.

The Lord: As anything is due to its very nature doomed to stop, is this destroyed?

Subhuti: No, Lord. [354]

The Lord: This future thought which is not yet being produced, is this due to its very nature doomed to stop?

Subhuti: No, Lord [as anything which is not being produced cannot be stopped].

The Lord: So, as it comes to such a point as by its own nature it is doomed to stop, will it now be destroyed?

Subhuti: No, Lord.

The Lord: As this essential nature of this thought involves neither production nor stopping, is this now being stopped?

Subhuti: No, Lord.

The Lord: As any dharma is, due to this essential original nature, stopped already in its own being, is this dharma being stopped?

Subhuti: No, Lord.

The Lord: Is this true nature of dharmas being stopped?

Subhuti: No, Lord.

The Lord: Does any Bodhisattva stand firm in this same way in which Suchness stands firm?

Subhuti: Yes, one does. [355]

The Lord: Is now Suchness not in danger of being changed away from overtowering immobility?

Subhuti: No, Lord.

The Lord: Unfathomable is Suchness.

Subhuti: It is beyond fathoming, O Lord.

The Lord: Is here and now any thought in Suchness?

Subhuti: No, Lord.

The Lord: Is thought [identical with] Suchness?

Subhuti: No, Lord.

The Lord: Is thought other than Suchness?

Subhuti: No, Lord.

The Lord: Can you see a Suchness?

Subhuti: No, Lord.

The Lord: One which courses like unto Suchness, does one course in the unfathomable?

Subhuti: Such a one courses nowhere at all. As any ideas as to one's own performance neither habitually proceed in one, nor befall one.

The Lord: Where does a Bodhisattva course as one courses in perfect wisdom? [356]

Subhuti: In ultimate reality.

The Lord: As coursing in ultimate reality does any Bodhisattva course in a sign?

Subhuti: No, Lord.

The Lord: Is the sign a sign as in something which one does not undo by one's meditational development?

Subhuti: No, Lord.

The Lord: Is this sign, to the Bodhisattva who courses in perfect wisdom, something which is undone by one's meditational development?

Subhuti: The Bodhisattva does not make any efforts, while coursing in the course of a Bodhisattva, to reach in this present birth any state in which all signs are forsaken. As one makes an effort to reach in this present birth any state in which all signs are forsaken, as any or all Buddha-dharmas are not complete in this one, one automatically is recognized as a Disciple. The skill in means of a Bodhisattva consists in this, as one cognizes any sign, both its mark and cause, and yet surrenders oneself completely to the Signless [realm of dharma, in which no sign has ever arisen].

Sariputra: Does a Bodhisattva's aspiration to perfect wisdom increase as in one's dreams one develops the three doors to deliverance, i.e. the Empty, the Signless and the Wishless?

Subhuti: As this increases through development by day, this also increases in one who dreams about this. As the Lord says dreams and waking are indiscriminate, essentially the same. As [357] a Bodhisattva which aspires to perfect wisdom, day by day courses in perfect wisdom, one also in one's dreams remains close to perfect wisdom, and develops even now in abundance.

Sariputra: In one's dreams as one does a deed, wholesome or unwholesome, is this added on to the heap or collection of one's karma?

Subhuti: The Lord teaches all dharmas are like a dream, and infinitely so, as in such [i.e. from the standpoint of infinite reality] this deed is not added to one's heap or collection of karma. On the other hand [from the standpoint of empirical reality], this deed is added to the heap and collection of one's karma when, upon waking up, one thinks the dream over, and consciously forms the notion as wanting to kill someone. How does one do this? During this dream one may dream of taking a life, and as one wakes up, thinks this dreamed of deed over like this: "It is good this being is killed! It is right this being is killed! It is just this being is killed! It is I who killed this being." Such thoughts are equivalent to the conscious notion this one wants to kill someone.

No Objective Supports and No Own-Being

Sariputra: As a result of conscious reflections, the deed of any particular person is added on to this persons collection of karma, so to this deed of Buddha, the Lord, as he thinks to himself and consciously forms this notion he wants to enter extinction, [358] will this not also be added to the Buddha's heap and collection of karma?

Subhuti: No, indeed not, Sariputra, as the Tathagata is beyond reflections and discriminations. Empty awareness beyond any objective support, raises to, or rather reveals result as neither deed nor thought, as such simply cannot. A deed 'arises' only with an objective support as basis and not without one [even IF such is merely assumed, as in the dream where, say, one kills another, and upon waking carries on as if having actually killed]. This result of false view, raises or reveals the assumption to reality, even though a mirage, a phantom spector now in both this objective reality, as well as the dream-world. This type of thinking arises with only a (personally) untested presumption for its objective support, not without one (and sadly in most cases, habitually left beneath any discursive perusal). As 'intellectual' acts can only refer to dharmas such as are seen, heard, felt, or known, in this unchecked thinking all results necessarily do miss the mark, and are inaccurately assumed as fact and truth, and thusly projected out onto the myriad worlds as such.

Without giving an objective support as such TO such as is here being done in THIS instant...in regards to some objects intellectual acts take on defilement or obscuration quite naturally as just seen, while with regards to others, these don purification through revelations of non-objective, non-productive contemplation AS pure awareness beyond any basis. Acts of will and deeds only arise with objective support, not without. Suchness thus comes to reveal 'itself', OF 'itself', and so neither adds to nor takes away from any dharmas whatsoever. Your 'heap and collection of karma', Sariputra, only reveals IT's true nature OF itself, as well.

Sariputra: As the Lord describes objective supports as isolated [without an inherent relation to a subject], how can an act of will arise only with objective support, and not without?

Subhuti: An act of will is raised only with an objective support, and not without, in the sense one treats an actually non-existent objective support as a sign, as an objective support. In fact also the act of will is isolated, and also the sign. And so are Karma-formations which are conditioned by ignorance, and so all the links of conditioned co-production, up to decay and death conditioned by birth, and vice-versa. Even so objective supports are isolated. The act of will is isolated from the sign [which seems to cause it], and it arises only in reference to the conventional expressions current in the world.

Sariputra: As in one's dream a Bodhisattva gives a gift, and dedicates it to full enlightenment, can this gift effectively called dedicated? [359]

Subhuti: We are face to face with Maitreya, the Bodhisattva, the great being. The Tathagata has predicted his supreme enlightenment. He is a direct eyewitness of this matter, he can dispose of this matter.

Sariputra: Maitreya, Subhuti the Elder has said: "Here is Maitreya, the Bodhisattva, the great being! He can dispose of this matter." Dispose of this matter, Venerable Ajita!

Maitreya: With reference to what the Venerable Subhuti says, what corresponds to these words 'Maitreya' and "he can dispose of this matter? Does my form reply? Or my feeling, perception, impulses, or consciousness? Does my outward appearance reply, or my shape? Or does emptiness of form reply, or emptiness of feeling, perception, impulses or consciousness? Obviously emptiness of form, etc., does not have any capacity to reply. [360] Nor do I see any dharma which can reply, or which may reply, or by which one does reply, nor any dharma which is predicted to supreme enlightenment.

Sariputra: Maitreya, do you really witness these dharmas in this way, in which you teach?

Maitreya: I do not. Even I do not, nor can I know these dharmas, do not apprehend, do not see these, in this way in which these words express, and these thoughts reflect. But certainly this body cannot touch these, speech cannot express these, mind cannot even consider these. These things indicate own-being of all dharmas, yet even these things are without any own-being.

Sariputra thought: Deeply wise, indeed, is this Bodhisattva Maitreya the great being. How he expounds the perfection of wisdom in which he courses for such a long time!

The Lord: Why does this thought occur to you? Can you, Sariputra, see this dharma endowed with which you have been made into an Arhat?
Sariputra: No, Lord. [361]

The Lord: In this same way this does not occur to a Bodhisattva which courses in perfection of wisdom, "

"this dharma is predestined to full enlightenment, that dharma will be predestined, this dharma is being predestined, that dharma will know full enlightenment." As one courses in such a way, one courses in perfect wisdom.

Five Places which Inspire Fear

Coursing thus, here is no fear. Impregnated with this strength which is gained [in these coursings in baselessness], this enables persistence in any endeavours to think such as: "This is not a condition such as not to

reveal enlightenment." Coursing thus, one courses unto perfect wisdom. This being as it is, a Bodhisattva is not afraid as when arriving in a wilderness infested with wild beasts. Here is laid bare one's honor to renounce everything to benefit all beings. Reacting with thoughts such as: "as these wild beasts may devour this fleshly thing, just this must be freely given. Perfection of giving as this becomes perfect selflessness and of it's direction turns all the more toward full realization. Coming to have revealed perfect luminosity, steps are taken in one's Buddha-field such as are seen no animals, as these are not regarded as 'animals' at all, and none have any concept of these as such, but rather, simply as beings living on divine food."

As well, a Bodhisattva is not afraid when finding one's self in a wilderness infested by robbers. As Bodhisattvas find pleasure in this wholesome practice of renouncing anything such as belongings and what ever, a Bodhisattva exudes non-attachment to even this body, having freely renounced all of which is necessary to life. Reacting to danger with a thought such as [362]: "As these beings need everything necessary to life, just this must be life's gift. As someone needs this life, here is felt no ill will, anger or fury on account of this. Against these no offensive action is taken, either by body, voice or mind. Life here is ever an occasion to bring these perfections of generosity, discipline, and patience to more limpid perfection, and clearing any and all obscurities to great perfection. As reality of great perfection, exuding such a manner in this Buddha-field...a wilderness infested with robbers is in no way whatsoever possible, or even conceivable. Diligence and concentration to this realization of perfect purity in any Buddha-field is so great as neither these nor any faults are known as such, or even conceivable in such."

As well, in a waterless waste also a Bodhisattva is not afraid. Such is neither alarmed nor terrified. This training resolves such as may result in quenching any thirst of any and all beings. Here one will not tremble as thinking that "as one dies of thirst one is reborn as a Preta." On the contrary, as one directs a thought of great compassion unto all beings, thinking [363]: "Alas, certainly these beings are in great need as in this world such deserts are even conceivable. As this reality of great perfection, one sees to this in this Buddha-field no such deserts exist, or are even conceivable, for such simply are not needed. One exudes suchness on any and all beings as surely these drink the most excellent water. Thus effort is exerted on behalf of all beings, so on any and all occasion(s) also the perfection of effort [diligence, vigor] is more perfected. So, in a foodless waste also a Bodhisattva is not afraid.

Such is protected with this thought: "As effort is firmly exerted, a Buddha-field is purified in such a way as approaching enlightenment, in this Buddha-field is no foodless waste...such is not even conceivable. The beings in this field are entirely happy, filled with happiness, possessed of all happiness. And thus all the intentions and plans of these beings are realized as reality. Just as with these Gods of the Thirty-three, any idea in these minds is sufficient to produce anything whatsoever these desire, so effort is exerted so these beings can realize and produce everything by merely thinking of it in their minds. In order that their legitimate intentions are fulfilled, in order that all beings, everywhere and anywhere, do not go short of any requirements of life, [364] so is this exerted effort for purity in thought, for the benefit of any and all beings, as at this occasion also the perfection of concentration is more perfect. As such a Bodhisattva is not afraid in a district infested by epidemics. But such considers, reflects and deliberates as 'here is no dharma which sickness can oppress, nor is this which is called "sickness" a "dharma." In this manner contemplate emptiness, and do not be afraid. Do not think this "is an excessively long time to realizing full enlightenment," do not tremble at such a thought. This thought-moment [which in reality is not produced] is an extreme limit with no beginning; in other words, this is absence of any limit. A Bodhisattva here avoids dwelling on difficulties as such thinks "great and long is this limit with no beginning as one single thought-moment, in other words, no absence, as no limit." Such 'prevents' a Bodhisattva from trembling at any thought such as "it will be a long time until full enlightenment". And this as well, Subhuti, as these and other fears and terrors, be they seen, heard, felt or known, do not cause a Bodhisattva to tremble, one knows "this [any] son or daughter of good family is capable of knowing full enlightenment." A Bodhisattva here dons the great armor of this thought [365]: "Thus act, thus exert firm effort and diligence such as any and all beings in this Buddha-field do not suffer any sickness, and do not even know what it is. In such a way the Tathagatas have taught and thus teach, and apply this as is taught and as such master the perfection of wisdom, for the benefit of all beings, such that on this occasion also the perfection of wisdom comes to fulfillment."

Prediction of the Goddess of the Ganges

So now a certain woman comes to this assembly, and sits down in it. She rises from her seat, puts her upper robe over one shoulder, salutes the Lord with folded hands, and says: "O Lord, as I am placed in these positions, I am not afraid. Without fear, I demonstrate dharma to all beings."

The Lord at this time smiles a golden smile. Its luster irradiates endless and boundless world systems, it rises up to the Brahma-world and returns, circulates three times round the Lord, and disappeares again in the head of the Lord. As she sees this smile, this woman seizes golden flowers, and scatters these over the Lord. Without being fixed anywhere, these remain suspended in the air. [366]

Ananda: What is this reason, O Lord, of his smile? It is not without reason the Tathagata manifests a smile.

The Lord: This Goddess of the Ganges, Ananda, is in a future period a Tathagata, 'Golden Flower' by name, -an Arhat, fully Enlightened, proficient in knowledge and conduct, Well-Gone, a knower of the world, unsurpassed, a tamer of any beings to be tamed, a teacher of Gods and people, a Buddha, a Lord. In the starlike aeon such appears in this world and realizes full enlightenment. As this one deceases here she ceases to be a woman, she is seen as a man. He is reborn in Abhirati, the Buddha-field of the Tathagata Akshobhya, in whose presence he leads the holy life. After his decease he passes from Buddha-field to Buddha-field, never deprived of the sight of the Tathagata. He goes on passing from Buddha-field to Buddha-field, from here to here, always choosing such as in which he is not without the Buddhas, the Lords. A universal monarch passes from palace to palace, and the soles of his feet never, during this entire life, tread upon the surface of the earth, [367] and he dies without ever, up to the time of his death, having trodden with his feet on the ground. Just so the Ganges Goddess passes from Buddha-field to Buddha-field, and she is never at any time deprived of the Buddhas and Lords, until the time of her full enlightenment.

Ananda thought: These Bodhisattvas which are with the Tathagata Akshobhya must actually be considered as the congregation of the Tathagata.

The Lord read Ananda's thoughts, and said: So it is, Ananda. These Bodhisattvas which lead this holy life in the Buddha-field of Akshobhya, the Tathagata, are known as having emerged from the mud, as having approached to the accomplishment of enlightenment. In addition, Ananda, the community of disciples of the Tathagata 'Golden Flower' are not bound by any measure. For his disciples are so many as here will be no measure of these. On the contrary, these are styled 'immeasurable, incalculable.' In addition, Ananda, at this time, on this occasion in such a Buddha-field is no wilderness infested with wild beasts, or with robbers, and no waterless wastes, and no districts infested by epidemics and no foodless wastes. [368] All these, and all other disagreeable places in this Buddha-field, in no way whatsoever either is, or is conceived. It is quite certain, as the Tathagata 'Golden Flower' realizes full enlightenment, all these kinds of places which inspire fear and terror no longer exists, or is even conceivable.

Ananda: Who is this Tathagata in whose presence this Goddess of the Ganges planted this wholesome root of the first thought of enlightenment, and turned it over to supreme enlightenment?

The Lord: This is under the Tathagata Dipankara. And she actually scattered golden flowers over the Tathagata as she requested of him [this prediction to] supreme enlightenment. It is as I strewed the five lotus flowers over Dipankara, the Tathagata, and acquired the patient acceptance of dharmas which fail to be produced, Dipankara predicted this future enlightenment with the words: "You, young man, in a future period are a Tathagata, Shakyamuni by name!" Here now, as she heard this prediction, this Goddess produced a thought to the effect of [369]: "Oh, certainly, as this young man I also like to be predicted to full enlightenment!" And in this way, Ananda, in the presence of the Tathagata Dipankara, this Goddess planted the wholesome root of the first thought of enlightenment, [and turns it over to] full enlightenment.

Ananda: Certainly, as one who makes the necessary preparations, as one who makes the grade this Goddess of the Ganges is predicted to full enlightenment.

The Lord: So it is, Ananda, as you say.

Chapter 20: ~DISCUSSION OF SKILL IN MEANS ~

Emptiness and Reality-Limit

Subhuti: How does a Bodhisattva coursing in perfection of wisdom come to reveal to self, another, and countless beings, these humbled revelations as the non-limitedness of emptiness, or, how does one enter into concentration on emptiness?

The Lord: One contemplates form, etc., [skandhas], as empty. However, one contemplates this with an undisturbed continuum of thought resulting from non-conceptual awareness thusly: as one contemplates this universal law..."form, feeling, perception, impulse and consciousness is empty,"...one doesn't regard any dharma [phenomena] as any 'thing' [phenomena] which as a result of emptiness is any separate entity [because it IS it's true nature]. So, as one does not, and logically cannot regard any nature -AS- any specific dharmas being any real thing, one cannot realize any reality-limit (which is 'a point' where reality 'as we know it' comes to an end, because the knowing itself thereof comes to be revealed as this non-limitedness, synonymous with all-knowledge, or emptiness.) As such, this can be viewed intellectually from many different angles and almost grasped, BUT still cannot be known and stated experientially in some conventional discursive fashion because 'where' this comes to be definitively known...is beyond thought, word, and concept...'where' no-thing exists. Here or about, one comes to say with the greatest conviction and knowing..."I know nothing!", and joins the ranks of the exceedingly rare minority who can say this with any truth whatsoever behind it.

Subhuti: In reference to the Lord saying, "a Bodhisattva does not realize emptiness," how does a Bodhisattva who stands firmly in [this continuing practice of] this concentration [on emptiness] not realize emptiness?

The Lord: A Bodhisattva contemplates emptiness which yields it's inherency of the naturalness of all modes [of the six perfections]. Yet, one does not contemplate this: "I shall realize," or "I should realize," but one contemplates this: "this is time for complete discomfiture, and not realization." [371] So, without losing oneself in this concentration, one ties one's thought to any objective support [for one's compassion] and determines to yield one self to the infinitely apparent perfect wisdom [which is essentially skill in means], and one determines within this, one will not realize emptiness [as it's realization is not any 'final goal']. Yet the Bodhisattva does not lose any dharmas which act as the 37 wings of enlightenment. [These are the 4 foundations of mindfulness, the 4 restraints, the 4 bases of accomplishment, the 5 faculties, the 5 powers, the 7 limbs and the 8 fold path.] One does not affect the extinction of outflows [which prevent renewed rebirths], yet one 'achieves' no limitations. As a Bodhisattva dwells in concentration as emptiness - which is one of the doors to deliverance - one also dwells in concentration on Signlessness, but without realizing the Signless. Endowed with dharma of this wholesome root which is thus in place, one contemplates "this is time for nurturing beings, and not for realization." Taken hold of by perfect wisdom one does not realize any reality limit.

Three Similes

The Lord: Suppose, Subhuti, one excellent, of noble qualities...very vigorous, of high social position, attractive and most fair to behold, of many virtues, in possession of all the finest virtues, virtues which spring from the very height of sovereignty, discipline and morality, learning, renunciation and so on. This person is judicious, able to express with ease, to formulate views clearly, to substantiate one's claims; one who always knows the suitable time, place and situation for everything. In archery this one has gone as far as one can go, is successful in warding off all manner of attack, most skilled in all arts, and foremost, through fine achievements, in all crafts. Of good memory, this one is intelligent, clever, steady and prudent, versed in all the treatises, has many friends, is wealthy, strong of body, with large limbs, with all faculties complete, [372] generous to all, dear and pleasant to many. Any work undertaken is managed to completion. This one also speaks methodically, shares great riches with the many, honors what should be honored, reveres what should be revered, worships what should be worshipped. Would such a person, Subhuti, feel every increasing joy and zest?

Subhuti: Yes indeed, O Lord.

The Lord: Now suppose as well, this person so greatly accomplished, takes one's family on a journey, one's mother and father, sons and daughters. By some circumstances, these find themselves in a great, wild forest. The foolish ones among them feel fright, terror and hair-raising fear. This one, however, fearlessly says to this family: "Do not be afraid! I shall soon take you safely and securely out of this terrible and frightening forest. I shall soon set you free!" Then more and more hostile and inimical forces rise up in this forest, would this noble person decide to abandon this family, and to take oneself alone out of that terrible and frightening forest - this one who is not one to draw back, who is endowed with all the force of firmness and vigor, who is wise, exceedingly tender and compassionate, courageous and a master of many resources? [373]

Subhuti: No, O Lord. This person, who does not abandon this family, has at one's disposal powerful resources, both within and without. On this one's side forces arise in this wild forest which are quite a match for the hostile and inimical forces, and these stand up for and protect these one's. These enemies and adversaries, who look for a weak spot, who seek for a weak spot, do not gain any hold over these one's. This one is competent to deal with the situation, and is able, unhurt and uninjured, soon to take out of that forest both this family and oneself, and securely and safely these reach a village, city or market-town.

The Lord: Just so, Subhuti, is it with a Bodhisattva which is full of pity and concerned with the welfare of all beings, which dwells in friendliness, compassion, sympathetic joy and impartiality, is taken hold of by skill in means and perfect wisdom, which has been taken over by one's wholesome roots, employing the kind of transformation which is the Buddha's sanction. Although one enters into this concentration which proffers just these doors to deliverance, -being concentrated contemplation on; emptiness, signlessness and wishlessness- this one nevertheless just does not realize any reality-limit, such as one has a tendency toward on levels of Sravaka Disciple, or on these of a Pratyekabuddha. This one has at this one's disposal very strong and powerful helpers, in perfect wisdom and skill in means. Since this one does not abandon all beings, this one is thus able to have revealed full enlightenmcnt, safely and securely.

At such a time as a Bodhisattva makes all beings an object for one's thought of friendliness, and with this highest friendliness ties oneself to these, at this time one rises above the factiousness of the defilements and of Mara, one rises above the level of Sravaka Disciple and Pratyekabuddha, [374] and one abides in this concentration [on friendliness]. This is not one who has attained the extinction of the outflows, yet achieves a complete consummation of emptiness, which [in this case] is endowed with these highest perfections. At such a time as a Bodhisattva dwells in this concentration on emptiness, which is but one door to freedom, one yet does not dwell in concentration as Signlessness, nor does this one realize concentration on the Signless. This is just like a bird which on its wings courses in the air. It neither falls to the ground, nor does it stand anywhere on any support. It dwells in space, just in the air, without being either supported or settled herein.

Just so a Bodhisattva dwells as this dwelling of emptiness, realizes this total permeance of emptiness. Just so this one dwells AS this dwelling of

Signlessness and Wishlessness, and such comes to be revealed as this specific consummation as Signless and Wishless. But one does not fall into emptiness, neither into Signlessness, nor Wishlessness, with one's Buddha-dharmas remaining incomplete. It is as with a master of archery, strong, well-trained, perfectly trained in archery. He first shoots one arrow upwards. He now sends after this another arrow which checks the fall of the first. By a regular succession of arrows he would not permit that first arrow to fall to the ground, and that arrow is kept in the air until he decides it falls to the ground. In this same way a Bodhisattva which courses in perfection of wisdom and which is upheld by skill in means, does not realize the farthest reality-limit until one's wholesome roots are matured, well matured as full enlightenment. Only as one's wholesome roots are matured, well matured as full enlightenment, [375] does this one realize this farthest reality-limit. A Bodhisattva which courses in perfection of wisdom, which develops revelations as perfect wisdom, here now contemplates and meditates on this limitless true nature of these dharmas, but still one does not realize perfect wisdom as goal or conquest. Such as these come to exude wise (or, purely natural) humility.

Doors to Deliverance and Vows about Beings

Subhuti: A doer of what is difficult is the Bodhisattva, a doer of what is most difficult, as one courses and dwells as emptiness, one enters into this concentration as emptiness, and yet does not realize any reality-limit! Exceedingly wonderful is this, O Well-Gone!

The Lord: So it is, Subhuti. For the Bodhisattva does not abandon beings. We have made these special vows to reveal this process to freedom from defilement and obscurations to buddha-nature for themselves, for all beings. As the mind of a Bodhisattva forms this aspiration not to abandon beings but to set this freeing technique and process in front of these beings, and in addition one aspires AS this concentration on emptiness, Signlessness, Wishlessness, this being the three doors of deliverance...such a Bodhisattva is known as one which is endowed with skill in means, and does not realize any reality-limit midway, before Buddha-dharmas are complete. It is just this skill means which protects such a one. Any thought of enlightenment, for a Bodhisattva, [376] consists in just this fact -- one does not leave beings behind. As one is thus endowed with this thought of enlightenment and with skill in means, one does not midway realize any reality-limit, hereby stopping as any result of any thing whatsoever. In addition to this, as a Bodhisattva either actually contemplates these limitless stations, being the three doors to deliverance, or aspires to contemplate these, in this mind one forms this following aspiration: "For a long time beings such as these have a notion of existence, and course in apprehension of basis. [birth, life, death and any and all dharmas in-between]. As in realizing these coursings toward full enlightenment, dharma only too naturally comes to be revealed and demonstrated to these beings so these too, may forsake whatever erroneous views may be harbored about any basis."

As a free agent one now enters this concentration on Emptiness, on Signlessness, on Wishlessness. A Bodhisattva revealing to oneself one's natural endowment with this thought of enlightenment and skill in means does not midway realize or give way to some reality-limit. On the contrary, one does not lose concentration on friendliness, compassion, sympathetic joy and impartiality. Upheld as skill in means, one increases pure dharma more and more. One's faith, etc., developes as keener and keener, one acquires siddhis, revealing to self and others the limbs of enlightenment, and this path. [Here are 7 Limbs: mindfulness, investigation of dharmas, vigor, tranquility, rapture, concentration, and evenmindedness] [377]

Even so, a Bodhisattva reflects this..."for a long time beings as these perceive dharmas, course in the apprehension of a basis,"...and develops this aspiration as the former one, entering concentration as emptiness. Also, one reflects this..."as perceiving a sign, these beings coursed for a long time in these signs",...and this one deals with this aspiration thusly, entering concentration as Signlessness. And, a Bodhisattva reflects: "For a long time these beings are perverted by these perceptions of permanence, of happiness, of some self, of loveliness." This one now acts in such a way as dharma is demonstrated so these may forsake these perverted views of any perception of permanence, of happiness, of self, of loveliness, and in order that these may learn this: "impermanent is all this, not permanent; ill is all this, not happiness; without self is all this, not with a self; repulsive is all this, not lovely."

Endowed with this thought of perfection of wisdom, [378] and with the previously described skill in means, here and now taken hold of by perfect wisdom, one does not realize any reality-limit midway, before all one's Buddha-dharma are complete. One dwells thus, and one enters on concentration as Wishlessness, but one does not lose one's concentration as friendliness, etc. Upheld by skill in means, one increases more and more one's pure dharmas. Faith, persistence, mindfulness, concentration, discernment [as the five faculties] develop as keener and keener, and one acquires siddhis, the limbs of enlightenment, and the path. A Bodhisattva raises the following thought: "These beings for a long time are in the habit of coursing in the apprehension of a basis, and even just now these do so. These are for a long time in the habit of coursing in the perception of signs, in perverted views, in perception of material objects, in perception of unreal objects, in wrong views, and even now these continue to do so. Thusly it may be that these faults in each and every way may cease to be in these, and these faults come to be revealed as inconceivable in them." As a Bodhisattva has all beings in mind in such a way, is endowed with this recollection of all beings, with this production of thought, and as skill in means, as one is taken hold of by perfect wisdom and, as endowed with all these qualities, one thus contemplates the true nature of these unfathomable dharmas - through Emptiness, or Signlessness, or Wishlessness, or through these being unaffected, unproduced, without birth, [379] without any positivity - it is quite impossible such a Bodhisattva, which is endowed with such pure cognition, could either fall into the Unaffected, or become intimate with anything belonging to the triple world. This cannot possibly be.

Irreversibility

A Bodhisattva is asked by another Bodhisattva wanting to win full enlightenment: "Over which dharmas does one come to consummation of realization? What kind of aspiration does one form in one's mind, aspirations which enable a Bodhisattva to not settle in realization of Emptiness, or Signlessness, or Wishlessness, or Unaffectedness, or non-production, or non-positivity, but to go on developing perfection of wisdom?" As the answering Bodhisattva answers - just emptiness is attended to, -just Signlessness, -just Wishlessness, -just Unaffectedness, -just non-production, -just no-birth, -just non-positivity, and does not make manifest this production of the thought of the non-abandonment of all beings, or not manifest or indicate skill in means in this answer, one can know this Bodhisattva is not in irreversibility predicted to full enlightenment by the Tathagatas previously. This one does not indicate this special dharma of an irreversible Bodhisattva [i.e. the non-abandonment of all beings], does not make much of this, does not make this manifest, does not wisely know this, does not include this in one's answer, and does not induce others to enter into this stage [of skill in means] which is the true stage of an irreversible Bodhisattva. [380]

Subhuti: And how can a Bodhisattva, in regard to this question, be regarded as irreversible?

The Lord: One is known as an irreversible Bodhisattva as, whether one hears this perfection of wisdom or not, one hits upon the correct answer.
Subhuti: Here are many who course towards enlightenment, but a few only could give the correct answer.

The Lord: As few only are these Bodhisattvas which are predicted to this irreversible stage on which this cognition is possible. But these who are predestined for it, these give the correct answer. One can be sure that these have planted splendid wholesome roots in the past, and the whole world, with its Gods, persons and Asuras, cannot possibly and ultimately overwhelm these.

Dream Experiences and the Mark of Irreversibility

So, as a Bodhisattva even dreams and beholds, "all dharmas are like a dream," but does not realize this experience, regarding it as final,...so too this is known as the irreversible mark of an irreversible Bodhisattva. This is another mark...as even in dreams, neither the level of Sravaka Disciple nor Pratyekabuddha, nor anything which belongs to any triple world, is seen or known as an object of any longing, or appears advantageous. It is another mark...as even in dreams, one sees oneself as a Tathagata, -in the middle of an assembly of many hundreds of thousands of niyutas of kotis of persons, [381] seated in a circular hall with a peaked roof, surrounded by a community of monks, revered by the community of Bodhisattvas, demonstrating dharma.

It is another mark, as, even in dreams, one rises into the air and demonstrates dharma to beings, as one perceives the halo round the Buddha, one conjures up monks who go into different directions to fulfil the functions of Buddhas on other world systems and demonstrate dharma here. Even as one dreams one has such perceptions.

It is another mark as one dreams and remains unafraid when a village, town, city, or kingdom is sacked; or sees a huge conflagration spreading; or sees wild beasts or other offensive animals; or one's head is about to be cut off, or as one is subjected to other great fears and terrors, and also one sees these fears and terrors to which other beings are subjected. In no case do fear and terror arise in one such as this, and one remains unafraid. And immediately as one awakes from this dream, reflects how "like a dream is all this which belongs to any triple world. And in this sense should I demonstrate dharmas, as one which demonstrates dharma correctly."

It is again another mark of irreversibility as a Bodhisattva, on seeing in dreams [382] the beings which are in these hells, reflects: "Thus as in this Buddha-field are no states of woe at all!" This also is known as a mark of an irreversible Bodhisattva as never having to be reborn in such states of woe.

And how does one know here are no states of woe in a Buddha-field of any particular Bodhisattva? As a Bodhisattva, on seeing in dreams the beings reborn in the hells, as 'animals', or as Pretas, sets up mindfulness and a Buddha-field without such states of woe, this is known as the mark which shows one can never again need to be reborn in the states of woe. Also, a Bodhisattva may dream a prophetic dream to the effect that a town or village is on fire, and as one wakes up considers thusly: "The attributes, tokens and signs in these dreams, are the attributes, tokens and signs which an irreversible Bodhisattva bears in mind. This Truth, as of utterance of this Truth, let this town fire or village fire, which is taking place here, be appeased, cooled, and extinguished." As the fire is extinguished, one can know [383] this Bodhisattva is predicted to full enlightenment by Tathagatas in this past; as it is not extinguished, one should know this is not so predicted. Again Subhuti, if instead of being appeased, this conflagration passes beyond all bounds and spreads from house to house, from road to road, one should know this Bodhisattva has in some past collected karma consisting in refusal of dharma, conducive to weakness in wisdom, or, specific abilities to maintain a state of naturalness. From this refusal and conductivity results karma which led to this experience in this present life [i.e. to this distress at being unable to control this fire], which is just a result of karma left over from refusal of dharma. For, as is known, a Bodhisattva's past lives condition the [absence or presence of the] mark of irreversibility later on. A Bodhisattva which succeeds in controlling this fire is, on this other hand, borne in mind as irreversible.

Irreversibility and the Magical Power of Veracity

And now Subhuti, are demonstrated attributes, tokens and signs by which an irreversible Bodhisattva is borne in mind. Listen well and attentively to this teaching.

Subhuti: So be it, O Lord, speak on.

The Lord: As a person, -man or woman, boy or girl, - is seized or possessed by a ghost, a Bodhisattva, which comes across one such as this, performs this Act of Truth, and says: "As it is true by Tathagatas of this past, [384] and it is true these intentions are perfectly pure, - to the extent this attention to this is perfectly pure, to this extent I leave behind thoughts of Sravaka Disciples and Pratyekabuddhas. It is this nature to reveal full enlightenment. Not to not revealfull enlightenment! Just revealing full enlightenment! Here is nothing which the Buddhas and Lords which reside in countless world systems do not cognize, see, feel and fully know. These Buddhas and Lords which know this earnest intention also reveal full enlightenment. As this is truth, as this is utterance of Truth, may this one depart which seizes and possesses this person with this ghostly seizure!" So, as a result of these words of this Bodhisattva, if this ghost does not depart, one can know the Bodhisattva has not had one's prediction yet; but as this being departs, one can know this Bodhisattva has this prediction to full enlightenment.

Chapter 21: ~(MORE OF) MARA'S DEEDS~

Pride and the Magical Power of Veracity

This Bodhisattva, as we see, says: "I am predicted to full enlightenment by the Tathagatas of this past. As this is the Truth, and my utterance of this Truth, let this ghost depart!"

Now as this happens, Mara -is seen to be- in his turn trying at this same time to induce the ghost to depart. And his efforts are particularly strong and energetic when he has to deal with a Bodhisattva which has but recently set out in the vehicle. It is the magical power of Mara which is seen to have driven the ghost away. But a recently set out Bodhisattva thinks one's own might drove the ghost away, and does not know nor consider that this just may be what is called Mara's might, as one's own negative forces within, driving one to thoughts of great advantage. The Bodhisattva now slackens in efforts.

As a result of this [apparent] victory over the ghost this Bodhisattva thinks to have had this prediction in this past, and despises other Bodhisattvas, sneers at these, ironically compliments, condemns and deprecates these. Pride goes on increasing, until quite firm and rigid. The pride, arrogance, hauteur, false pride, conceit keeps this one away from all-knowledge, from supreme cognition of a Buddha, from cognition of the Self-Existent [386], from cognition of all-knowing, from supreme enlightenment. As this one meets with Bodhisattvas which are good friends, -virtuous in character, resolutely intent on the sublime, earnestly intent, skilled in means, endowed with irreversible dharma, - in this one's conceit these are despised, as such does not tend to, love and honor these. So, this recently set out Bodhisattva tightens what's seen as the bond of Mara still further. One can expect this one to belong to one of two levels, either of Sravaka Disciple, or of a Pratyekabuddha. In this way, in connection with magical power of the enunciation of a Truth, Mara the Evil One is seen to be allowed to cause an obstacle to full enlightenment in any Bodhisattva which has recently set out in the vehicle, which has little faith, has learned little, lacks any good friend, is not upheld by perfect wisdom, and lacks in skill in means. This also can be known as Mara's deed to any Bodhisattva.

Pride in Connection with the Annunciation of the Name

Here and now, Subhuti, these deeds of Mara are seen to operate also in connection with the annunciation of a Bodhisattva's name. And how? Mara is accredited with using even the annunciation of the name, and of the other details connected with it, to tempt a Bodhisattva. He comes to the Bodhisattva in all kinds of disguises, and says: "You have your prediction from Tathagatas in other times. The proof is this name you have, even as a Buddha, and these are the names of your mother, your father, your brother, your sister, your friends, maternal relatives, kinsmen and relations." He proclaims these names backwards through seven generations. He tells you that you are born in this region, this country, this village, town or marketplace. [387] As you have any particular quality, he tells you that you have that same quality also in other times. Whether this Bodhisattva is dull by nature, or keen in faculties, Mara tells this one that such is the same in other times as well.

Or, he will take other qualities which one has in this present life: As, say, a forest dweller, or one who begs for food from door to door without accepting invitations, or wears clothes made of rags taken from a dust heap, or never eats any food after midday or eats a meal in one sitting, or sleeps at night wherever one may happen to be, or possesses no more than three robes, or lives in and frequents cemeteries, or one dwells at the foot of a tree, or even in sleep remains in a sitting posture, or lives in an open, unsheltered place, or wears a garment made of felt, or has few wishes, is easily contented, detached, frugal, soft in speech, or a person of few words, -in each case, Mara announces that also in other times this same one is endowed with the same quality, and that for certain the Tathagatas of the three times must have predicted this one to full enlightenment and to the stage of an irreversible Bodhisattva, for now this one has the just mentioned qualities of an austere ascetic, and must now in all certainty also have endowments with these from other times.

It may be now a Bodhisattva comes to feel conceit as one thinks of the annunciation of these names and circumstances from other times, and of present austere penances as a rigid ascetic. One may actually think one had this prediction in other times as now one has these qualities of a rigid ascetic. And Mara confirms this one in this view. [388] In the guise of a monk, or nun, or lay brother, or lay sister, or Brahmin, or householder, or mother, father, brother, sister, friend or relative, Mara is seen as coming to the Bodhisattva and telling this one that in other times one has had this prediction to full enlightenment and to this irreversible stage of a Bodhisattva for the simple reason that now one has these qualities of a rigid ascetic, which, according to Mara, are the qualities of an irreversible Bodhisattva. But...the Bodhisattva does not have the attributes, tokens and signs of an irreversible Bodhisattva which is described. This is surely a being seen as beset by Mara, unlike these other Bodhisattvas [which are good friends]. For this one does not have the attributes, tokens and signs which are actually characteristics of an irreversible Bodhisattva.

So, as a result of the annunciation of the circumstances of other times one feels conceit. In this conceit, overcome by great and rigid conceit, defeated by what's seen as the magical power of Mara, one despises brother and sister Bodhisattvas, sneers at and deprecates these. One can recognize this as a deed -seen as being done- of Mara, which makes uses of the annunciation of the circumstances, said to be from other times of a Bodhisattva. [389]

Also Subhuti, Mara -is seen to- operate in connection with the prediction of the name which a Bodhisattva will have as a Buddha. In the guise of a monk he comes to a Bodhisattva and predicts: "this will be your name when you have won full enlightenment." And Mara, strangely enough, is seen to predict the name which the Bodhisattva had already guessed when pondering over the name one would bear after full enlightenment. If the Bodhisattva is weak in wisdom, [which is pure and natural sensibilities more or less refined] and without skill in means, this one reflects that, strangely enough, the name which that monk has mentioned is the same guessed by oneself.

The Bodhisattva compares the name thought out by oneself with the name proclaimed by that monk, who is seen as either beset by Mara, or was conjured up by Mara or his host, and finds that the two agree, and concludes oneself has in other times also been predicted to full enlightenment by Tathagatas by name. But one has not got the attributes, tokens and signs of an irreversible Bodhisattva as are described. Since lacking in them, one feels conceit as a result of this prediction of name. In this conceit [390] one despises the brother and sister Bodhisattvas, and thinks that as one has had this prediction, these others have not. This pride, arrogance and conceit which makes one despise these other Bodhisattva keeps one far away from all-knowledge and the cognition of a Buddha. Not upheld by perfect wisdom, lacking in skill in means and the good friend, taken hold of by the bad friend, one would, we must expect, belong to one of two other levels, that of a Sravaka

Disciple, or that of a Pratyekabuddha.

Now, even if after one has spent a long time, a good long time in erring about and in wandering about [in birth-and-death], one would again come to want to know full enlightenment by resorting to just this perfection of wisdom; and if one were to go to these good friends and regularly approach them; and if, in one's newfound outlook on life one would, first of all, censure former ideas, vomit them up, abhor them, throw them back, see their error, - even then it is still difficult for this one to realize buddha-nature. So serious is the offense of conceitedness, for it is a result of pandering to the self-aggrandizing and deluded needs of one's self for immediate gratification.

Among the monks who belong to the vehicle or level of the Sravaka Disciples four unforgivable offences are so serious that, as someone has been guilty of one of them, that one ceases to be a monk, a Shramana, a son or daughter of the Shakya. More serious than those four unforgivable offences is the production of a proud thought, when, on the occasion of the prediction of one's name, a Bodhisattva has despised other Bodhisattvas, and produced a thought which is very unwholesome, which is more serious than the four unforgivable offences. Not only this, but it is more serious even than the five deadly sins, this production of thought connected with pride, [391] produced on the occasion when a Bodhisattva's future name [as a Buddha] is announced. That thought is more serious than the five deadly sins. In this way, even through the mere annunciation of a Bodhisattva's name very subtle deeds -seen to be- of Mara may arise. These are recognized for what these are, and avoided, both by the Bodhisattva oneself, and by others.

Faults in Connection with Detachment

Furthermore, -what is seen as- Mara the Evil One, comes to any Bodhisattva and exhorts and informs these in connection with the quality of detachment which Tathagatas have appraised as detachment, and that this means one should dwell in a remote forest, in a jungle, in mountain clefts, burial grounds, or on heaps of straw, etc. But this is not taught as the detachment of a Bodhisattva, that one should live in a forest, remote, lonely and isolated, or in jungle, mountain clefts, burial grounds, on heaps of straw, etc.

Subhuti: As this is not the detachment of the Bodhisattva, what then is this detachment of a Bodhisattva?

The Lord: A Bodhisattva dwells detached as one is detached from the mental activities associated with Disciples and Pratyekabuddhas [392].

As one is taken hold of by perfection of wisdom and skill in means, and as one dwells in the dwelling of friendliness and of great compassion towards all beings, one dwells detached even as one dwells in the neighborhood or village. Thusly ordained is this detachment from the mental activities associated with Disciples and Pratyekabuddhas: A Bodhisattva dwells detached as one passes day and night dwelling in this detachment. As any Bodhisattva dwells in this dwelling while one lives in remote dwelling places, in remote forests, in the jungle, in mountain clefts and burial grounds, thus one dwells detached. But as to the detachment recommended by Mara, the Evil One, -i.e. the dwelling in remote forests, jungles, mountain clefts and burial grounds, -as this detachment is actually contaminated or tainted by the mental activities associated with Disciples and Pratyekabuddha, just so, as one does not apply as one practices the perfection of wisdom, one does not fulfil these conditions necessary to realize all-knowledge. As a result, one dwells in a contaminated dwelling, in a mental activity which is not wholly pure. By consequence of this, one despises other Bodhisattvas who dwell in villages, but which are uncontaminated by mental activities associated with Sravaka Disciples and Pratyekabuddhas, who dwell in dwellings of wisdom with many devices, and with great compassion.

As one's deeds of body, voice and mind are not quite pure, one is a dweller in contamination, not a dweller in detachment, although one may dwell in the remote forest. At first one despises these which live in the neighborhood of a village, though these dwell in the dwelling of wisdom, with devices and great compassion, though these are habitually quite pure in what these do with their body, voice or mind, though these are detached from mental activities associated with Disciples and Pratyekabuddhas, uncontaminated by them [393]; after this one finds one cannot gain the Trances, Concentrations, Attainments, Emancipations and Super-knowledges, and these qualities do not reach fulfillment in this person. The reason for this is that this one is without skill in means.

Even though a Bodhisattva may dwell in deserted forests hundreds of miles wide, with no other company than beasts of prey, antelopes, flocks of birds, uninfested even by the smaller wild animals, by Yakshas and Rakshasas, and untroubled by the fear of robbers, and even though one may settle here for one year, or for one hundred years, or even for hundreds of thousands of niyutas of kotis of years, or for more than that; -if one does not know this detachment as explained, and through which detachment and explanation a Bodhisattva dwells as one who has set out with earnest intentions, who has achieved earnest intentions; even now one completely devoted to life in the remote forests fails to gladden the heart of hearts, as one does not know this [detachment], as one is without skill in means, as one leans on this detachment, clings to it, is bent on it, indulges in it. For the detachment of any Bodhisattva which is described does not appear in this one's detachment. But from a place high up in the air Mara can be seen as saying to the dweller in the remote forest that this dweller does well, that one's detachment is the one which Tathagatas have described, and one can go on dwelling in just this detachment, and in consequence of it one quickly realizes full enlightenment. [394]

As one leaves this isolated place in the forest, and comes back to a village, one despises Bodhisattvas here, monks who are well behaved, chaste, lovely in character, uncontaminated by mental activities associated with Sravakas, Disciples and Pratyekabuddhas, and living their lives quite pure in body, voice and mind. This one tells these they surely do not dwell in a detached dwelling, but in a contaminated and crowded one. Any Bodhisattvas here, who dwell in a detached dwelling, this one warns against contaminated and crowded dwellings, tries to commit them to a detached dwelling [as this one conceives it].

One such as this also attempts to make claims, and demanding their respect for one's own isolated residence...is proud, and tells these: "Superhuman beings have exhorted me, superhuman beings have come to inform me! This [isolated place in the forest] is the dwelling in which I dwell. What dweller in a village has ever been exhorted and informed by superhuman beings?" In this way this one despises the persons who belong to the vehicle of the Bodhisattva. This one is known as a Candala of a Bodhisattva, as a defamer of Bodhisattvas, as a mere pretender of a Bodhisattva, as a counterfeit Bodhisattva, as filth of a Bodhisattva, as a robber in the guise of a Shramana, a robber of persons belonging to the vehicle of the Bodhisattvas, a robber of the world with its Gods. Such a one is surely not yet tended, loved or honored. For such persons have fallen into conceit. [395] These even succeed in corrupting other kindred spirits, weaklings who have but recently set out in the vehicle. These are regarded as yet obscured of nature, as devoid of any ability as yet to allow teachers to find their effectiveness within one such as this, devoid of any realization of the qualities of holiness.

Although a Bodhisattva does not yet tend such persons, neither does one not love or honor these, as a true Bodhisattva is one who can neither abandon beings, nor all-knowledge, nor full enlightenment, as one aspires earnestly to reveal full enlightenment, and indicate to countless others how to bring about this revelation themselves as well as the weal of all beings.

On the contrary, one who has raised oneself to a height which is such as one considers the weal of all beings, also does, so one may see through these and other deeds -seen to be- of Mara, always maintain one's mind as anxious to expound the path to beings who have not yet got it, a mind which does not tremble and which is not submerged in the wanderings through these triple worlds; one has revealed first of all an attitude of friendliness, and an attitude of compassion, one has revealed the great compassion and is moved by sympathy, one has thoughts of joy and in sympathy with the beings who progress, whether or not such is obvious, and one is impartial, for the true nature of dharmas is such as it cannot be apprehended; [with all this in mind] one forms the resolution: "Thus in any time any and all the faults seen to be of Mara's deeds are in no way whatsoever either conceived, or produced; or, appearing as produced, these at once pass away again. Thus train oneself!"

This is also known as a Bodhisattva's courageous advance towards one's own higher knowledge. So much for this which a Bodhisattva knows about Mara's deeds in connection with the quality of detachment.

Chapter 22: ~THE GOOD FRIEND ~

The Good Friends

A Bodhisattva which sets out with earnest intention from the very beginning tends, loves and honors good friends.

Subhuti: Who are these good friends of a Bodhisattva?

The Lord: The Buddhas and Lords, and also the irreversible Bodhisattvas who are skillful in the Bodhisattva-course, and which instruct and admonish one in the perfections, who demonstrate and expound perfection of wisdom. The perfection of wisdom in particular is regarded as a Bodhisattva's good friend. All the six perfections, in fact, are good friends of a Bodhisattva. These are one's Teacher, one's path, light, torch, illumination, one's shelter, refuge, place of rest, one's final relief, island, mother, father, and these lead one to this sublime revealing of undifferentiated awareness and this inherent pure cognition herein, to understanding, to full enlightenment. For it is in these perfections this perfection of wisdom is accomplished. Simply from the six perfections is revealed all-knowledge of Tathagatas which, in a period which stands completely clear of time as it is known in these triple worlds, come to realize full enlightenment and enter Nirvana...and so also the all-knowledge of Tathagatas which in all periods of these three times simultaneously realize enlightenment, and so these Tathagatas which just now reside in incalculable, immeasurable, infinite, inconceivable world systems. I also, Subhuti, am a Tathagata which in this present period is revealing full enlightenment, and reveal also this all-knowledge coming forth from these six perfections. For the six perfections contain the thirty-seven dharmas which act as wings to enlightenment, these contain four Brahma-dwellings, four means of conversion, and any Buddha-dharma whatsoever, any Buddha-cognition, cognition of the Self-Existent, any unthinkable, incomparable, immeasurable, incalculable, unequalled cognition, any cognition which equals the unequalled, any cognition of all-knowing. So Subhuti, simply the six perfections of any Bodhisattva [398] are known as one's good friends. These are one's Teacher, etc., to: these lead one to cognition, to understanding, to full enlightenment. In addition, a Bodhisattva which trains in these six perfections is a true benefactor to all beings which are in need of one. But as one wants to train in these six perfections, a Bodhisattva must above all hear this perfection of wisdom, take it up, bear it in mind, recite, study, spread, demonstrate, expound, explain and write of and about this, and investigate this profound meaning, content and method, meditate on this, and ask questions regarding this. For this perfection of wisdom directs these six perfections, guides, leads, instructs and advises these, this is their genetrix and nurse. Because, if these are deprived of the perfection of wisdom, the first five perfections do not come under any concept of perfections and these are not called "perfections". As a Bodhisattva trains in just this perfection of wisdom, one comes to reveal a state which is such as one cannot be led astray by others, and stands naturally and firmly in this.

Emptiness, Defilements, and Purification

Subhuti: How is perfect wisdom marked? [399]

The Lord: It has non-attachment for mark.

Subhuti: Is it feasible to say that same mark of non-attachment, which exists as regards perfect wisdom, exists also as regards all dharmas?

The Lord: So it is, Subhuti. For all dharmas are isolated and empty. Here as well this same mark of non-attachment, which indicates perfect wisdom as isolated and empty, also indicates all dharmas as isolated and empty.

Subhuti: As all dharmas are isolated and empty, how is the defilement and purification of beings conceivable? For what is isolated cannot be defiled and purified, what is empty cannot be defiled or purified, and what is isolated and empty cannot know full enlightenment. Nor can one get at any dharma outside emptiness which has known full enlightenment, which will know it, or which does know it. How do we so understand the meaning of this teaching! Show us, O Lord, show us, O Sugata!

The Lord: What do you think, Subhuti. Do beings course for a long time in I-making and mine-making? [400]

Subhuti: So it is, Lord.

The Lord: Are also I-making and mine-making empty?

Subhuti: These are, O Lord.

The Lord: Is it just do to this I-making and mine-making these beings wander about in birth-and-death?

Subhuti: So it is, Lord.

The Lord: It is in this sense the defilement of beings is conceivable. To whatever extent beings take hold of things and settle down in these, to this extent is defilement in place. But no one is here defiled. And to whatever extent one does not take hold of things and does not settle down in these, to this extent does one deconceptualize I-making and mine-making. In this sense does one come to continuously participate in revealing and hence forming this realization of the purification of being. So see, Subhuti, to whatsoever greater or lesser extent these do not take hold of things and do not settle down in things, in direct proportion to this extent here is realized, or rather, here is revealed, purification. But no one is here purified. As a Bodhisattva courses thus, one courses in perfect wisdom. It is as this sense which we gradually and steadily come to reveal to our selves as...it is this which we are but indications of...in our day to day practice, that we form this concept of any and all defilement, and deconceptualize I-mine concepts -as becoming "some kind of purification" of beings- in spite of the fact all dharmas are isolated and empty. As such, here is neither question of defilement to rise above or send away, nor even purity in which to seek absolution. Here is no thing whatsoever, which 'I' have...and nothing which is mine. To be sure, Subhuti, none of this.

Subhuti: This is truly wonderful! And a Bodhisattva which courses thus, courses in perfect wisdom as one now does not course in form, or other skandhas. As one courses thus, [401] a Bodhisattva is not crushed by worlds with various Gods, beings and Asuras. As one courses thus, a Bodhisattva comes to reveal the coursing of all persons belonging to the vehicle of Sravaka Disciples and Pratyekabuddhas as it is, and gains an insuperable equanimous position. For Buddhahood is insuperably equanimous, and so is Tathagatahood, this state Self-Existent beyond any existent self, this state of all-knowledge in which is nothing knowledgeable. A Bodhisattva, which day and night passes 'time' dwelling on these mental activities associated with perfect wisdom, is quite near full enlightenment and quickly comes to reveal such.

Attentions to Perfect Wisdom, and the Pearl of Great Price

The Lord: So it is, Subhuti. Suppose, Subhuti, all beings in Jambudvipa simultaneously acquire a human personality, and upon raising any thoughts to full enlightenment, abide in [402] these thoughts of enlightenment all life long. Just so...now [after all this preparation], these give gifts to all beings, -do these Bodhisattvas on the strength of this beget much merit?

Subhuti: These do, O Lord.

The Lord: Truly again, Subhuti, any son or daughter of good family begets a much different merit, who, as a Bodhisattva, dwells for even one single day only in mental activities connected with perfection of wisdom. For, as one goes on dwelling day and night in these mental activities, one is more and more worthy of the bestowal of sacrificial gifts to any and all beings. Few beings whatsoever have minds and intentions so full of friendliness as these and, except for Buddhas, the Lords, and Tathagatas of course, are matchless, without any likeness, endowed with unthinkable dharmas. So, how do these sons or daughters of good family at first aspire to such merit?

Such ones are endowed with a kind of wise (or, exceedingly natural) insight which allows one to view any and all beings as on their way to being slaughtered. This being as it is, great compassion on all occasions take hold of such as these. [403] We survey countless beings with this heavenly eye, and what we see fills us with great agitation. So many beings carry this burden of karma which lead to immediate retribution in hells. Others acquire unfortunate rebirths [which keeps these away from the Buddha and their own revelations of Buddha-nature, and these teachings]. Still others are doomed to be killed, or are enveloped in a net of false views, or fail to find this path, while again others which gain fortunate rebirths lose it again, and yet again.

So, one attends to these with a thought: "I shall become a savior to all these beings, I seek release for these from all suffering!" But one makes neither this, nor anything else, into a sign to which one is partial. This also is this light of a Bodhisattva's natural wisdom, this same light by which one cognizes and reveals full enlightenment. Bodhisattvas which dwell in these dwellings are worthy of the gifts from the worlds which these inhabit, and do not turn back upon recognition of full enlightenment. These purify gifts and offerings of any and all which accord to these the requisites of life, when their thoughts are well directed toward perfect wisdom, as these are near to all-knowledge.

So here a Bodhisattva dwells in mental work accorded to perfect wisdom, as one does not consume one's alms fruitlessly, as one points out the path to any and all beings, [404] sheds light over a limitless range, is able to set free from birth-and-death any and all beings who subject themselves to these ones and apply themselves attentively, and is able to cleanse the organs and faculties of perception and vision of all beings.

As one dwells in mental activities directed towards these goals, one brings to mind and maintains mental activities which accord with perfection of wisdom. As one decides to bring these to mind, one's mind works welfare for any and all beings. But as well, one gives no room to other mental activities, such as lack in perfect wisdom. As one so accords [as the mental work, which is essentially loving concern for beings, impels one thusly], one spends days and nights in mental activities which accord with perfection of wisdom.

Suppose a man, well versed in jewelry and the different varieties of jewels, newly acquires a very precious gem. This makes him very glad and elated. As he again lost this precious gem, he is most sad and distressed. Constantly and always mental activities associated with this jewel proceed in him, and he regrets being parted from it. He does not forget it, until he either regains this gem, or another one of like quality and kind. Just so a Bodhisattva who again loses sight of the precious jewel of perfect wisdom; [405] with a clear perception of this preciousness of perfect wisdom, and convinced one is not definitely parted from it, one does, with a thought not lacking in mental work on perfect wisdom, and which is directed to the state of all-knowledge, search about everywhere until one regains this Sutra, or gains an equivalent one. All this time this is one which is not lacking in mental activities which accord with the recognition of the precious jewel of perfection of wisdom, one who is not lacking in mental activities which accord with recognition of this great jewel of all-knowledge.

Subhuti: But, since the Lord teaches all dharmas and all mental activities are lacking in own-being, and empty, -how can a Bodhisattva now be as one not lacking in mental activities which accord with perfect wisdom, or with all-knowledge?

The Lord: As the mind of a Bodhisattva works on this fact that all dharmas are through their own-being isolated and empty, and agrees this is so, now such a one is one not lacking in mental activities which accord with perfect wisdom and with all-knowledge. As perfect wisdom is empty, such neither increases nor decreases.

Emptiness and Growth in Enlightenment

Subhuti: So, how can a Bodhisattva cognize, with no increase in perfect wisdom, full attainment of enlightenment, how can one know full enlightenment?

The Lord: In actual fact a Bodhisattva which courses in perfect wisdom neither increases or decreases. Just as perfect wisdom is empty, without increase or decrease, just so also a Bodhisattva is empty, without increase or decrease. It is this fact, -i.e. just as perfect wisdom is empty, [406] without increase or decrease, -a Bodhisattva arrives at cognition of enlightenment, and thus is full enlightenment revealed. As a Bodhisattva is taught, and is not afraid, does not lose heart, this one is known as a Bodhisattva who courses in perfect wisdom.

Subhuti: Does now perfect wisdom course in perfect wisdom?

The Lord: No, Subhuti.

Subhuti: Does emptiness of perfect wisdom course in perfect wisdom?

The Lord: No, Subhuti.

Subhuti: Can one now apprehend outside any emptiness of perfect wisdom, any dharma which courses in perfect wisdom?

The Lord: No, Subhuti.

Subhuti: Does emptiness course in perfect wisdom? [407]

The Lord: No, Subhuti.

Subhuti: Can one apprehend in emptiness any dharma which courses in perfect wisdom?

The Lord: No, Subhuti.

Subhuti: Does emptiness course in emptiness?

The Lord: No, Subhuti.

Subhuti: Does form, etc., course in perfect wisdom?

The Lord: No, Subhuti.

Subhuti: Can one apprehend outside form, etc., any dharma which courses in perfect wisdom?

The Lord: No, Subhuti.

Subhuti: So, O Lord, how does a Bodhisattva course in perfect wisdom?

The Lord: Do you now, Subhuti, see any real dharma which courses in perfect wisdom?

Subhuti: No, Lord. [408]

The Lord: Do you see perfect wisdom, in which the Bodhisattva courses, as a real thing?

Subhuti: No, Lord.

The Lord: Do you see as real any dharma which offers no basis for apprehension? Is this dharma by any chance produced, or can this be produced, or is this being produced, is this stopped, can this be stopped or is this being stopped?

Subhuti: No, Lord.

The Lord: This insight gives any Bodhisattva patience in regards to dharmas which fail to be produced. As one is endowed with this, one is sure to reveal full enlightenment. One is bound to progress towards self-confidence of a Tathagata. This is quite impossible for a Bodhisattva, which courses, strives and struggle in this way, and progresses in this direction, to not reach this supreme cognition of a Buddha, the cognition of the all-knowing, the cognition of a great Caravan Leader.

Subhuti: Can this true nature of all dharmas, which consists in the fact that these fail to be produced, can this be predestined to full enlightenment?

The Lord: No, Subhuti.

Subhuti: How in this case does the prediction of this dharma to full enlightenment take place?

The Lord: Do you see as real this dharma which has a prediction to full enlightenment? [409]

Subhuti: No, Lord. I do not see any real dharma which is at any time predestined to full enlightenment. Nor do I see any real dharma which is known by the enlightened, which can be known to these, or by means of which these can even reveal full knowledge. It is such as any and all dharmas cannot be apprehended, that this does not occur to me to think, "this dharma is known to the Enlightened, this dharma can be known to such as these, by means of this dharma these recognize full knowledge."

Chapter 23: ~SAKRA~

The View of Bodhisattvas

At this time Sakra, Chief of Gods, is seated amid this assembly, and says: To be sure, deep is this perfection of wisdom, hard to see, difficult to understand!

The Lord: So it is, Kausika. As infinite asspace is perfect wisdom infinite. As isolated none can come close to see, as empty is perfect wisdom beyond thought and understanding.

Sakra: These beings which hear this perfection of wisdom, take it up, study, spread, and write it, are endowed with more than a puny wholesome root!

The Lord: So it is. Imagine all the beings in Jambudvipa are endowed [411] with [the ability to observe] the ten ways of wholesome action, do these on the strength of this endowment beget much merit?

Sakra: These do, O Lord.

The Lord: A person who hears, studies, spreads and writes this perfection of wisdom begets merit other than these, as merit beyond any reach of greatness, and indeed beyond even merit itself. The just mentioned heap of merit, due to the morality of all beings in Jambudvipa, is not compared with anyso called merit which is due to the wholesome root of one who hears, studies, spreads and writes this deep perfection of wisdom.

Here and now, a monk said to Sakra, Chief of Gods: You are conceived of and recognized in essence, Kausika, by a person who hears, studies, spreads and writes this deep perfection of wisdom!

Sakra: I am even conceived of in essence and recognized by these sons or daughters of good family who raise but one single thought to enlightenment: [412] how much more so, as, in addition, these train to Thusness, progress to thus, make endeavours regarding thus; thus on their journey these conceive in essence and cognize the whole world with its Gods, beings and Asuras. On their journey these not only conceive and cognize in essence the world with its Gods, beings and Asuras, but also all the Streamwinners, Once-Returners, Never-Returners, Arhats and Pratyekabuddhas. These conceive and cognize also in essence Bodhisattvas which are great almsgivers but lack as yet in perfect wisdom and skill in means; and equally these with morality as perfectly pure, which possess a vast quantity of morality, with observation of the moral rules as unbroken, flawless, unstained, complete, perfectly pure and unspotted, but also as yet lack in perfect wisdom and skill in means; and equally any which reveal from within themselves patience and peaceful calm, [413] with thoughts free from hostility, which think no thought, nor harbor any feelings of malice even while burned at the stake, but who lack in perfect wisdom and skill in means; and equally any which exert perseverance, which persist in trying, are free from sloth, and remain uncowed in all these do with body, voice and mind, but which as yet lack perfect wisdom and skill in means; and equally these who are fond of the trances and delight in these, which are strong and powerful in the trances, which are established in the trances, which are masters of trances, but which as yet lack in perfect wisdom and skill in means. For, as one courses in perfection of wisdom as this is expounded, a Bodhisattva conceives of and recognizes in essence the worlds with their Gods, beings and Asuras, conceives of and recognizes in essence any and all which belong to the vehicle of Sravaka Disciples and Pratyekabuddhas, also the Bodhisattvas which are not skilled in means. And all these mentioned cannot surpass one such as this, for such is this nature and profound balance struck by total equanimity. For a Bodhisattva which courses in perfection of wisdom as this is expounded, which complies with this...takes up such a position so the lineage of all-knowing is not interrupted, and does not keep aloof from Tathagatas. This one's journey, as one progresses in this way, shortly reveals to one such as this the terrace of enlightenment; [414] one training oneself in this way, rescues beings which are sunken into the mud of defilement. Training oneself this way, one trains in this training of a Bodhisattva, and not in the training of Sravaka Disciple or Pratyekabuddha.

Rewards of Perfect Wisdom

And the four Great Kings, the World Guardians, come to any Bodhisattva who trains this way in the perfection of wisdom, and these say to this one: "Train yourself quickly in this course of a Bodhisattva, O you born of good family! Nimbly train yourself! Here are the four begging bowls which you receive as you are seated on the terrace of enlightenment, as one which has revealed full enlightenment." Not only the four World Guardians come to a Bodhisattva which trains in perfect wisdom as is being expounded, but I also come, not to mention other Gods. Constantly as well, Tathagatas bring one to mind. All the worldly ills which might befall the Bodhisattva which courses in perfect wisdom, such as attacks from others, etc., are prevented from affecting this one in any way. This also, O Lord, is a quality which a Bodhisattva which courses in perfect wisdom gains in this very life.

Ananda just now thinks: Is this speech of Sakra, Chief of Gods, due to his own insight, or to the Buddha's might?

Sakra, through the Buddha's might, read his thoughts, and said: To the Buddha's might, Ananda, to the Buddha's sustaining power is this attributed. For I myself [415] am quite incapable of uttering anything relevant on the subject of Bodhisattvas.

The Lord: So it is, Ananda. What Sakra, Chief of Gods, is saying is due to Tathagatas might, to this sustaining power.

Chapter 24: ~CONCEIT~

Conditions Which are seen as Opening a Bodhisattva to Mara's Influence

As a Bodhisattva trains in perfect wisdom, makes endeavours about this and develops this, all the Evil Maras in the great trichiliocosm are seen as being in a state of uncertainty: "Does this Bodhisattva prematurely realize the reality-limit of the level of Sravaka, Disciple, or Pratyekabuddha, or know full enlightenment?" Even so, as a Bodhisattva dwells as this dwelling for perfect wisdom, beings believe with firm resolve that it is the Evil Maras which are pierced by a dart of sorrow. As a Bodhisattva ever courses toward perfecting wisdom, makes endeavours about this and develops this, the Evil Maras are resolutely believed to be thinking of how to hurt such a one as this.

For instance, beings resolutely believe these Maras try to invoke fear by letting loose a shower of meteors in all directions, causing an impression the horizon is all aflame. As a result, these beings believe with unquestioning certainty that these Maras hope now for the Bodhisattva to cower, for one's hair to stand on end, so even one single thought concentrated toward full enlightenment or any benevolent equanimity might get extinguished. [417] But Mara, the Evil One, does not hurt these Bodhisattvas. Some he is seen and resolutely believed to hurt, and yet others, not? Such fallaciousness in resolute belief. Such idleness of intent and action. Such unfortunate arrogance.

Ananda: What kind of a Bodhisattva is Mara seen as, or believed in as confounding, and herein called to blame for hurting?

The Lord: Mara is thus seen as, or believed in as confounding, or herein called to blame for hurting a Bodhisattva which in time, as this perfection of wisdom is taught, does not produce a thought of firm belief in what is the actual nature of these various dharmas, all-knowledge. Mara is thus firmly believed to gain entry. Such is this fallaciousness of resolute belief. He is believed to have already hurt Bodhisattvas which, as this deep perfection of wisdom is being taught, are seized by uncertainties, feel perplexed, and think, "perhaps this perfection of wisdom is so, perhaps it is not so"...or Bodhisattvas which are seen to be lacking a good friend, which are believed to have been taken hold of by bad friends who, as perfecting of wisdom is taking place, either do not hear or do not understand about very deep stations in nature, or wisdom, and choosing to remain in ignorance of these, do not ask how this perfecting of wisdom is developed; or, Bodhisattvas which cling to someone who upholds any dharma which, not being true of any of these dharmas, thus says: "I am an adherent to this one [or mental state], and in all things this one I follow does not abandon me. [418] Here are many other Bodhisattvas whom I might adhere to, but these do not suit me. I have taken this one as my fitting companion and this suits me."

Moreover, a Bodhisattva might, as this deep perfecting of nature as wisdom is taking place, say to another Bodhisattva: "Deep, indeed, is this perfecting of wisdom! What point is here in your listening to this? For even as I apply myself to this in the way in which Tathagatas have taught in other Sutrantas, even so I do not get to the bottom of this, nor derive any enjoyment from this. What is any point in anyone's hearing and writing this?"

In this way one projects one's lack of understanding, and herein appears to be making attempts to estrange other Bodhisattvas. Thus, it is seen as being Mara coming also to such a Bodhisattva...to hurt and gain entry herein. Furthermore, Ananda herein is this thought to be Mara as the one being contented, elated or enraptured. Mara is accredited in one's thinking as being the one who is overjoyed, exultant and glad, thrilled, delighted and jubilant in any case in which a Bodhisattva in one's own laxity despises other Bodhisattvas, thinking: "I dwell in the dwelling of detachment, but not so these; theirs is not this dwelling in detachment." And blindly is it thought of as being Mara also who is so joyful as this Bodhisattva keeps far away from revealing full enlightenment. On the contrary, in this imagined joy and contented ecstasy of one who allows themselves to think thus, is Mara seen to be this most excellent teacher of the exceedingly tenuous nature of one's disconcerted application of right concentration, mindfulness and effort.
Besides this, as a Bodhisattva takes on a name or clan, or as ascetic qualities are proclaimed, one may regard this as a sufficient reason to despise other Bodhisattvas, well-behaved and lovely in character though these are. [419] But this one has no depth of practice and does not apply qualities of irreversible Bodhisattvas which course toward perfect wisdom, nor their attributes, tokens or signs. As this one does not exude the irreversible qualities, such a one gives rise to defilement, seeing as this one thinks to attempt exalting one's self and self's concepts above others, and deprecates others, and thinks these are not equal to such dharmas, as oneself is. The Evil Maras, which are anyone's unpracticed, untrained inclinations toward such, then foresee that the realms of Mara will not remain empty, and the great hells, the animal kingdom, the world of the Pretas, and the assemblies of the Asuras are overcrowded. And what is thought of as Mara, and blamed on this Evil One, is seen as becoming even more determined, and thinking something such as: "With this kind of start any Bodhisattvas such as this are

soon smothered by gain and honor. These are plausible talkers, and with their plausible talk these catch hold of many people. Many people decide to listen to these, imitate what these speak of and show, and consequently do not train in Thusness, do not progress in this, do not make endeavours about this, and as well, these further increase defilements. So it is a fact all these deeds -of body, voice or mind- which these undertake with perverted mentality impels these to a rebirth in conditions which are unserviceable and do not provide selfless service, disagreeing as disagreeable, unpleasing as well as unpleasant. Consequently, what is seen to be the realms of Mara are overcrowded, i.e. the great hells, the animal world, the world of the Pretas, and [420] the assemblies of the Asuras." As this Bodhisattva considers this sequence of events, one believes it to be Mara the Evil One who is contented, elated, enraptured, overjoyed, exultant and jubilant. It is not Mara, however, who is given to sloth, this contented unawareness or ecstatic jubilation.

Furthermore, Ananda, as a Bodhisattva fights with any person belonging to the vehicle of the Sravakas, or Disciples, disputes and quarrels with these, abuses and reviles these, feels ill-will and hatred for these, a person comes to think to themselves that Mara thinks "surely, this son or daughter of good family keeps away from all-knowledge, this one remains far away from this." Now also, Mara is thought of as being even more jubilant as any person belonging to the vehicle of the Bodhisattvas fights with someone else which also belongs to this vehicle of the Bodhisattvas, for he thinks that "both these Bodhisattvas remain far from all-knowledge." But as a Bodhisattva which has one's prediction fights with another Bodhisattva which also has this prediction, and cherishes malice for one such as this - for many aeons this one does, as this one may have such an attitude of mind, put on the armor [which enables any to struggle against it], -unless, of course, one has abandoned all-knowledge completely. [421]Still in this, one here sees that it is not Mara, but one's own inclinations, attitudes and disconcertedness, seen as being Mara, which brings these unfortunate circumstances to bear...as well, it will be one's own right intentions and efforts, mindfulness and concentrations which comes to reveal these circumstances as dissolved in equanimity and perfect wisdom.

The Bodhisattvas Right Attitude Towards other Bodhisattvas

Ananda: Can one escape from these attitudes of mind, or is one definitely condemned to go on putting on the armor for all this length of time?
The Lord: Ananda, a dharma is demonstrated which includes the possibility of escape, -for persons of the Sravaka, Disciple-vehicle, for persons of the Pratyekabuddha-vehicle, for persons of the Bodhisattva-vehicle. As to this

person which belongs to the vehicle of the Bodhisattvas and quarrels with someone else which also belongs to the vehicle of the Bodhisattvas, -as one does not confess one's fault, does not promise restraint in future, harbors a latent bias towards hate, and dwells tied to bias, -this person does not allow for the teaching of escape [i.e. from the consequence of action], but is definitely condemned to go on putting on the armor for any and all lengths of time. But, to any one which confesses any and all fault, resolves true restraint throughout any of the three times, and reflects as follows: "This nature is to drive away bias, to pacify and appease the quarrels, disputes and conflicts of all beings, yet I myself engage in disputes! It is indeed a loss to me, and not a gain, as I answer back as I am spoken to. As I am to any and all beings a bridge across the sea of birth-and-death, I nevertheless say to another, 'the same to you,' or return a harsh and rough answer. This is not a way in which to speak. In fights, quarrels and disputes, here I behave as a senseless idiot, or dumb sheep. As I hear someone using offensive, abusive, insulting words towards me, this heart does not cherish malice for these or others. It is not [422] disciplined for me to mete and perceive faults assumed by me or another of others, or to think what is being said or even thought about any faults of others is worth listening to. As well, neither are any which mete and perceive thusly thought of as such. For as I am earnestly intent and intentioned, I do not do harm to others. As I indicate joy and contentment by pointing out any and all things which allow for joy and contentment, I head this way, as these, toward Nirvana, -yet nevertheless I bear ill will! I truly resolve to not bear ill will even against these which I perceive as having offended against me, and I truly resolve to avoid rage, and I truly resolve by making diligent and persistent effort in this direction. Even as my life is in danger I truly resolve not to allow a rage, or even a frown to appear on my face." -To such a Bodhisattva, Ananda, I teach escape. This is the attitude which a Bodhisattva adopts also towards persons who belong to the vehicle of the Disciples. Never to allow anger with any being, this is the attitude of mind one adopts towards all beings. What attitude now does a Bodhisattva have towards other persons avowed to this vehicle of the Bodhisattvas? The same as towards any Teacher. One has the attitude that, "these Bodhisattvas are my teachers. Surely, these mount on this same vehicle as I, have ascended by this same path, are of like intention with me, are set out in this same vehicle as I. Here these are trained, this is the method by which I train. But as some of us dwell in a dwelling tainted [by the ideas of Maras, Disciples and Pratyekabuddhas], [423] I do not do likewise. As, however these dwell in an uncontaminated dwelling, in mental activities which accord unto all-knowledge, now I also train as these. No obstacles can arise to any Bodhisattva which trains oneself in this way in all-knowledge, and one quickly reveals full enlightenment.

Chapter 25: TRAINING

How a Bodhisattva is Trained in All-Knowledge

Subhuti: In which training, O Lord, does a Bodhisattva train to be trained in all-knowledge?

The Lord: A Bodhisattva trains in Extinction, in Non-production, in Non-stopping, in No-birth, in the absence of positivity, in Isolatedness, in Dispassion, in Space, in the element of dharma, and Nirvana.

Subhuti: How do these amount to a training in all-knowledge?

The Lord: Do you think, Subhuti, this Suchness which is (also) Tathagatas, which is the prime cause of Tathagata being a Tathagata, can this become extinct?

Subhuti: No, Lord. For extinction cannot become extinct, extinction being inextinguishable. [425]

The Lord: Suchness of Tathagata is primordial essence of Tathagata, as a Tathagata, is this now produced, or stopped, or born; or does this become or cease to become; or does this become isolated; or impassioned or dispassionate; or does this become like space, or does this become of the nature of dharma?

Subhuti: No, Lord.

The Lord: Does this Suchness then, or even now, enter Nirvana?

Subhuti: No, Lord.

The Lord: Now...Subhuti, any Bodhisattva which trains oneself trains thus, "Suchness does not, indeed cannot get extinct"...as one trains thus, one realizes this perfection of all training. One cannot be crushed by what is seen or thought to be Mara, or by what is seen or thought to be Mara's associates or by Mara's host.

Soon one reveals to oneself this condition of irreversibility which becomes realized by others. Soon one sits on this terrace of enlightenment. One courses in one's own range. [426]

One is trained in the dharmas by which one is revealed as a facilitator and guide to realization, in great friendliness, great compassion, great sympathetic joy, as well as great and equanimous impartiality. One trains as turning the wheel of dharma with three revolutions and twelve aspects. One trains to indicate these revelations and the realization herein to no limit of beings. One trains to ensure non-interruption of this lineage of Tathagatas. One trains by opening this door and indicating such, as well as revealing this deathless element. Any being not training thusly is however, incapable of this sublime training. A weakling cannot train in this training.

As these which train thusly are the very cream of beings which indicate realization to any and all beings, these persevere and reach this state of elevated awareness for these beings. A Bodhisattva which trains thus is not reborn in the hells, nor among animals, nor in the realms of the Pretas, nor among the Asuras, nor in outlying districts [among barbarous populations], nor in the families of outcasts or fowlers, of hunters, fishermen or butchers, nor in any families of a kind in which one is addicted to the lower deeds. This one is not blind, deaf, or one-eyed; neither a cripple nor hunch-backed, nor a being with withered hand or arm, nor limping, nor lame, or stunned, [427] not tremulous, quivering or shaky; this one's limbs are not puny, nor incomplete, nor abnormal; such a one is not weak, nor have a bad complexion or shape; these faculties are not inferior nor incomplete, but are in every way perfect; and this one also has a melodious voice. Such a one as this is not a person who takes life, or who takes what is not given, or who goes wrong about sense-desires, or who speaks falsely, or maliciously, or harshly, or who prattles indistinctly, or who is covetous, or who harbours ill will in one's heart, or who has wrong views, and does not earn a livelihood in some wrong fashion. This one is not reborn among the long-lived Gods, does not take up bad moral practices, does not take hold of unreal dharmas, and does not get reborn through the influences of trances and [formless] attainments. For here is skill in means, and endowed with this, one does not get reborn among the long-lived Gods. But what is this skill in means of a Bodhisattva? This is just this perfection of wisdom. And this one applies oneself to this skill in means in such a way as, endowed with this, a Bodhisattva enters into these trances without being reborn through the influence of these trances. [428] As one trains thus, any Bodhisattva incurs the perfect purity of these powers, of these grounds of self-confidence, of these Buddha-dharmas. One reaches all this.

Subhuti: As we all know, O Lord, all dharmas are by nature perfectly pure. But now, with regard to this, whichever dharma does any Bodhisattva incur and reach perfect purity of these powers, these grounds of self-confidence and these Buddha-dharma?

The Lord: Well it is which you ask, Subhuti. For all dharmas are just by [their essential original] nature perfectly pure. A Bodhisattva which trains in perfection of wisdom does not lose heart and remains uncowed although all dharmas are by nature perfectly pure, now this is this perfection of wisdom. But the foolish neither know nor see these dharmas are really so constituted, and these neither know nor see the true nature of dharmas, even as this comes to be revealed. On behalf of such beings and things the Bodhisattva struggle on and exert vigour so any who do not know may be enabled to know, so any who do not see may choose to see. In this training these train, and here [in the world of appearance] a Bodhisattva realizes these powers through making these available to countless beings, these grounds of self-confidence, and all Buddha-dharmas. As these train thus, Bodhisattvas wisely (naturally come to) know these throbbing thoughts and actions of any and all beings, of any and all persons as these persons really are. And now, in this we go beyond the knowledge of the thoughts and actions of others. We traverse this ground upon which no foot gains footing, no words can mention, no thought can think, and neither can any eye behold. [429]

The Fewness of Bodhisattvas

On this earth, few are places free from stones, few the spots where gold and silver are found. Much more numerous are saline deserts, arid deserts, places covered with grass, or thorns, or steep chasms. Just so, in the worlds of beings few Bodhisattvas exist which train in this training in all-knowledge, i.e. in the training toward perfect wisdom which is perfect nature. Much more numerous are these which train in the training characteristics of Sravakas,

Disciples and Pratyekabuddhas.

Furthermore, Subhuti, in the worlds of beings few do deeds which lead to the authority of a universal monarch. Much more numerous are these which do deeds which lead to the authority of a commander of a fort. Just so, in these worlds of beings few are Bodhisattvas which are mounted on this path of perfect wisdom and/or nature, and which now are resolved to reveal and realize full enlightenment. Much more numerous are these which mount on the path of Sravakas, Disciples and Pratyekabuddhas.

Furthermore, few only do deeds which permit these to become Sakra, Chief of

Gods. Much more numerous are those whose deeds lead to the world of [the minor] Gods. Just so, few beings only are Bodhisattvas which train in this training as the perfecting of wisdom. Much more numerous are these Bodhisattvas which train in the training of Sravakas, Disciples and Pratyekabuddhas. [430]

Furthermore, few beings only do deeds which permit these to become Brahma. Much more numerous are any whose deeds lead to Brahma's assembly. Just so, few beings only are irreversible to full enlightenment. Much more numerous are Bodhisattvas which turn away from full enlightenment.

Here now, Subhuti, in the worlds of beings few beings exist which set out toward full enlightenment. Fewer are these which progress toward Thusness. Still fewer are these very few which make endeavours about and toward perfecting wisdom. Still fewer even are these very very few Bodhisattvas which are irreversible from full enlightenment. A Bodhisattva which aspires to be numbered among these very, very few irreversible Bodhisattvas now train in just this perfection of wisdom, and make endeavours about this. Moreover, Subhuti, no harsh thoughts arise to a Bodhisattva which thus trains in perfecting this nature as wisdom, nor any doubting thought, or an envious or mean thought, or an immoral thought, or a thought of ill will, or a lazy thought, or a distracted thought, or a stupid thought.

The Perfection of Wisdom Comprehends All Perfections

It is thus as a Bodhisattva trains in the perfection of wisdom, [431] all the perfections are automatically incorporated, taken up, followed and included. The view of individuality includes all the sixty-two views, and even so, for a Bodhisattva which trains in this perfection of wisdom, all the perfections are included in this. As long as someone's life-faculty is present, all faculties are included in this. Even so for a Bodhisattva which trains in this perfection of wisdom all the wholesome dharmas are included in this. As someone's life faculty is not present, all faculties are not present. Even so, for a Bodhisattva which trains in perfect wisdom, any unwholesome dharmas are stopped as only non-cognition is stopped, and all these perfections are included in this, and automatically revealed and realized.

Merit from Perfect Wisdom

Here and now, Subhuti, a Bodhisattva which has aspirations to reveal and realize all perfections trains in this perfection of wisdom. As one trains in this perfection of wisdom, a Bodhisattva trains in this which is unfathomable perfection as is any being. And herein lies this answer to this greatest of mysteries. For one's merit is different and unfathomable. Subhuti, consider all beings in the great trichiliocosm, are these many?

Subhuti: Even in Jambudvipa alone, here are many beings, how many more are here in this great trichiliocosm?

The Lord: As one single Bodhisattva, during one's entire life, furnishes all these beings with robes, alms bowl, lodging, medicinal appliances for use in sickness, and all which brings these happiness, -[432] does such a Bodhisattva on the strength of this beget a great deal of merit?

Subhuti: One does, O Lord.

The Lord: Yet Subhuti, a different and unthinkable merit still does this Bodhisattva beget as a result of developing this perfection of wisdom, of buddha-nature, for even the duration of a finger-snap. So greatly profitable is this perfection of wisdom of Bodhisattvas, as she feeds these revelations of this supreme enlightenment. A Bodhisattva here now trains in perfecting wisdom as this aspiration to full realization, revealed as this supreme position common to all beings, as a protector of any which are helpless and helps these to reach this sphere of the Buddha, to emulate the humaness of the Buddha, to sport as a Buddha's sport, to roar a Buddha's lion roar, to reach the accomplishment of a Buddha, and to explain this dharma in this great trichiliocosm. As a Bodhisattva trains in this perfection of wisdom, I do not see the accomplishment in which one does not train.

Bodhisattvas and Disciples

Subhuti: Is now a Bodhisattva also trained in this accomplishment of a Sravaka, a Disciple?

The Lord: He also trains in this. But one does not train with intentions of always continuing with these accomplishments of a Sravaka, or Disciple, or with any idea of making this or anything one's own. [433] Not thus does one train. One also knows qualities of the Disciples, but does not abide with these. One assimilates these, without opposing these. One trains with the intention as one demonstrates and reveals also these virtues of the Disciples. As one trains thus, a Bodhisattva is revealed in a condition here as one worthy of receiving gifts from the world with its Gods, beings and Asuras. These surpass others which are worthy of gifts, associated with Disciples or Pratyekabuddhas. And all-knowledge is near to such one's as these. As one trains thus, a Bodhisattva does not part from this perfection of wisdom, but courses in this, is not lacking in the dwelling of this perfection of wisdom. As one courses thus a Bodhisattva is known as "unfailing, definitely unfailing" with regard to all-knowledge, and does not settle on any level of a Sravaka, Disciple or Pratyekabuddha. One such as this is near to full enlightenment. As, however, such may occur to this one "this is the perfection of wisdom which brings this all-knowledge," -now, one which has such a notion does not course in this perfection of wisdom. On the contrary any such as this have no notion whatsoever of perfecting wisdom. Do not perceive or review "this is the perfection of wisdom," or "this is the perfection of wisdom," or "this feeds all-knowledge." As one courses thus, a Bodhisattva courses in this perfection of wisdom.

Chapter 26: ~LIKE ILLUSION ~

Sakra Praises the Bodhisattvas

So now it occurs to Sakra, Chief of Gods: A Bodhisattva, even as one courses only just so far, surpasses all; how much more so as one knows full enlightenment! A great gain accrues to these beings, a good life do these live as thoughts stride in all-knowledge; how much more so as these have realized thoughts unto full enlightenment! To be emulated are these, the very cream of all beings, which realize full enlightenment!

So here, Sakra, Chief of Gods, conjured up Mandarava flowers, saluted these reverently, scattered these over Tathagata, and said: May any persons who are avowed to the vehicle of Bodhisattvas, and who have revealed and realized thoughts to full enlightenment, succeed in their resolve to know full enlightenment, and beyond this, to transfer any and all beings which are borne along by the great flood of birth-and-death to the smooth yonder shore! May this thought of enlightenment which these wish for, think over and take hold of, bring to fulfillment any dharmas of a Buddha, and dharmas in accord with all-knowledge, dharmas of the Self-Existent, insuperable dharmas! I have not even the slightest suspicion such Bodhisattvas, which are endowed with great compassion, might turn away from full enlightenment, [435] or these persons who are avowed to the vehicle of the Bodhisattvas and who are set out for full enlightenment might turn away from this. On the contrary, I am sure this resolve to reveal and realize full enlightenment increases more and more in these, as these survey the ills which afflict beings on the plane of birth-and-death. For through great compassion these desire the welfare of this world with its Gods, beings and Asuras, are of an aspiration to benefit this, are full of pity for this, these, who are endowed with this attitude of mind, dwell in the attitude of mind which is expressed in this resolution..."we have crossed over, we help beings to cross over! Freed, we free them! Recovered, we help these to recover! Gone to Nirvana, we lead these to Nirvana!" "Gat¨| Gat¨| Paragat¨| Parasamgat¨| Bodhi Svaha!"

Jubilation, Turning Over, and Merit

Any son or daughter of good family who rejoice at this production of thought of any Bodhisattvas, who are just now set out in the vehicle, as well as at this production of thought of any which realize progression as always, on course, as well as at this irreversible nature of any which realize irreversibility, as well as at this nature of any which inevitably realize one birth only, -to what extent is their merit a different one?

The Lord: One might be able, Kausika, to grasp the measure of Sumeru, king of mountains, or of a world system, up to a great trichiliocosm, with the help of a tip of straw, but one can not possibly grasp any measure of merit coming to these sons or daughters of good family, or to a Bodhisattva, from the production of this thought connected with that jubilation. [436]

Sakra: Seen as and thought of as beset by Mara are any beings which do not hear of this immeasurable merit of jubilation over the career of a Bodhisattva -which begins with the first thought of enlightenment [tathagatagarbha] and which ends with full enlightenment [Tathagata] -which do not know it, which do not see it, which do not bring this jubilation to mind. These are seen as partisans of Mara, deceased in Mara's realms. For any which bring to mind these thoughts, which turn these over into the supreme enlightenment, rejoice at these, such do so in order to bring to realization Mara's realm, as this truly is. One does O Lord, rejoice at the various stages of thought which these Bodhisattvas raise to enlightenment. [437] Sons and daughters of good family abandon neither the Tathagata, nor Dharma, nor Community, these rejoice in the stages of the thought of enlightenment!

The Lord: So it is, Kausika. And sons or daughters of good family who have rejoiced in the stages of the thought of enlightenment, these do - whether these belong to the vehicle of the Bodhisattvas, or of the Pratyekabuddhas, or of the Disciples - soon please the Tathagatas, and not displease such as these.

Sakra: So it is, O Lord. Here and now, these are reborn as a result of the wholesome roots [which these plant] as hearts are filled with jubilation, here these are treated with respect, revered, worshipped and adored. These never see any unpleasant sights, nor hear any unpleasant sounds, nor smell any unpleasant smells, nor taste any unpleasant tastes, [438] nor come into contact with anything unpleasant to the touch. One realizes these things to be reborn in the wholesome roots of countless beings, roots which bring happiness to all beings. The thoughts of jubilation of any beings which, as producing an aspiration towards enlightenment, rejoice over the successive stages of the thought of enlightenment [enlightened thought] in persons who aspire to the vehicle of Bodhisattvas, as these thoughts increase, are nourishers of full enlightenment. As these realize and reveal full enlightenment, and just so these lead countless beings to Nirvana.

The Lord: So it is, Kausika, as you say through Tathagatas might. The wholesome roots of countless beings are rejoiced over, planted and consummated as a consequence of these actions of sons or daughters of good family who rejoice over the successive stages of the thought of enlightenment in these persons who belong to this vehicle of the Bodhisattvas.

The Nature of Illusion

Subhuti: But how can a thought which is like illusion know full enlightenment?

The Lord: Subhuti, do you see the thought which is like illusion as a separate real entity?

Subhuti: No, Lord.

The Lord: Do you see illusion as a separate real entity?

Subhuti: No, Lord. [439]

The Lord: So, as you see neither illusion, nor the thought which is like illusion, as a real separate entity, do you now perhaps see this dharma which knows full enlightenment as something other than illusion, or as something other than the thought which is like illusion?

Subhuti: No, Lord. I do not. In consequence, to which dharma can I point, and say "it is" or "it is not?" To a dharma which is absolutely isolated one cannot attribute "it is" or "it is not." Also any absolutely isolated dharma can not know full enlightenment. Here now, O Lord, perfect wisdom is absolutely isolated. But any dharma which is absolutely isolated, this is not a dharma which can be developed, nor does this bring about or remove any dharma. So, how can a Bodhisattva, by resorting to an absolutely isolated perfection of wisdom, know full enlightenment? Even full enlightenment is absolutely isolated. [440] As, O Lord, the perfection of wisdom is absolutely isolated, and as full enlightenment is absolutely isolated, how can the isolated become known through the isolated?

The Lord: So it is, Subhuti. It is just as this perfection of wisdom is absolutely isolated that absolutely isolated full enlightenment is known [by this]. But as a Bodhisattva forms such a notion as "the perfection of wisdom is absolutely isolated," this is not the perfection of wisdom. It is thus certain, thanks to perfecting wisdom a Bodhisattva can know full enlightenment, and one cannot know this without resorting to this. The isolated cannot be known by the isolated, and nevertheless a Bodhisattva knows full enlightenment, and does not know this without resorting to the perfection of wisdom.

Subhuti: As I understand the meaning of the Lord's teaching, a Bodhisattva in this way courses in an unfathomable object.

The Lord: A doer of what is hard is the Bodhisattva which courses in an unfathomable object, and which yet does not realize such object [or: gain], i.e. on the level of Sravaka, Disciple or Pratyekabuddha.

Subhuti: As I understand the meaning of the Lord's teaching, here is in this way no Bodhisattva at all which is any doer of what is hard. [441] As this very dharma is not got at which is realized, nor anything whatsoever which can be revealed or realized, nor anything whatsoever by means of which one can realize. So, as this is being taught, as a Bodhisattva is not despondent, cowed or stolid, does not turn back, and remains unafraid, this one courses in perfect wisdom. As one does not review this as a certain fact as one courses, one such courses in perfect wisdom. As one does not review this as a real fact one is near to full enlightenment, one such as this courses in perfect wisdom. As it does not even occur to one that one is keeping aloof from the level of Disciples and Pratyekabuddhas, this one courses in perfect wisdom. This does not occur to space, "I am near to this, or, I am far from that," for space cannot make such discriminations, just so it cannot in truth occur to a Bodhisattva which courses in perfect wisdom..."full enlightenment is near to me, the level of Sravaka, Disciple or Pratyekabuddha is far from me."

The perfection of wisdom does not make any discriminations. It is as with a man created by magical illusion to which (!) it does not occur "the conjurer is near to 'me', but this assembled crowd of spectators is far from 'me'." For illusory men make no such discriminations. [442] It is as with the reflection of an object in a mirror or in water, to which it does not occur "the object which produces the reflection is near to 'me', but these who come along and cast the reflection in the mirror or in water, are far from 'me'." For this reflection of an object makes no discrimination. Just as Tathagata, as one which forsakes all constructions and discriminations, finds nothing dear or not dear, just so a Bodhisattva which courses in perfecting wisdom, for here is no discrimination on the part of perfect wisdom. Just as Tathagata is one which forsakes all constructions and discriminations, even so perfect wisdom forsakes all constructions and discriminations. It does not occur to a fictitious creature which Tathagata magically conjures up "the level of Sravakas, Disciples and Pratyekabuddhas is far from 'me', full enlightenment is near to 'me'," for any fictitious creature can not make any discriminations. In the same way a Bodhisattva which courses in perfect wisdom does not think "the level of Sravakas, Disciples and Pratyekabuddhas is far from 'me', full enlightenment is near to 'me'," and this simply due to an absence of any and all discrimination on the part of the perfection of wisdom. [443] A fictitious creature [which has been conjured up by the Tathagata] to do a certain work [in converting beings], performs this work, but remains without discrimination, just due to being so constituted as it lacks all discrimination. Just so a Bodhisattva performs the work for the sake of which one develops this perfection of wisdom, but this perfection of wisdom remains without discrimination, due to the fact as it is so constituted it lacks all discrimination. An expert mason, or mason's apprentice, makes of wood an automatic man or woman, a puppet which can be moved by pulling the strings. Whatever action it is made to perform, this action it performs, yet this wooden machine has no discrimination. Just due to the fact as it is so constituted that it lacks all discrimination. Just so a Bodhisattva performs this work for the sake of which one develops this perfection of wisdom, but this perfection of wisdom remains without discrimination, just due to the fact as this perfection of wisdom is so constituted it lacks all discriminations.

Chapter 27: ~THE CORE~

The Bodhisattvas Courage in Difficulties

Sariputra: Translucently...in this core and substance of things course these Bodhisattvas coursing in perfect wisdom!

Subhuti: Translucently as well, Sariputra...devoid of any center or boundary, in dharmas devoid even of substantiality course theseBodhisattvas coursing in perfect wisdom.

Here and now, these thoughts occur at once to many thousands of Gods of the realm of sense-desire: Homage is due to these beings which raise thoughts to, and are consummating these thoughts in full enlightenment, these coursing in this most profound perfection of wisdom, and as these are coursing thus, do not realize any boundary to reality, be this on the level of a Sravaka, Disciple, or even of a Pratyekabuddha. In this way also are Bodhisattvas known as doers of what is hard, as these course in this true nature of dharma, but do not realize this as such, for of this truth is herein no thing to be revealed, and indeed, nothing to realize. This is, again...Suchness. We, as any and all dharmas, are this already, prior to and beyond even any thought to seek for it...and once we begin to seek, are no longer that which we seek, for we think of this, then, as some thing other than what this is.

Subhuti read their thoughts, and said to them: This is not hard for these Bodhisattvas that these do not realize any reality-limit. This, however, is hard for these, this is most hard for these, [445] as these put on this armor of this resolution to lead countless beings to Nirvana, but now absolutely such beings do not exist. And since these do not exist, these cannot be got at.

Owing to isolatedness of beings, these who are disciplined thus absolutely do not exist. It is in this spirit the Bodhisattva set out toward revealing full enlightenment, and decides to discipline beings. For isolatedness of beings is known only as is the design of isolatedness of space [as dharmakaya]. In this way also Bodhisattvas are doers of what is hard, as these put on this armor for the sake of beings who do not exist, who cannot be got at. One decides to put on space exactly the same as one decides to put on this armor for the sake of beings. And yet this armor, as non-extinguishable space IS put on by Bodhisattvas for the sake of beings. But this non-apprehension of beings, in [ultimate and] absolute reality, is taught by Tathagatas. And this non-apprehension of beings is inferred from this very isolatedness, and from the isolatedness of any who are so disciplined is the isolatedness of a

Bodhi-being inferred. As a Bodhisattva, while this is being taught, does not lose heart, one can know this one courses in this perfection of wisdom. For from the isolatedness of a being is known the isolatedness of form, feeling, perception, impulse, and consciousness...and this the same of all dharmas. [446] Thus is the isolatedness of all dharmas viewed. As this isolatedness of all dharmas is thus taught, a Bodhisattva does not lose heart, and due to this, one courses in this perfection of wisdom.

The Lord: For what reason does a Bodhisattva not lose heart as the isolatedness of all dharmas is thus taught?

Subhuti: Due to isolatedness no dharma can ever lose heart. For one cannot get at any dharma as loses heart, nor at any dharma which makes a dharma lose heart.

The Lord: So it is, Subhuti. It is quite certain a Bodhisattva courses in perfect and natural wisdom as this is being taught, demonstrated, expounded and pointed out...one does not lose heart, is neither cast down nor depressed, is not cowed or stolid, does not turn one's mind away from this, does not have one's back broken, and remains unafraid.

The Bodhisattva Protected by the Gods, and against Mara

Subhuti: So it is. As a Bodhisattva courses thus, one courses in perfect wisdom. And the Gods round Indra, around Brahman, round Prajapati, round Ishana, and the crowds of men and women round the Rishis, from a distance pay homage with hands together to a Bodhisattva coursing thus. [447]

The Lord: And not only these, but also all the other Gods, up to the Akanistha Gods, pay homage to such a one. And with the Buddha-eye, Tathagatas within any present moment residing in countless world systems behold these Bodhisattvas thus coursing in perfect wisdom, and these help such a one, and bring one to mind. This is quite certain, Subhuti, these Bodhisattvas coursing in perfect wisdom, and being helped and brought to mind by Tathagatas, are borne in mind as irreversible from full enlightenment being revealed and realized as such. No obstacle seen or thought of as being put up by Mara or anyone else can stop these. Even as all beings in the great trichiliocosm are seen as being evil Maras, and each one of these conjure up just as many diabolic armies, [448] even these all together have not the strength to obstruct on one's way to full enlightenment any Bodhisattva brought to mind by the Buddhas and coursing in perfect wisdom. And this remains true even as all the beings in all the countless trichiliocosms are seen as evil Maras, and as each one of these conjures up just as many diabolic armies. The endowment with these two dharmas safeguards a Bodhisattva against all attacks which are seen and thought of as coming from the Maras, or their hosts: 1) One can not abandon any being, and 2) One surveys all dharmas as reflected from emptiness. Two other dharmas have this same effect: 1) As one speaks so one acts, and 2) One is brought to mind by the Buddhas, the Lords.

As a Bodhisattva courses thus, the Gods also decide to go up to one such as this. These decide to ask questions and counter-questions, [449] to honor, and to strengthen one's determination by saying: "Soon, child of good family, shall you know full enlightenment! Here now, go on dwelling in this dwelling of perfect wisdom! Thus you offer safety to the helpless, defense of the defenseless, a refuge to these without refuge, a place of rest to these without resting place, the final relief of these who are without this, an island to any without one, a light to the blind, a guide to the guideless, a resort to any without one, and you guide to the path any who have lost this, herein you become a support to one's who are without support."

The Buddha's Praise the Bodhisattva

The Buddhas, Lords who reside in countless world-systems, and who demonstrate dharma surrounded by a congregation of monks and attended by a multitude of Bodhisattvas, proclaim the name, clan, power, appearance and form of a Bodhisattva which courses and dwells in perfect wisdom, and is endowed with the virtues of roaming in perfect wisdom, perfecting wisdom. And these demonstrate Dharma, and exult over this Bodhisattva, proclaiming name, clan, power, color and form. Just here and now I demonstrate dharma, and I proclaim the name, etc., of the Bodhisattva Ratnaketu, and of the Bodhisattva Sikhin. [450] I exult over these, and also over the other Bodhisattvas which just now lead the holy life with Tathagata Akshobhya. In a similar way, the Buddhas in other Buddha-fields proclaim the name, etc., of Bodhisattvas just now leading the holy life here in this Buddha-field, and which dwell in the dwelling of perfect wisdom. And these exult over such as these.

Subhuti: Do the Buddhas honor all Bodhisattvas in such a manner?

The Lord: No, Subhuti. But only one's which are irreversible and free from all attachment.

Subhuti: Apart from the irreversible Bodhisattvas, do the Buddhas in such a manner honor any other Bodhisattvas?

The Lord: Yes, here are others. These are persons belonging to the vehicle of the Bodhisattvas, who are strong in assimilating what may be seen as an enemy. These are [451] just now engaged in learning this course of a Bodhisattva under Tathagata Akshobhya, and the Bodhisattva Ratnaketu, courses here on the pilgrimage of a Bodhisattva, and dwells, engaged in learning it. In addition, these Bodhisattvas which course in perfect wisdom, and resolutely believe "all dharmas fail to be produced" without, however, so far acquiring definitely the patient acceptance of dharmas which fail to be produced; as well as these which resolutely believe "all dharmas are calmly quiet," without, however, having entered into accord with the irreversible domain over all dharmas; any Bodhisattvas which dwell in this dwelling are honored by the Buddhas in the above manner. [452] Bodhisattvas of whom the Buddhas proclaim the name, etc., and over whom these exult, have forsaken the level of the Sravakas, Disciples and Pratyekabuddhas, and one can well see these come to be on the level of the Buddha. And these are predicted to full enlightenment. For Bodhisattvas of whom the Buddhas proclaim the name, etc., and over whom these exult, also stand in irreversibility.

Enlightenment and Suchness

In addition to this, Subhuti, Bodhisattvas stand in irreversibility as, upon hearing this deep perfection of wisdom being taught, these resolutely believe in this, are not stupefied, do not hesitate or doubt; as in this resolute belief "so it is, as Tathagata teaches" these go on listening to this in greater detail; and as these make up their minds to listen in still greater detail to this perfection of wisdom in the presence of Tathagata Akshobhya; and as these resolutely believe from just hearing this perfection of wisdom in the presence of persons avowed to this vehicle of the Bodhisattvas which in this Buddha-field lead the holy life. [453] Thus I teach merely to hear perfection of wisdom achieves much. How much more is achieved by any who resolutely believe in this, who, upon this, take up a position in relation to Thusness and progress toward Thusness, and who, upon this, stand firmly in Suchness and who, standing firmly in Suchness and in all-knowledge, demonstrate dharma.

Subhuti: As, O Lord, one cannot get at any different dharma, distinct from Suchness, what is this dharma which stands firmly in Suchness, or which knows full enlightenment, or which even can demonstrate this dharma?

The Lord: One cannot get at any different dharma, distinct from Suchness, which stands firmly in Suchness. This very Suchness, to begin with, is not apprehended, how much less one which stands firmly in Suchness. Suchness does not know full enlightenment, and no dharma is got at which knows full enlightenment, can do so, or does do so. Suchness does not demonstrate dharma, and this dharma cannot be got at which is demonstrated. [454]

Emptiness and Dwelling in Perfect Wisdom

Sakra: Deep, O Lord, is perfecting of wisdom. Doers of what is hard are these Bodhisattvas which aspire to full enlightenment. Indeed, no dharma stands in Suchness, no dharma knows full enlightenment, no one demonstrates dharma. And yet this does not cow these, nor do these hesitate, nor are these stupefied.

Subhuti: You say, Kausika,"doers of what is hard are Bodhisattvas which, as dharmas as deep as these are being taught, feel neither hesitation nor stupefaction." But, as all dharmas are empty who can herein feel hesitation or stupefaction? Who herein, can even begin to raise a question of hesitation or stupefaction?

Sakra: Whatever the holy Subhuti is expounding, this he expounds with reference to emptiness, and he does not get stuck anywhere. The holy Subhuti's demonstration of dharma does not get stuck anywhere, no more than an arrow shot into the air. Now perhaps, O Lord, I, as I take into consideration Subhuti the Elder, and teach as he thus teaches and expounds, may be one who correctly preaches Tathagata-truth, a preacher of Dharma, and one who declares also the logical sequence of dharma.

The Lord: So it is, Kausika. As you come to teach and expound as he does, you come to be one who correctly preaches Tathagata-truth, a preacher of dharma, and one who declares also the dharma's logical sequence. For whatever [455] the Elder Subhuti makes clear, this he makes clear with reference to emptiness. As the Elder Subhuti does not, to begin with, even review or apprehend perfection of wisdom, how much less one coursing in perfection of wisdom. Enlightenment, even to begin with he does not get at, how much less at one who knows full enlightenment. Even all knowledge, he does not get at, how much less at one who reaches unto all-knowledge. Even Suchness he does not get at, how much less at one who becomes a Tathagata. Even non-production he does not get at, how much less at one who fully has awoken to enlightenment. Even the powers Subhuti does not get at, how much less at one who possesses the powers. Even the grounds of self-confidence he does not review, how much less at one who is self-confident. Even the dharma he does not get at, how much less at one who demonstrates dharma. For Subhuti the Elder dwells in this dwelling of the isolatedness of all dharmas, in this dwelling of the baselessness of all dharmas. And this is quite certain this dwelling in isolatedness and baselessness of all dharmas, on the part of Subhuti the Elder, is of infinitesimal value compared with the dwelling of a Bodhisattva coursing in perfect wisdom, perfecting herein and dwelling in this. You see Kausika, except for the dwelling of Tathagata this dwelling of a Bodhisattva coursing in perfect wisdom, which dwells in it, surpasses all other dwellings. [456] This dwelling is described as the foremost of all dwellings, as the best, the choicest, the most excellent, the most sublime, the highest, the supreme, the unequalled, the incomparable. It surpasses the dwellings of all Sravakas, Disciples and Pratyekabuddhas. So here now, Kausika, a son or daughter of a good family who have this aspiration to arrive at the highest possible degree of perfection of all beings, to arrive at the best state, the choicest state, the most excellent state, the most sublime state, the incomparable state, -these do with diligence aspire to dwell in this dwelling of Bodhisattvas which course in perfect wisdom, which dwell in this.

Chapter 28: AVAKURNAKUSUNA

The Prediction of Avakirnakusuma

So, at this time, one of the Gods of the Thirty-three seized Mandarava flowers, magnificent Mandarava flowers, and comes here to the Lord. And just at this time, six thousand monks are assembled and seated in this assembly. They rise from their seats, put their upper robes over one shoulder, place their right knees on the earth, and salute the Lord with their hands together. Through the Buddha's might their hands are now filled Mandarava flowers, with magnificent Mandarava flowers. They scatter these flowers over the Lord, and speak: "We, O Lord, course in this perfection of wisdom!" Here and now, as this occasion progresses, the Lord is smiling. Such is the nature of the Buddhas and Lords that, when a smile is made to manifest [in an assembly of Bodhisattva], multiple colors of rays issue from the Lord's mouth, -rays of blue, yellow, red, white, crimson, crystal, silverfish and golden. These rays illuminate endless and boundless world systems with their luster, rising right up even to this world of Brahma, again returning from this world to the Lord, circulate thrice round the Lord, and now vanish again into the head of the Lord. [458] Here and now the venerable Ananda rises from his seat, put his upper robe over one shoulder, placed his right knee on the earth, placed his hands together and offered them and his entire being to the Lord, and said: It is not without reason the Tathagata manifests a smile. What is the reason for your smile, O Lord?

The Lord now speaks and says: These six thousand monks, Ananda, in a future period, in the Starlike aeon, do finally come to know full enlightenment, and within this demonstrate dharma to beings. These all bear the same name. With Avakirnakusuma for their name these Tathagatas are teachers in the world. These all have an equal congregation of disciples. These all live the same length of time, i.e., twenty thousand aeons. Each one of these have an extensive holy writ, which spreads widely among Gods and beings. In each case their good law abides for the same length of time, for twenty thousand aeons. And showers of flowers, of all the five colors, descends upon all of these - wherever they may leave a home which they had in a village, town or marketplace, or wherever they may turn once again the wheel of dharmas, wherever they may dwell, wherever they may appear [among people]. [459] [NOTE: the name 'Avakirnakusuma', literally means, 'covered with flowers', said in this prediction to be a group of future Buddhas.]

Praise of Perfect Wisdom

So here, Ananda, in any of these three times, Bodhisattvas aspiring to dwell in this highest dwelling, beyond limit, aspiring to dwell in this dwelling of Tathagata, dwell in this dwelling of perfect wisdom. With any Bodhisattvas coursing in perfecting this wisdom within, and actually becoming this and adapting this as oneself, ones such as these can be quite certain of having, before one is reborn here among people, deceased among people or among the heavenly hosts of the Tushitas. For it is among people and Tushita Gods this perfection of wisdom circulates to this full extent. One can be certain Tathagatas behold such Bodhisattvas as course in this perfection of wisdom, learn this, bear this in mind, study, speak of, repeat, or merely write this, and also instruct any other Bodhisattvas, admonish, instigate and encourage these.

You can know that ones such as these have planted and continue planting wholesome roots within and beyond any known limits, or any limits yet to be established...and these do this within this view and thought of Tathagatas. These do, not only in the presence of Sravakas, Disciples, and Pratyekabuddhas plant wholesome roots so as to train self and others in perfect wisdom, but, without any doubt these Bodhisattvas training in this perfection of wisdom and remaining unafraid, plant wholesome roots with Tathagatas. [460]

Any taking up this perfection of wisdom, bear this in mind, study, speak of, repeat and write this, which pursue this, - in its meaning, contents and method - one can be quite certain these have been face to face with Tathagatas. As Bodhisattvas do not revile this perfection of wisdom, neither oppose, deny nor reject this, one can know these fulfill their inclinations indicated under Jinas, these Buddhas of this past.

As a Bodhisattva does not go back on one's vow to reveal and have revealed, to realize and bring to realization full enlightenment, this one does not give the wholesome root which one plants in the all-presence of Tathagatas, over to Discipleship or Pratyekabuddhahood as one's reward. As a rule, as a matter of imperishable principle struck by the complete interdependence of any and all dharmas, such Bodhisattvas are grateful and practice this perfection of wisdom with no stopping whatsoever, even beyond these forms, feelings, perceptions, impulses or any consciousness of such dharmas. One can know this, to be sure. The spontaneity of Suchness reveals this thoughtless, timeless cognition borne of pure awareness...identical to space.

Transmission of the Sutra to Ananda

So, here now, Ananda, again and again I entrust and transmit to you this perfection of wisdom, laid out in letters, so this is available for learning, bearing in mind, discoursing, studying and spreading wide, so this lasts long, so this does not disappear. As, Ananda, you forget all the demonstrations of dharma which you learn directly from me - the perfection of wisdom being this lone exception - as you cast these away, and allow these to be forgotten, this is but a slight offence against Tathagatas.

But consider as you forget, cast away and allow to be forgotten only one verse of this perfection of wisdom, or merely a part of a verse, this is a serious [461] offence against Tathagatas, and this displeases me. And as you learn this perfection of wisdom, and you forget this, cast this away, allow this to be forgotten, you fail in the respect, reverence and worship afforded Tathagatas, past, future and present, all together. Here and now, Ananda, remember it is a serious offence against Tathagatas, whereas you learn this perfection of wisdom, you forget this, cast this away, and allow this to be forgotten, this displeases me. For Tathagatas say "this perfection of wisdom is mother, this sourceless source, the generatrix of past, future and present Tathagatas, the nurse in all-knowledge." Here and now, Ananda, do I entrust and transmit to you this perfection of wisdom, so it does not disappear.

This perfection of wisdom is learned, borne in mind, studied, repeated, written and developed. Attend this well, and spread this well. And as one learns this, one carefully analyzes this grammatically, letter by letter, syllable by syllable, word by word. [462] As the dharma-body of past, future and present Tathagatas is this dharma-text authoritative. In this same way in which Ananda behaves towards me, at present residing as a Tathagata - with solitude, affection and respect - in this same virtuous spirit, do you learn this perfection of wisdom, bear this in mind, study, repeat, write and develop this, respect, revere and worship this. This is a way for you or any to worship, this is a way to show affection, serene faith and respect for the past, future and present Buddhas and Lords.

As I, a Tathagata, am dear and pleasant to you Ananda, and you do not abandon me, here and now may this perfection of wisdom be dear and pleasant to you, and may you not abandon this, may you not forget even one single word of this, so this does not disappear. For long I speak to you about this bestowal of perfection of wisdom, for one kalpa, or for the remainder of a kalpa, for one hundred kalpas, for up to hundreds of thousands of kotis of kalpas, and more. But to cut this short, in this same way in which I am your teacher, so is this perfection of wisdom. In this same way in which the past, future and present Buddhas and Lords are teachers of the world with its Gods, beings and Asuras, just so is this perfection of wisdom.

Here and now, Ananda, [463] with a measureless bestowal I entrust and transmit to you this perfection of wisdom, which is beyond any measure whatsoever, for the benefit and happiness of the world with its Gods, beings and Asuras. As one does not want to abandon these Jewels of Tathagata, Dharma, or noble Sangha, as one does not want to abandon enlightenment of past, future and present Buddhas and Lords, - does one not abandon this perfection of wisdom! And here is this further admonition - as these who learn this perfection of wisdom, bear this in mind, study, repeat, write and develop this, these assist in enlightenment of the past, future and present Buddhas and Lords. For, whoever assists this perfection of wisdom as it is either thought to be, or seeming to crumble away, such a one assists in enlightenment of the past, future and present Buddhas and Lords. From this perfection of wisdom does enlightenment of Buddhas and Lords come forth. And this holds good of all Tathagatas, whether past, future or present.

Here and now, a Bodhisattva which has aspiration to know full enlightenment and to train in the six perfections listens to this perfection of wisdom, studys, repeats and writes this, [464] and one trains in this very perfection of wisdom, and makes endeavours around, about, and within this. This perfection of wisdom is mother, this sourceless source and generatrix of Bodhisattvas. It is due to this perfection of wisdom any Bodhisattvas ever train in the six perfections, and at any time progress to full enlightenment. It is due to just this perfection of wisdom Bodhisattvas progress in the six perfections, as all these perfections come to nourish this which provides dissolution of defilements and revelations toward supreme enlightenment as these are indicated and revealed from this perfection of wisdom.

Here and now, Ananda, again and again, for a second time, for a third time, do I entrust and transmit this perfection of wisdom to you, so it does not disappear. For this perfection of wisdom is the inexhaustible storehouse of the dharma of Tathagatas. The dharma which Buddhas and Lords demonstrate to beings in this past period, in these worlds of birth-and-death with no beginning or end, all this is indicated and revealed from just this storehouse of dharma, from this perfection of wisdom. As well, this dharma which the Buddhas and Lords demonstrate to beings, reveals also full enlightenment in any future period, for any such as have a view which leads beyond these measureless worlds of birth-and-death, also as is indicated and revealed from just this storehouse of dharma, this perfection of wisdom. And also the Buddhas and Lords just now residing in countless world systems, and demonstrating dharma, these also derive revelation from just this storehouse of dharma, this perfection of wisdom. As inexhaustible, here and now is this storehouse of dharma, this perfection of wisdom, still and after all. [464a]

As, Ananda, you demonstrate dharma on the Disciple-level to persons who take vows to the vehicle of the Disciples, and as a result of your demonstration of dharma all the beings in the great trichiliocosm realize Arhatship, you do not do your duty as my disciple as in this way you keep moving as I the wheel of dharma, and demonstrate dharma. But as, on this other hand, you demonstrate and reveal but one single verse of dharma associated with this perfection of wisdom to a Bodhisattva, I am pleased with you, who as my disciple turns as I the wheel of dharma, and demonstrate dharma. As you consider this demonstration of dharma of yours through which the beings in this great trichiliocosm all are induced to attain Arhatship, and of these Arhats the meritorious work founded on giving, on morality, and on meditational development continues, does all this constitute a great heap of merit?

Ananda: It would, O Lord.

The Lord: A person who has taken vows to the vehicle of the Disciple begets a different and immeasurable merit as this one demonstrates to Bodhisattvas the dharma associated with the perfection of wisdom. This merit is different as it is a Bodhisattva who demonstrates to another Bodhisattva [a verse of] dharma associated with this perfection of wisdom, -for even one single day only, for a morning, for an hour, for half an hour, for a minute, nay for a second, for a moment, or for an incidence of a single moment. For this gift of dharma on the part of any Bodhisattva is different from all the wholesome roots of all who avow to the vehicle of the Sravakas, Disciples, or Pratyekabuddhas. It is quite impossible for a Bodhisattva who is thus endowed as a Bodhisattva with wholesome roots, who thus brings to mind this wholesome root, to turn away from full enlightenment. This cannot be.

Akshobhya's Buddha-Field

Now on this occasion, the Lord exercises his wonderworking power. The entire assembly - monks, nuns, laymen and lay women, Gods, Nagas, Yakshas, Gandharvas, Asuras, Garudas, Kinnaras, Mahoragas, humans and ghosts - these all, through the Buddha's might, [465] see this Tathagata Akshobhya surrounded by the congregation of monks, accompanied by a retinue of Bodhisattvas demonstrating dharma, in an assembly vast like the ocean, deep and imperturbable, surrounded and accompanied by Bodhisattvas which are endowed with unthinkable qualities, all of these Arhats, -with outflows exhausted, undefiled, fully controlled, quite freed in their hearts, well freed and wise, thoroughbreds, great Serpents, their work done, their task accomplished, their burden laid down, their own weal accomplished, with the fetters which bound these to become, extinguished, their hearts well freed by right understanding, in perfect control of their entire hearts.

Here and now the Lord again withdrew his wonderworking power. The Lord Akshobhya, a Tathagata, no longer appeared, and all the Bodhisattvas and great Disciples, and the Buddha-field no longer comes within the range of vision of the members of the Lord's assembly. For the Tathagata drew in his wonderworking power. The Lord said to Ananda: In this same way, Ananda, all dharmas do not come within the range of vision. Dharmas do not come within the range of vision of dharmas, dharmas do not see dharmas, dharmas do not know dharmas. All dharmas are of such a nature as these can be neither known nor seen, and are incapable of doing anything. All dharmas are inactive, these cannot be grasped, as these are as inactive as space. All dharmas are unthinkable, similar to illusory men. All dharmas are unfindable, as these in a state of non-existence. As one courses thus a Bodhisattva courses in perfect wisdom and does not settle down in any dharma. [466] As one trains thus, a Bodhisattva trains in perfect wisdom. As a Bodhisattva aspires to reveal, to realize great enlightenment, which is perfection of all training, one thus trains in and as perfecting wisdom.

As the training in perfect wisdom is described as the foremost of all trainings, as the best, the choicest, the most excellent, the most sublime, the highest, the utmost, the unequalled, the incomparable, this is said to bring benefit and happiness to all the worlds, this is described as a protector of the helpless, it is ordained and extolled by the Buddha. The Tathagatas, as a result of training in this perfection of wisdom, of having stood in this training, can lift up this great trichiliocosm with one big toe, and just let it drop again. It does not occur to Buddhas and Lords that "this great trichiliocosm has been lifted up, has been dropped again," for the perfect wisdom is endowed with immeasurable and incalculable qualities. As a result of training in this training of perfect wisdom, the Buddhas and Lords reach a state of non-attachment to past, future and present dharmas. Of all the possible trainings in the past, future and present period, this training in perfect wisdom is foremost, the best, the choicest, the most excellent, the most sublime, the highest, the utmost, the unequalled, the incomparable.

Extinction, Non-Extinction, and Perfect Wisdom

Perfect wisdom is unlimited, inexhaustible and boundless, [467] for limits, exhaustion, and bounds are absent in perfect wisdom. To attribute limits, exhaustion and bounds to perfect wisdom is like attributing these dharmas to space. As this perfection of wisdom is unlimited, inexhaustible and boundless, I do not teach anything such as this perfection of wisdom has any limits, can be exhausted, or that this has any bounds. As well, the sum total of these words contained in this Sutra is not identical with perfection of, perfecting of, or even perfect, wisdom. Perfect wisdom, although called such as this is, is nonetheless not subject to any physical, verbal or mental limitations, it is without any limits whatsoever.

Ananda: For what reason does the Lord not teach any limits to perfect wisdom?

The Lord: It is due to the fact this is inexhaustible and isolated. As one cannot apprehend any isolatedness of any isolated dharma, how much less can one here apprehend any definite circumference to any, or all of this? Thus, beyond any and all measurement this perfection of wisdom is unlimited, without any limits whatsoever. The Tathagatas throughout and beyond all time draw strength from just this perfection of wisdom, [468] and yet this is neither exhausted, nor does this become extinct. This also means Tathagatas of any future also draw strength from just this perfection of wisdom, and yet this is neither exhausted, nor does this become extinct. These Tathagatas also just now residing in countless world systems, these also draw strength from just this perfection of wisdom, and yet it neither becomes exhausted nor extinct. I also, as a Tathagata just now, also draw my strength from just this perfection of wisdom, and yet this neither becomes exhausted, nor extinct. One can exhaust this perfection of wisdom no more than one can exhaust space. So, this perfection of wisdom is quite inexhaustible.

Here now it occurs to Venerable Subhuti: Beyond fathoming is this station which the Tathagata teaches. Let me now question the Tathagata about this station. And Subhuti said to the Lord: How inexhaustible, O Lord, is perfect wisdom?

The Lord: This cannot become extinct, since, like space, this cannot be extinguished, just as all dharmas are not produced, can this not be exhausted.

Subhuti: How does a Bodhisattva consummate this perfection of wisdom?

The Lord: Through non-extinction of form, feeling, perceptions, impulses, and consciousness. [469] Through non-extinction of ignorance, of karma-formations, of name and form, of the six sense-fields, of contact, of craving, of grasping and attachments, of becoming, of birth, of decay and death, of grief, lamentation, pain, sadness and despair. In this manner the Bodhisattva surveys conditioned coproduction in such a way as one avoids any duality of the extremes. One surveys it without seeing any beginning, end or middle. To survey conditioned coproduction, one acquires cognition of all-knowing. Here is non-acceptance and so, non-rejection, non-attachment and so, non-detachment. For a Bodhisattva which, while coursing in perfect wisdom through this consummation of non-extinction, and surveying conditioned coproduction, cannot stand on the level of Sravaka, Disciple, or Pratyekabuddha, but must stand in all-knowledge. Some Bodhisattvas turn away from supreme enlightenment, as, due to not having resorted to these mental activities [which aspire to and result in consummation of non-extinction] and to skill in means, these do not know how a Bodhisattva coursing in perfect wisdom consummates perfect wisdom through the consummation of non-extinction, [470] nor how conditioned coproduction is surveyed in this perfection of wisdom through consummation of non-extinction. Any Bodhisattvas at any time turning away from full enlightenment do so as these do not resort to skill in means. Any Bodhisattvas at any time not turning away from full enlightenment, do so due to this perfection of wisdom. In this way a Bodhisattva which courses in perfection of wisdom consummates perfect wisdom through consummation of non-extinction. A Bodhisattva which thus surveys conditioned coproduction, does certainly not review any dharma as is being produced without a cause nor does one review any dharmas as permanent, stable, eternal, not liable to reversal, nor does one review any dharmas as a doer or a feeler. This is the surveying of conditioned coproduction on the part of a Bodhisattva which consummates this perfection of wisdom through the consummation of non-extinction, and which courses in this perfection of wisdom. At the time a Bodhisattva, consummating the perfection of wisdom through the consummation of non-extinction, surveys conditioned coproduction, at this time one does not review form as a real separate entity, nor feelings, perceptions, impulses or consciousness; nor ignorance, karma-formations, etc., to decay and death, [471] sorrow, lamentation, pain, sadness, and despair; nor does one review any fact "this is my Buddha-field" as real, nor the fact "that is another Buddha-field," nor does one review as real any dharma by which one distinguishes between this and other Buddha-fields. This, Subhuti, is the perfection of wisdom of the Bodhisattvas, the great beings.

Advantages Derived from Perfect Wisdom

As a Bodhisattva courses in perfect wisdom, what is thought of as, and therefore seen as Mara the Evil One feels struck with the dart of great sorrow, just as a person does when one's mother or father have died.

Subhuti: Is this affliction confined to one Mara, or does it affect many Maras, or does it extend to all the Maras in the great trichiliocosm?

The Lord: At any time as Bodhisattvas dwell in the dwelling of perfect wisdom all the Maras in the great trichiliocosm are thought of as feeling struck with the dart of great sorrow, and these cannot sit still on their respective thrones. [472] For all these worlds, with these Gods, beings and Asuras, cannot gain entry to a Bodhisattva which dwells within this dwelling of perfect wisdom, so can these not gain a foothold which would allow this taking possession of, this hurting, or this turning one away from full enlightenment. So now, Subhuti, a Bodhisattva which aspires to reveal and realize full enlightenment of self and others as already in place, courses in perfect wisdom.

In a Bodhisattva coursing in perfect wisdom the perfection of giving arrives at its most perfect development, and so do perfections of morality, patience, vigour, and concentration. In such a one all six perfections arrive at the most perfect development, and also all varieties of skill in means. Whatever is thought of as, or seen as deeds of Mara arising in a Bodhisattva coursing in perfect wisdom, such a one naturally knows these as these are taking place, and one gets rid of these again.

A Bodhisattva aspiring to acquire all the varieties of skill in means courses in perfect wisdom, and develops this. At any time in which a Bodhisattva courses in perfect wisdom, and continuously aspires for this, one brings to mind not only the Buddhas and Lords residing in countless world systems, but also all-knowledge which comes forth from perfection of wisdom.

One now produces the thought, "I also aspire to reach dharmas which these Buddhas and Lords reach!" [473] For a day, or even down to the time taken up by a finger snap, a Bodhisattva which courses in perfect wisdom raises such thoughts and aspires to these. But a Bodhisattva which even for one day, or even for the duration of a fingersnap, aspires for this perfection of wisdom begets different merit, indeed receives winds other than a Bodhisattva which leans on a basis, and for countless aeons gives gifts. Such a Bodhisattva stands in irreversibility as one's winds carry one through to revelations of non-extinction and nothing as such to become extinct, timelessness, and this realization which is borne through any and all reality-limits, even unto this dharmakaya as pure and undifferentiated awareness, the same as space. One such as this speaks of this as if it were indeed such a finger snap, for this has no beginning and in no-time is beyond even any duration. A Bodhisattva coursing in perfect wisdom and which, even for a day, or even for the duration of a finger snap, raises such thoughts, is, we know, brought to mind by Tathagatas. How much more so one who daily pursues such thoughts. What future destiny can one expect a Bodhisattva to have which Tathagatas have brought to mind? No other destiny except full enlightenment can one expect of these. One such as this cannot possibly be reborn in the states of woe. One can expect such a one to be reborn in these heavens, and even here one is not without the Tathagatas, and here one comes to mature beings. These are the qualities and advantages of a Bodhisattva coursing in perfection of wisdom, and aspiring for perfect wisdom, and raising such thoughts, [474] even for the length of a finger snap. How much greater is the advantage of one who pursues such thoughts daily, as for instance Bodhisattva Gandhahastin who just now leads this holy life in the presence of Tathagata Akshobhya.

The Prajna Paramita Sutra on the Buddha-Mother's Producing the Three Dharma Treasures, Spoken by the Buddha

Chapter 29: ~Approaches~

What is more, Subhuti, a Bodhisattva approaches the perfection of wisdom as follows: Through non-attachment to any and all dharmas. From the non-differentiatedness of any and all dharmas. From the fact all dharmas cannot possibly come about. In the conviction "any and all dharmas are equal in remaining unaffected by change." One recognizes by innate wisdom as pure buddha-nature, all dharmas as without self, give us no hint [about their true nature or intentions]. In the conviction "any and all talk about dharmas [is extraneous to them], consists in mere words, mere conventional expressions, - but these conventional expressions do not refer to anything real, are not derived from anything real, nor are these conventional expressions anything real." In this conviction "any and all dharmas lie outside conventional expression and discourse, and it is not these which are conventionally expressed or uttered." The Bodhisattva approaches the perfection of wisdom from unlimitedness of any and all dharmas. [476] By penetration into any and all dharmas. From the fact any and all dharmas are perfectly pure in their original nature. From the fact any and all dharmas are beyond words. Even the different kinds of forsaking are equal [in value and kind], since any and all dharmas can never be stopped. Suchness is everywhere sameness, since any and all dharmas are already realized Nirvana. In this conviction "any and all dharmas do not come, nor do these go; these cannot be generated, these are unborn...this non-birth being absolute." One such as this observes neither oneself nor others. In this conviction "any and all dharmas are holy Arhats, perfectly pure in this original nature." In this conviction "any and all dharmas laid down this burden, as no burden has ever been taken on by these." Such ones approach perfection of wisdom from the fact any and all dharmas have neither place nor locality. For form, feeling, perception, impulses, and consciousness, are without place and locality, in accordance with the own-being of original nature which is no-being. One is exhilarated by the cessation of any and all dharmas. One feels neither content nor discontent. One is neither impassioned nor dispassionate. For form, etc., in their nature reality, in their own-being, are not either impassioned or dispassioned. In the conviction "the original nature [of any and all dharmas], is perfectly pure." In the conviction, "all dharmas are non-attached, free from both attachment and non-attachment." [477] In the conviction "any and all dharmas are essentially enlightenment, as these are equally understood by Buddha-cognition." From the Emptiness, Signlessness and Wishlessness of all dharmas. In the cognition "any and all dharmas are essentially a healing medicine, as controlled by friendliness and accord." In the conviction "all dharmas are dwellers in friendliness, dwellers in compassion, dwellers in sympathetic joy, dwellers in impartiality." In the conviction "all dharmas are identified as this supreme universal spirit, as in simply being no faults can arise, as in essential being all faults remain unproduced." In the conviction "all dharmas are equally neither hopeful nor hostile."

One approaches this boundlessness of perfection of wisdom through [the analogy of] boundlessness of the ocean; through [the analogy of] multicolored brilliance of Meru. One approaches boundlessness of perfection of wisdom: from boundlessness of form, feeling, perception, impulses, consciousness; through [analogy of] boundless illumination shed by the circle of the sun's rays; from boundlessness of all sounds; from boundlessness of the final achievement of any and all dharmas of a Buddha; from boundlessness [of the excellence] of the equipment of any worlds of limitless beings with merit and cognition; from boundlessness of element earth; and so from boundlessness of elements water, fire, air, space and consciousness. [478]

One approaches unlimitedness of perfection of wisdom from unlimitedness of the collection of wholesome and unwholesome dharmas; from unlimitedness of the collection of all dharmas.

One approaches boundlessness of perfection of wisdom: through acquisition of boundlessness of concentration on all dharmas; from boundlessness of all Buddha-dharmas; from boundlessness of all dharmas; from boundlessness of emptiness; from boundlessness of thought and constituents; from boundlessness of thoughts and actions.

One approaches measureless perfection of wisdom from measureless wholesome and unwholesome dharmas. One approaches resounding declarations of perfection of wisdom through the [analogy of the] roaring of the lion's roar.

One approaches the fact that perfection of wisdom cannot be shaken by outside factors from the fact that any and all dharmas cannot be shaken by outside factors. For form, etc., is like the ocean. Form, and each skandha, is like firmament; like brilliant and multicolored Meru; like production of the rays of the disk of the sun; boundless like all sounds; boundless like the whole world of beings; boundless like final achievement of the dharmas of a Buddha; boundless like equipment with merit and cognition of all beings in all worlds; [479] this is like earth, like water, fire, air, space and consciousness; this has no definite boundary like collection of all wholesome and unwholesome dharmas; this has no definite boundary like collection of all dharmas. Form is departure [into Buddhahood], the own-being of form is Buddha-dharma which is essentially Suchness of form; etc., to: consciousness is departure [into Buddhahood], the own-being of consciousness is the Buddha-dharma which is essentially Suchness of consciousness. Form, and each skandha, is boundless true nature of any and all dharmas; Suchness as empty, boundless true nature [of things]; boundlessness of thought and constituents; which merely appears to give rise to thought and action; which is apprehended as wholesome or unwholesome until non-apprehension; it is as the lion's roar; it cannot be shaken by outside factors.

In such ways a Bodhisattva approaches perfect wisdom. [480] As the Bodhisattva approaches perfect wisdom in this way, apperceives this, enters into this, understands this, reflects on this, examines, investigates, and develops this, -with acts of mind which abandon any and all deception and deceit, any and all conceit, any exaltation of self, any and all laziness, any deprecation of others, notion of self, any notion of a being, gain, honor and fame, the five hindrances, envy and meanness, and any and all vacillation, - so this is not hard for one to gain full perfection of all virtues, of the Buddha-field and of supreme dharmas of a Buddha.

Chapter 30: SADAPRARUDITA

Sadaprarudita Sets Out to Find Perfect Wisdom

Furthermore, Subhuti, one searches for perfect wisdom as the Bodhisattva Sadaprarudita, at present leading the holy life in the presence of the Tathagata Bhishmagarjitanirghoshasvara.

Subhuti: How does Bodhisattva Sadaprarudita search for perfection of wisdom?

The Lord: First of all Sadaprarudita, the Bodhisattva, searches for perfect wisdom in such a way as to have no regard for body or life, and gain, honor and fame do not interest him. In the seclusion of a remote forest, a voice in the air said to him:

"In the East, son of good family, hear the perfection of wisdom! And on your way do not pay attention to weariness of your body, do not give in to any fatigue, pay no attention to food or drink, day or night, or to cold or heat. Do not make any definite plans, either about inward, or about outward things. Do not look to the left or right, to the South, East, West or North, upwards or downwards, or in any of the intermediate directions. Neither be shaken by self or individuality, nor by form or other skandhas. [482] For one shaken by these, is turned away from Buddha-dharmas. As one is turned away from Buddha-dharmas, one wanders in birth-and-death. And as one wanders in birth-and-death, one does not course in perfect wisdom, and cannot reach perfection of wisdom."

Sadaprarudita said to the voice: This is how, from this point on, I am and act accordingly. As I aspire to indicate light to all beings, as I aspire to procure the dharma of a Buddha.

The Voice answered: "Well spoken, son of good family!"

The Bodhisattva Sadaprarudita again listens to the voice, and he hears this:

"Son of good family, this search for perfect wisdom takes place as you produce the firm conviction all dharmas are void, signless and wishless. Be not affected by signs, existence, and false views anywhere, or at anytime here appears being, or are beings appearing. Be not affected by thoughts of bad friends. Good thoughts of friends, however, tend, love and honor. These demonstrate dharma, and teach 'all dharmas are void, signless and wishless, not produced, not stopped and non-existent.'

"As you progress like this, you are studing or applying this perfection of wisdom either from a book, direct experience, or from the mouth of a monk speaking dharma. Treat as the Teacher any person from whom you come to hear perfection of wisdom, be grateful and thankful, and think [483]: 'This is my good friend. As I hear this perfection of wisdom from this one, I gradually come to realize irreversibility from full enlightenment, I draw nearer to Tathagatas, and come to be reborn in Buddha-fields in which Tathagatas are not lacking, and, avoiding unfortunate rebirths, I accomplish auspicious rebirth!' As you weigh up such advantages, you are bound to treat a monk speaking dharma as the Teacher. Do not follow this one with motives of worldly gain, but for love of dharma, out of respect for dharma, and the benefit of any and all beings.

"Also, see through things which are thought of or seen as Mara's deeds for here always is appearing Mara, the Evil One, who may seem to suggest your teacher tends, enjoys and honors things which are seen, heard, smelled, tasted or touched, while in actual fact the teacher does so from skill in means, and has really risen above these. Here now, do not lose confidence in the teacher, but say to yourself: 'I do not yet know skill in means as the teacher naturally does. The teacher tends, enjoys and honors such dharmas in order to indicate proper discipline to beings, in order to bring to realization wholesome roots for them. For no attachment to such objective supports exist in or for Bodhisattvas.' At this, contemplate this true reality of dharmas, which is to say, as all dharmas are without defilement OR purification. As all dharmas are empty of own-being [484], such can 'have' no properties as appear to be these attributes of a living being, such can 'have' no life, no individuality, no personality, such are as illusion, a dream, an echo, a reflected image. As you thus contemplate this true reality of all dharmas, and follow what is spoken of Dharma, you go forth in, and as, perfection of wisdom. But watch out for seeing yet another deed of Mara. As you may be disheartened at what the preacher of dharma has said, let this not make you averse to perfection of wisdom; but with a mind which desires only dharma, which respects only dharma may you, unwearied, follow any monk which preaches Dharma."

After receiving this admonition from this voice, the Bodhisattva Sadaprarudita now journeys East. Before long it occurs to him that he had not asked the voice how far he ought to go. He stands still just at this, crying, sorrowful and lamenting. For seven days he stays in this very spot waiting to be told how far to go to hear this perfection of wisdom, and all this time he pays no attention to anything else, and takes no food, but simply pays homage to perfect wisdom, waiting to be told...how far he needs to go, and how to do this.

Any person, Subhuti, who loses their only child are very sad and unhappy, [485] and can think of one thing only, the child and the sorrow felt due to this. Even so this Bodhisattva Sadaprarudita can at this time think of nothing else, except "when then shall I hear this perfection of wisdom?"

Description of Gandhavati, and of Dharmodgata's Life

As Sadaprarudita thus sorrows and pines away, a Tathagata-frame [suddenly] stands here before him, gives his approval and says: "Well spoken, son of good family! The Tathagatas of these three times, while these are still Bodhisattvas as you are now, also search for perfect wisdom in the same spirit in which you just now search for this. In this same spirit of vigor and determination, of zeal and zest, -do you go East! Five hundred leagues away from here, is a town called Gandhavati. It is built of seven precious things. It is twelve leagues long and twelve leagues broad, and enclosed by seven walls, seven moats and seven rows of palm trees. It is prosperous and flourishing, secure from attack, contains abundant provisions and is full of beasts and beings. Five hundred rows of shops run through the town from one end to the other, beautiful to behold like a well-colored painting, arranged one by one in regular succession, and in between them well-constructed sites and passages are erected, respectively for vehicles drawn by animals, for palanquins, and for pedestrians, so that there is plenty of room for all. The walls all round this town are made of the seven precious substances. [486] Their well-founded copings slope into the golden river Jambu. And on each coping grows a tree, made of the seven precious things, laden with various fruits, also made of precious things. A network of small bells is fastened on strings, and thus surrounds the entire city. When stirred by the wind, the small bells give out a sweet, charming and delightful sound, just like the sound from five musical instruments when they are played in harmony by the Gandharvas, skilled in songs. And this sound causes beings to divert, enjoy and amuse themselves. The moats all around the city are full of water which flows gently along, neither too cold nor too hot. The boats on this river are brilliant with the seven precious things, beautiful to behold, and existence is a reward of past deeds of inhabitants who, aboard these, divert, enjoy and amuse themselves. The water is everywhere covered with blossoms of the blue lotus, of the pink lotus, of the white lotus and with other most beautiful and fragrant flowers. Here is not any species of flowers in the great trichiliocosm which is not found. All around this city are five hundred parks, beautiful to behold, brilliant with the seven precious things. [487] Each park has five times five hundred large lotus ponds, covered with beautiful blossoms, each of the size of a cartwheel, fragrant, -blue, yellow, red and white. The sounds of geese, cranes, ducks, curlews and other birds fill the air over the ponds. And the existence of these parks which none regard as their own private property is a reward for past deeds of these beings, for these have coursed for a long time in perfection of wisdom, their minds faithfully devoted to this Guide of the Buddhas and bent on listening to her and understanding her, and for a long time these remain intent on deep and even truly fathomless dharmas.

"And here, in this city of Gandhavati, at a place four roads meet, is the house of the Bodhisattva Dharmodgata, - one league all round, with the seven precious things, beautiful to behold, enclosed by seven walls and seven rows of palm trees. Here are four parks near the house, for the enjoyment of these who live in it. These are called Nityapramudita, Asoka, Sokavigata, and Pushpacitra. Each park has eight lotus ponds, called Bhadra, Bhadrottama, Nandi, Nandottama, Kshama, Kshamottama, Niyata and Avivaha. One side of each pond is gold, the second of silver, [488] the third of vaidurya, the fourth of crystal. The ground at the bottom consists of quartz, with golden sand over it. Each pond has eight stairs to it, decorated with steps, made of variegated jewels. In the gaps between the steps, inside the golden river Jambu, grows a plantain tree. The ponds are covered with various kinds of water flowers, and the air above these is filled with the sounds of various birds. Round these ponds grow various flowering trees, and as these are stirred by the wind, their flowers drop into the ponds. The water in the ponds has the scent, color, taste, and feel of sandalwood.

"In this mansion lives Bodhisattva Dharmodgata, with his retinue, among these sixty-eight thousand women. He diverts, enjoys and amuses himself, he feels and tastes the five kinds of sense-pleasure. All the inhabitants of this city, both women and men, divert, enjoy and amuse themselves, these have constant joy in the parks and on the ponds and feel and taste the five kinds of sense-pleasure. The Bodhisattva Dharmodgata, however, with his retinue, diverts, enjoys and amuses himself only for a certain time, and so now also he always demonstrates perfection of wisdom. And the citizens of this town built a pulpit for the Bodhisattva Dharmodgata in the central square of the town. It has a golden base, a cotton mattress is spread on this, and a woolen cover, a cushion and a silken cloth are put on top of this. High up in the air, half a Kos high, here an awning, shining with pearls, even and firm. All [489] round this pulpit flowers of the five colors are strewed and scattered, and the pulpit itself is scented with various perfumes. So pure is the heart of Dharmodgata, so great the respect of his hearers for dharma.

"Seated on the pulpit the Bodhisattva Dharmodgata demonstrates perfection of wisdom. The citizens of this town listen to his teaching with great respect for dharma, with trust in dharma, with faith in what is worthy of faith, with minds that are lifted up in faith. In addition many hundreds, many thousands, many hundreds of thousands of living beings, Gods and people, assemble here to listen. Some of these explain perfection of wisdom, some repeat it, some copy it, some follow it with wise attention. All these beings are no longer doomed to fall into states of woe, and are irreversible from full enlightenment. Son of good family, go to Bodhisattva Dharmodgata! From him you hear perfection of wisdom. For he is for a long time your good friend, he summons you, and even now instigates and encourages you to realize full enlightenment. He also, in these three times, searches for perfection of wisdom in this same way in which you search even now. Go forth, son of good family, go on day and night, giving your undivided attention to this unending task, this never-ending blessing which we learn quite naturally to neither accept as a basis, nor develop aversion to as a means to some end! Before long you hear perfection of wisdom!"

As the Bodhisattva Sadaprarudita hears this, he is contented, elated, joyful, overjoyed and jubilant. [490] A man, hit with a poisoned arrow, can not think of anything else except: "Where do I find a surgeon, a skilled physician, who can pull out this arrow, and free me from this suffering." Just so Bodhisattva Sadaprarudita at this time pays no attention to any dharma except:

"As I see this son of good family from whom I hear perfection of wisdom, as I hear this dharma, I forsake all attentions to any basis." Without leaving the place he is Sadaprarudita now hears Bodhisattva Dharmodgata demonstrating perfection of wisdom.

The List and Significance of the Concentrations

As a result he produces perception which does not lean on any dharma, nay, not even perception itself. And he is face to face with many doors to concentration. The names of the concentrations are as follows: "This surveys own-being of any and all dharmas," "The non-apprehension of own-being of any and all dharmas," "Non-difference of any and all dharmas," "Spectator of unchangeability of any and all dharmas," "Illuminator of any and all dharmas," "From any and all dharmas darkness vanished," "This shatters cognition of any and all dharmas," "This tosses any and all dharmas about," "The non-apprehension of any and all dharmas," "Bedecked with flowers," "Within this body this consummates any and all dharmas," "Having abandoned illusion," "Calling forth images reflected in a mirror," "Calling forth sounds of all beings," "Without any dirt," "Gladdening all beings," "A follower of vocal sounds of all beings, from skill in means," [491] "Consummation of the whole variety of letters, words and vocal sounds," "This state which comes from feeling no rigidity," "Inexpressible in essential nature," "Realization of unobstructed emancipation," "Visit from the king," "Grammatical analysis of speech into words and letters," "Insight into any and all dharmas," "This leaves the sphere of any and all dharmas beyond," "Unobstructed limit of any and all dharmas," "Fashioned as a firmament," "As a thunderbolt," "The king is near," "The unrivalled king," "Victorious," "One cannot avert this eye," "Fixed on this element of dharma," "Come out of this element of dharma," "Granter of consolation," "This roars like a lion," "No world for beings to be reborn in," "Free from dirt," "Undefiled," "Lotus-array," "Annihilation of hesitation," "Follower of any and all substantial excellence," "Situated beyond any and all dharmas," "Attainment of super-knowledges, powers and the grounds of self-confidence," "Piercer of any and all dharmas," "Seal of desisting from becoming on the part of any and all dharmas," "The ocean in which any and all dharmas lose any becoming," "Spectator of any and all dharmas without distinction," "This leaves behind this jungle of any and all views and actions," "Without darkness," "Without a sign of any and all dharmas," [492] "Free from any and all attachment," "Without a trace of laziness," "This sheds light on deep dharmas," "Fashioned like Meru," "Irresistible," "This shatters what is seen as the circle of Mara's army," "No inclination for anything in the triple world," "Emission of rays," "Sight of the Tathagata," "Spectator of all Tathagatas."

Established in these concentrations, he now sees Buddhas and Lords in the countless world systems in the ten directions, as these reveal this very perfection of wisdom to Bodhisattvas. And these Tathagatas applaud and comfort him, and these say to him:

"We also in these three times as Bodhisattvas, search for perfection of wisdom in just this same way. We also as we search, come to acquire by revelation, these concentrations which you acquire just now. Even after we acquire these we go on our route, established in and transmitting perfection of wisdom and irreversible dharmas of a Buddha. But as we peruse original essential nature and search for any true own-being of these concentrations, we do not see any real dharma enter into these, or emerge from these, course toward enlightenment, or know full enlightenment. This absence of imaginings about any dharma whatsoever...this is perfection of wisdom. As we stand in firm absence of any and all self-conceited imaginings we naturally reveal our bodies of golden color, these thirty-two marks of Tathagatas, these eighty accessory marks, and these splendid haloes around us, and reveal of us this unthinkable and yet, supreme cognition of Buddhas, this wisdom of Buddhas, this supreme concentration of Buddhas, and this perfection of all these dharmas and qualities of Buddhas, and quite simply as all in all...this nature of Buddhas. [493] Even Tathagatas cannot grasp any measure, nor define any boundary, of this perfection of qualities, -how much less Sravakas, Disciples and Pratyekabuddhas. Here and now fill your mind with respect for these dharmas of Buddhas, so you increasingly aspire toward these, so you become more and more zealous for these. The supreme enlightenment is not hard to realize for one aspiring towards this, who is zealous for this. For the good friend also arouses intense respect and affection, and to be sure, serenely keep your confidence in such. For it is as we are taken hold of by these good friends Bodhisattvas quickly come to reveal, realize, and know full enlightenment."

Sadaprarudita asked the Tathagatas: Who is our good friend?

A Tathagata replied: "The Bodhisattva Dharmodgata for a long time matures you toward this supreme enlightenment, he upholds you, he is your preceptor in perfecting this perfect wisdom, in skill in means, and in these dharmas of Buddha. It is he who has upheld you, and for this friendly deed you honor him in gratitude and thankfulness, and bear in mind what he does for you. As, son of good family, you for one aeon, or for two aeons, or for up to one hundred thousand aeons, or more, carry about the Bodhisattva Dharmodgata like a turban on your head, furnish him with everything which makes beings happy, and present him with as many forms, sounds, smells, tastes and touchables as are in the great trichiliocosm, [494] - even so you cannot have repaid this son of good family for what he does for you. This has happened through his might as you have acquired these concentrations, that you hear of perfection of wisdom and of skill in means, and that you gain this perfection of wisdom."

Sadaprarudita and the Merchant's Daughter

As these Tathagatas comfort Bodhisattva Sadaprarudita, they again disappear. But Sadaprarudita emerged from his concentrations, and asked himself, "whence do these Tathagatas come, and whither do these go?" Since he no longer sees these Tathagatas, he worries and pines away for these. He thinks to himself: "The holy Bodhisattva Dharmodgata has acquired the revelations of these dharanis in awareness and realization, and likewise he possesses the five superknowledges, he has performed his duties under the Jinas of these three times, he is my patron and good friend, who for a long time has done good all about me. When I come to him I must ask him about this matter, ask him to explain whence these Tathagatas come, and whither these go." Sadaprarudita here nursed affection and confidence, esteem and respect for Bodhisattva Dharmodgata. He now reflects: "With what kind of honoring gift can I now approach the Bodhisattva Dharmodgata? But I am poor, and have nothing of any value [495] with which I could express my respect and reverence for him. It is not seemly for me to come without anything at all. But I am poor, and this now makes me sad and regretful."

Such are these feelings, such these attitudes of reverence, with which this Bodhisattva Sadaprarudita proceeded on his journey. In due course he reaches a town, goes to the midst of the marketplace, and decides to sell his own body, and with the price hereof do honor to the Bodhisattva Dharmodgata. "As through the long night of past time, in this measureless cycle of birth-and-death, thousands of bodies of mine are shattered, wasted, destroyed and sold, again and again. I experience measureless pains in the hells for the sake of sense pleasures, as a result of sense pleasures, but never yet on behalf of dharmas of this kind, never yet for this purpose of doing honor to beings of such a kind." Sadaprarudita now goes to the middle of the marketplace, lifted up his voice, and cried: "Who wants a man? Who wants a man? Who wants to buy a man?"

Here now Mara the Evil One is thought of as, and indeed seen in the view of many to have thought to himself: "Lets obstruct this Bodhisattva Sadaprarudita. For as he succeeds in selling himself out of concern for dharma, and as he goes on to honor the Bodhisattva Dharmodgata, and to ask him, with regard to perfection of wisdom and skill in means just how a Bodhisattva coursing in perfect wisdom realizes full enlightenment, he is bound to reach this ocean of sacred knowledge, and become inaccessible to Mara and his host, [496] and reaches the perfection of all qualities, as he works the weal of all beings, and takes these away from my sphere, and others again he takes away as he realizes full enlightenment."

Mara, the Evil One, is thought of and seen to so dispose the Brahmins and householders in this town, so that these cannot hear the voice of Sadaprarudita. As Sadaprarudita cannot find a buyer for himself, he goes to one side, wailed, shed tears, and said: "Alas, it is hard on us this, as we do not find a buyer even for our body, so we could by selling our body, honor the Bodhisattva Dharmodgata." [in case anyone wonders...the name 'Sadaprarudita' means 'perpetual tears'(!) -- in Tibetan this name is - rtag tu ngu -]

So now, Sakra, Chief of Gods, thinks to himself: "Let me weigh up the Bodhisattva Sadaprarudita. Does he now, filled with earnest intention, renounce his body out of concern for dharma, or does he not?" Sakra conjured up the guise of a young man, goes to the Bodhisattva Sadaprarudita, and says to him: "Why do you, son of good family, stand here dejected, pining away and shedding tears?" [497] Sadaprarudita replied: "I want to sell myself, but I cannot find anyone to buy my body." Sakra, in the form of the young man, said: "On behalf of what do you want to sell yourself?" Sadaprarudita replied: "From love for Dharma I sell myself, so as to worship Dharma, and to honor the holy Bodhisattva Dharmodgata. But I do not find a buyer for this body of mine. I now think to myself, alas, I must be a person of exceedingly small merit indeed." The young man said: "I myself do not need a man. But my father is due to offer sacrifice. For this I require a man's heart, his blood and the marrow of his bones. These you give me, and I shall pay for these." Sadaprarudita now thinks to himself: "I exceedingly easily get as I desire. Now I know my body is sufficiently perfect for realizing perfect wisdom, skill in means and the dharmas of a Buddha, since in this young man I now find a buyer for my heart, blood and marrow." As his mind is bristling with joy, and all ready, he says: "I give you my body, as you have need of it!" The young man asked: "What price do I give you?" Sadaprarudita answered: "Give me whatever you do!" [498] Sadaprarudita took a sharp sword, pierced his right arm, and made the blood flow. He pierced his right thigh, cut the flesh from this, and strode up to the foot of a wall in order to break the bone.

A merchant's daughter, from her upper window, sees this, and she thought to herself: "Why does this son of good family do this to himself? Let me go to him, and ask him." She goes to Sadaprarudita, and said: "Why do you inflict such fatal treatment on yourself? What do you do with this blood, and with this marrow of your bones?"

Sadaprarudita said: "As I have sold them to this young man, I go to worship perfection of wisdom, and to do honor to the holy Bodhisattva Dharmodgata." The merchant's daughter said: "What is the kind of quality, what is the excellence of the qualities, which you create in yourself by your wish to honor the Bodhisattva Dharmodgata as you sell your own heart, blood and marrow?"

Sadaprarudita replied: "Dharmodgata now explains to me perfection of wisdom and the skill in means. [499] In these I train myself, and, as a result, I become a refuge to all beings; and, as I at this point realize full enlightenment, I acquire a body of golden color, thirty-two marks of the Tathagata, eighty accessory marks, the splendor of a halo the rays of which extend throughout infinitude, great friendliness, great compassion, great sympathetic joy, great impartiality, four grounds of self-confidence, four analytical knowledges, eighteen special dharmas of a Buddha, and I acquire five superknowledges, an unthinkable purity of conduct, and unthinkable purity of concentration, an unthinkable purity of wisdom, and ten powers of a Tathagata. I fully awake to the supreme cognition of a Buddha, and acquire the supremely precious jewel of Dharma, which I share with all beings."

The merchant's daughter replied: "It is wonderful, son of good family, how exalted and sublime are these dharmas which you proclaim. For the sake of even one of these dharmas should one be willing to renounce one?s bodies even for countless aeons, how much more so for the sake of many of these. These dharmas which you proclaim please me also, and seem good to me. But see, son of good family, I give you whatever you require, and with this you may [500] honor the Bodhisattva Dharmodgata! But do not inflict such treatment on yourself! I also go with you to the Bodhisattva Dharmodgata! I also, together with you, plant wholesome roots, which help to realize such dharmas!"

Sakra, Chief of Gods, now throws off his disguise as a young man, and in his own proper body he stood before the Bodhisattva Sadaprarudita, and says to him: "I applaud your firm sense of obligation. In these three times Tathagatas have so great an aspiration for Dharma, and it is this which helps these to full enlightenment and to gain the precious jewel of Dharma, as these first course in the vehicle of a Bodhisattva, and ask questions about perfection of wisdom and skill in means. I have no need for your heart, blood or marrow. I only come here to test you. Now choose a boon. I give you any boon whatsoever!"

Sadaprarudita answered: "Give me supreme dharmas of a Buddha!" Sakra, Chief of Gods, replied: "This lies not within my province. This lies within the province of Buddhas, the Lords. Choose another boon!" Sadaprarudita replied: "Do not trouble your mind about the mutilated condition of my body! I now make it whole again by the magical power of enunciation of Truth. As I am in truth irreversible, and predicted to full enlightenment, and am known to the Tathagatas by my unconquerable resolution, -may through this Truth, through this utterance of the Truth, this my body be again as it is before!" [501] This very moment, instant and second, through the Bodhisattva's might and through the perfect purity of the Bodhisattva's resolution, the body of the Bodhisattva Sadaprarudita became as before, healthy and whole. And Sakra, Chief of Gods, and Mara, the Evil One, reduced to silence, just vanished from this place.

The merchant's daughter then said to Sadaprarudita: "Come on, son of good family, let us go up to my house. I ask my parents to give you riches with which you can express your desire to worship this perfection of wisdom, and to honor the Bodhisattva Dharmodgata, a desire which is due to your love for dharma." The Bodhisattva Sadaprarudita and the merchant's daughter go together to her house. Upon arriving, Sadaprarudita remains standing on the threshold, while the merchant's daughter goes into the house, and now she says to her parents: "Mummy and daddy, give me a part of your wealth! I go away with the five hundred maidens you gave me for servants! Together with Bodhisattva Sadaprarudita I go to the Bodhisattva Dharmodgata, in order to worship him. And he demonstrates dharma to us, and in this way we acquire the dharmas of a Buddha." [502] Her parents replied: "Who is this Bodhisattva Sadaprarudita, and is he here just now?"

The merchant's daughter said: "This son of good family stands at the threshold of the door to our house. He set out determined to know full enlightenment, in other words, he aspires to set all beings free from immeasurable sufferings of birth-and-death." She told her parents all she saw and heard, [503] how Sadaprarudita sold his body, and mutilated it, and how, as she asked him for a reason, he praises and reveals to her unthinkable qualities of a Buddha and immeasurable dharmas of a Buddha, which he has in mind as his goal. She goes on to say, "As I hear of unthinkable qualities of a Buddha, I feel exceeding joy and elation. I think to myself: "It is wonderful to such extent as this son of good family is a doer of what is hard, and how much he loves the dharma to endure oppression and pain in this body. It is due to this love for dharma he renounces himself. How can we fail to worship dharma, and to make a vow to reach such stations, we who have vast and abundant possessions?" [504] So I said to this son of good family: "Do not inflict such fatal treatment on yourself! I give you abounding riches, which you may use to worship and honor the holy Bodhisattva Dharmodgata, I also go with you to this Bodhisattva, as I can worship him, too. I also accomplish these supreme dharmas of a Buddha which you proclaim!" Mummy and daddy, allow me to go, and give me the riches I ask for!

Her parents replied: "It is wonderful how well you relate the hardships of this son of good family. Unthinkable, for sure are the dharmas for the sake of which he endures these hardships, these must be the most distinguished in the whole world, a source of happiness to all beings! We give you our possessions to go. We also like to come with you, to see, to salute, to honor, to worship the Bodhisattva Dharmodgata." The daughter replied: "Do as you say. I do not oppose any who in truth do right."

The Meeting with Dharmodgata

Thus this merchant's daughter set out to worship and honor the Bodhisattva Dharmodgata. [505] She takes five hundred carriages and orders her five hundred servant girls to get ready. She takes abundant riches, and ample provisions, mounts upon one carriage together with the Bodhisattva Sadaprarudita, and proceeds East, surrounded by the five hundred maidens on their five hundred carts, accompanied by a huge retinue, and preceded by her parents. After some time the Bodhisattva Sadaprarudita sees the city of Gandhavati from afar. In the middle of the marketplace he sees the Bodhisattva Dharmodgata on his pulpit, demonstrating dharma, surrounded and revered by an assembly of many hundreds, of many thousands, of many hundreds of thousands. The moment he sees him he is filled with that kind of happiness [506] which a monk feels as with one-pointed attention he obtains the first trance. He looks upon him and thinks to himself: "It is not seemly to approach this Bodhisattva Dharmodgata seated on a carriage. Let me here and now alight from it!" He alights from this carriage, and the merchant's daughter with her five hundred maidens follow suit. Sadaprarudita, with the merchant's daughter and her five hundred maidens go up to the Bodhisattva Dharmodgata's seat amidst a magnificent display of religious aspirations. For the Bodhisattva Dharmodgata at this time created, for perfection of wisdom, a pointed tower, made of the seven precious substances, adorned with red sandalwood, and encircled by an ornament of pearls. Gems are placed into four corners of the pointed tower, and performed the functions of lamps. Four incense jars made of silver are suspended on its four sides, and pure black aloe wood is burning in these, as a token of worship for the perfection of wisdom. And in the middle of this pointed tower a couch made of the seven precious things is put up, and on it a box made of four large gems. Into this, the perfection of wisdom is placed, written with melted vaidurya on golden tablets. And this pointed tower is adorned with brightly colored garlands which hang down in strips.

The Bodhisattva Sadaprarudita and the merchant's daughter with her five hundred maidens look upon this pointed tower, so magnificently decorated as a display of religious aspirations. These see thousands of Gods, with Sakra, Chief of Gods, scattering over this pointed tower heavenly Mandarava flowers, heavenly sandalwood powder, heavenly gold dust, and heavenly silver dust, [507] and these hear the music of heavenly instruments. Sadaprarudita now asks Sakra, Chief of Gods: "For what purpose do you, together with many thousands of Gods, scatter over this pointed tower, which consists of precious substances, heavenly Mandarava flowers, etc., and why do the Devas up in space play heavenly music on their instruments?"

Sakra answered: "Do you not know the reason, son of good family? This is perfection of wisdom, the mother and guide of the Bodhisattvas. As Bodhisattvas train in this, these soon reach perfection of wisdom of all qualities, and, consequent on this, all dharmas of a Buddha and knowledge of all modes."

Sadaprarudita replied: "Where is this perfection of wisdom, the mother of Buddhas and guide of Bodhisattvas?"

Sakra answered: "The holy Bodhisattva Dharmodgata placed this in the middle of this pointed tower, as he has written this on golden tablets with melted Vaidurya, and sealed this with seven seals. We cannot easily show this to you."

Here just now the Bodhisattva Sadaprarudita and the merchant's daughter, with her five hundred maidens, all pay worship to the perfection of wisdom - with the flowers which these brought along, and with garlands, wreaths, raiment, jewels, incense, flags and golden and silvery flowers [508] and, one after another, these deposited their portion in front of this, for the greater honor of the Bodhisattva Dharmodgata. These now worship the Bodhisattva Dharmodgata by scattering flowers, garlands, wreaths, raiment, jewels, incense, flags, and golden and silvery flowers over him, and played heavenly music on their instruments - motivated by an aspiration to worship Dharma.

The flowers now rise high above the head of the Bodhisattva Dharmodgata and form a pointed tower of flowers. And these flowers of various colors, golden and silvery, stand high in the air, as a canopy. And also the robes, raiment and jewels stand high up in the air, as a pavilion in the clouds. As the Bodhisattva Sadaprarudita and the merchant's daughter with her five hundred maidens behold this wonder, these think to themselves: "This is wonderful to see such wonderworking power this Bodhisattva Dharmodgata possesses, how great a might, how great an influence. So far he courses but in the course of a Bodhisattva, and now already he possesses such power to work wonders. How much more does he have after he has known full enlightenment?" [509] The merchant's daughter and the five hundred maidens here feel a longing for the Bodhisattva Dharmodgata. All of one mind, these resolutely raise their hearts to the supreme enlightenment, and say: "May we, through this wholesome root, be Tathagatas in this future period!

May we come to course in the course of Bodhisattvas, and may we receive these very dharmas which this Bodhisattva Dharmodgata receives! And may we just so honor and respect the perfection of wisdom as this Bodhisattva Dharmodgata honors and respects this, and may we reveal this to many just as he does! And may we be as endowed with perfect wisdom and skill in means, and as accomplished in these as this Bodhisattva Dharmodgata is!"

The Bodhisattva Sadaprarudita, and the merchant's daughter with her five hundred maidens, as these worship the perfection of wisdom and honor the Bodhisattva Dharmodgata with their heads, respectfully salute him with hands together, and stand on one side. The Bodhisattva Sadaprarudita now tells the whole story of quest for perfection of wisdom, beginning with the voice he hears in the forest, which bid him go East. [510] He told Dharmodgata how he stands in many concentrations, and how the Buddhas and Lords of the ten directions comforted and applauded him, and had said: "Well done, son of good family! These concentrations issue from perfection of wisdom. By firmly standing in the perfection of wisdom we achieve all the dharmas of a Buddha." He goes on to relate: "The Tathagatas now vanished, and I emerged from this state of concentration. I asked myself, 'whence now these Tathagatas come, and whither these go?' I think to myself, 'the holy Bodhisattva Dharmodgata receives the dharanis, [511] he possesses five superknowledges, he does his duties under the Jinas of these three times, he plants wholesome roots, and is trains well in the perfect wisdom and skill in means. He can explain to me this matter as it really is, and tell me whence these Tathagatas come and whither these go.' Now I am come to you, and I ask you, son of good family: 'Whence these Tathagatas come, and whither these go?' Demonstrate to me, son of good family, this coming and going of these Tathagatas, so we may cognize this, and so we may be not lacking in vision of the Tathagatas."

Chapter 31: ~DHARMODGATA~

The Coming and the Going of Tathagatas

Dharmodgata: Tathagatas certainly do not come from anywhere, nor do these go anywhere. Suchness does not move, and Tathagata is Suchness. Non-production neither comes nor goes, and Tathagata is non-production. One can conceive of neither coming nor going of reality-limit, and Tathagata is reality-limit. This same can be said of emptiness, of anything which exists in according to facts, or of dispassion, of stopping, of element of space. Tathagata is not outside these dharmas. Suchness as these dharmas is Suchness as any and all dharmas, and Suchness as Tathagata is simply Suchness as any and all Tathagatas. Here is no division within Suchness. Simply before even one, throughout and after all is Suchness. Such is neither two, nor three, nor one divided into many. Suchness does not even pass beyond counting, as it can not be counted to begin with and thus certainly is here nothing to end with. Neither is Suchness one, nor other than one by which to determine any singularity, nor two nor three nor apart from these. Nothing of or by any concept whatsoever can Suchness relate to or be related to, yet Suchness is greatest of anything conceivable and infinitely beyond, even...'this'.

A man, scorched by the heat of summer, during the last month of summer [513], at noon might see a mirage floating along, and might run towards it, and think "here I shall find some water, here I shall find something to drink." What do you think, you children of good family, does this water come from anywhere, or does this water go anywhere, to or from the Eastern great ocean, or the Southern, Northern or Western?

Sadaprarudita: No water exists in this mirage. How can its coming or going be conceived? This man again is foolish and uninformed as, on seeing the mirage, he forms the idea of water, as here is no water. Water in its own being certainly does not exist in that mirage, any more than merely in his thought that it does.

Dharmodgata: Equally foolish are any and all these who adhere to Tathagatas through form and sound, and who in consequence imagine coming or going of any or all Tathagatas. A Tathagata can neither be seen nor determined from any form body. Dharma-bodies [Dharmakayas] are such Tathagatas, and the real nature of dharmas neither comes nor goes. Here is no real coming or going of the body of an elephant, horse, chariot or foot-soldier, tree or even a rock, which has been conjured up when magicians perform. Just so, here is neither coming nor going of Tathagatas which, as with all things, neither have any granting given nor even, any conjuring whatsoever. A sleeping person might in dreams see one Tathagata, or two, or three, or up to one thousand, or still more [514]. On waking up, however, they no longer see even one single Tathagata. What do you think, dear children of good family, have these Tathagatas come from anywhere, or gone to anywhere? As Tathagata means 'one thus gone', in this relative sense in so doing one cannot thus come. But, what's not too frequently understood, is that Tathagata also means 'one thus come', and likewise in so doing can one not be thus gone. Yet, such is this fact in principle and truth, that in, or as Suchness Tathagatas neither come nor go, at once within and throughout these three times...and at once here stand on naught but pure undifferentiated awareness as space outside of and through any and all dharmas. Such is this difference of purely equanimous stance the same as this fathomless station of all dharma.

Sadaprarudita: One cannot conceive as in any dream any dharma whatsoever as having the status of a full and perfect reality, for any dream is deceptive.

Dharmodgata: Just so Tathagatas teach all dharmas are as a dream. These who do not come to naturally and wisely know all dharmas as these really are, which is to say, as a dream, as Tathagata points out, these adhere to Tathagatas through their name-body and form-body, and in consequence these imagine Tathagatas come and go. These who in ignorance of true nature of dharmas imagine a coming OR going of Tathagatas, these are just foolish common people...not as yet diligent to truth, and presently as is as good as any and all times these belong to birth-and-death with six places of rebirth, and these are far from these revelations of perfection of wisdom, far away from dharmas of a Buddha - yet experience these dharmas within each and every breath, as close as pure life itself.

On the contrary, however, these who know all dharmas as a dream, i.e., as they really are, are in agreement with the teaching of Tathagata, these do not imagine the coming or going of any dharma, nor its production or stopping. These naturally know Tathagatas true nature, and do not imagine coming or going of Tathagatas. And these who naturally know true nature of Tathagata, these course near to full enlightenment and these course in this perfection of wisdom. These disciples of Lords do not consume alms fruitlessly, [515] and these are worthy of the world's results and dedications. The gems which are in the great ocean do not come from any place in the East, or West, or any other of the ten directions, but these owe existence to wholesome roots of beings. These are not produced without cause, or, are not without cause to be produced. Such simply manifest due to these causes and conditions. Yet still, as dependent on cause, condition and reason, these gems are coproduced and stopped by conditions, these do not pass on to any place anywhere in the world in any of the ten directions. And nevertheless, as these conditions exist, the gems are augmented; as these conditions are absent, no augmentation takes place. Just so the perfect body of Tathagatas does not come from any place anywhere in the ten directions, and it does not go to any place anywhere in the world with its ten directions. But the body of Buddhas and Lords is not without cause. It is brought to perfection by conduct and action in time, and it is produced dependent on causes and conditions, coproduced by subsidiaries, produced as result of karma done in this past. It is, however, not in any place anywhere in the world with its ten directions. But when these conditions exist, the accomplishment of the body takes place; when these conditions are absent, the accomplishment of the body is inconceivable.

As the sound of a boogharp is being produced, it does not come from anywhere. As it is stopped, it does not go anywhere, nor does it pass on to anywhere. But it is produced conditioned by this totality of causes and conditions for it to occur, -namely the boat-shaped hollow body of the harp, the parchment sounding board, the strings, the hollow arm of the boogharp, the bindings, the plectrum, the person who plays it, and this person's exertions and coming to knowledge of the music to be played thereon. [516] In this way this sound comes forth from the boogharp, dependent on causes, dependent on conditions. And yet that sound does not come forth from that hollow body of the harp, nor from the parchment sounding board, nor from the strings, nor from the hollow arm, nor from the bindings, nor from the plectrum, nor from the person who plays it, nor from this person's exertions OR knowledge. It is just the combination of all of these which makes the sound conceivable. And as it is stopped, the sound also does not go anywhere.

Just so the perfect body of Buddhas and Lords is dependent on causes, dependent on conditions, and it is brought to perfection through exertions which lead to many wholesome roots. But the augmenting of Buddha-body does not result from one single cause, nor from one single condition, nor from one single wholesome root. This is also not without cause. This is coproduced by a totality of many causes and conditions, but does not come from anywhere. So, also as this totality of causes and conditions cease to be, this does not go to anywhere. Thus is viewed the coming and going of Tathagatas, and this conforms to true nature of all dharmas. And it is just as this is naturally re-cognized as Tathagatas, and also all dharmas, are neither produced nor stopped, you are fixed on full enlightenment, and you definitely course in perfection of wisdom and in skill in means.

As this disquisition of the fact Tathagatas neither come nor go is being taught, the earth and the entire great trichiliocosm shakes in six ways, stirs, quakes, gets agitated, resounds and rumbles. And all the realms thought to be and seen as of Mara are stirred up and discomfited. All the grasses, shrubs, and herbs and trees in the great trichiliocosm bend in the direction of the Bodhisattva Dharmodgata. [517] Flowers come up out of season. From high up in the air a great rain of flowers comes down. And Sakra, Chief of Gods, and the Four Great Kings scatter and pour heavenly sandalwood powder and heavenly flowers over the Bodhisattva Dharmodgata, and say: "Well spoken, son of good family. Through your might we hear a sermon which issues from ultimate reality, which is contrary to the whole world, and which gives no ground to any beings which are established in any of the views which involve the assumption of an individuality, or have settled down in any of the views which assume the existence of something which is not."

Sadaprarudita now asks Dharmodgata: "What is the cause, what is the reason why this great earthquake is manifested in the world?"

Dharmodgata: In consequence of your asking for this disquisition on the non-coming and non-going of Tathagatas, and through my exposition of this, eight thousand living beings acquire patient acceptance of dharmas which fail to be produced, eighty niyutas of living beings raise their hearts to full enlightenment, and of sixty-four thousand living beings the dispassionate, unstained dharma-eye is purified for vision of dharmas.

Sadaprarudita's Self Sacrifice

The Bodhisattva Sadaprarudita now has a supreme, most sublime feeling of zest and joy: "It is a gain to me, a very great gain by asking for perfection of wisdom, and for this disquisition, I have wrought the weal of so many beings. [518] This alone brings me merit sufficient for the accomplishment of full enlightenment. Unquestionably I become a Tathagata." In his zest and joy he rose seven palm trees high into the air, and, standing at the height of seven palm trees, he reflected: "How can I, standing here in the air, do honor to the Bodhisattva Dharmodgata?" Sakra, Chief of Gods, now sees him, and reads his thoughts, presents him with heavenly Mandarava flowers, and says to him: "Honor the Bodhisattva Dharmodgata with these heavenly flowers! For we feel in this we honor the man who helps you. Today your might wroughts the weal of many thousands of living beings. Rare are the beings who, like you, have the strength, for the sake of all beings through countless aeons to bear such great burden."

The Bodhisattva Sadaprarudita now takes the Mandarava flowers from Sakra, Chief of Gods, and scatters these over the Bodhisattva Dharmodgata. He presents the Bodhisattva Dharmodgata with his own body, and said to him: "I give you myself as a present, and I am your attendant and servant from today onwards." And with hands together he stands before Dharmodgata. [519] The merchant's daughter and her five hundred maidens said to the Bodhisattva Sadaprarudita: "We in our turn make a present of ourselves to you, son of good family. Through this wholesome root we also become recipients of just these dharmas, and together with you we again and again honor and revere the Buddhas and Lords, and the Bodhisattvas, and we remain near to you." Sadaprarudita replied: "As you, maidens, in accordance with my own earnest intention, give yourselves with earnest intention to me, I accept you." The maidens replied: "We are in accord with you, and with earnest resolution we give ourselves as presents to you, to do with us as you may." Here and now the Bodhisattva Sadaprarudita presented the merchant's daughter and her five hundred maidens, embellished and adorned, together with their five hundred well-decorated carriages, to the Bodhisattva Dharmodgata, and said: "All these I present to you as attendants and servants, and also the carriages for your own use." Sakra, Chief of Gods, applauded him and said: "Well done, son of good family! A Bodhisattva renounces any and all property. Through this thought of renunciation one soon realizes full enlightenment, and the worship one pays thus to exponents and preachers of Dharma enables one to hear about perfection of wisdom and skill in means. [520] Also in these three times Tathagatas, as these still are Bodhisattvas, do, by this fact these renounce everything, procure a claim to realization of full enlightenment; and these also ask questions about perfect wisdom and about skill in means." The Bodhisattva Dharmodgata accepted Sadaprarudita's gift, so his wholesome root might reach fulfillment. Immediately afterwards he returned this to Sadaprarudita. After this all, now the Bodhisattva Dharmodgata goes into his house. The sun is about to set.

The Bodhisattva Sadaprarudita thinks to himself: "It does not indeed appear seemly for me, who comes here out of love for dharma, to sit or to lie down. I remain either standing or walking, until the Bodhisattva Dharmodgata again comes out of his house, in order to reveal dharma to us."

The Bodhisattva Dharmodgata remains for seven years immersed in one uninterrupted state of trance, and he dwelt in countless thousands of concentrations, peculiar to Bodhisattvas, which issue from perfection of wisdom and skill in means. For seven years Sadaprarudita adopted any other posture than sitting or lying down, and he did not fall into sloth and torpor. For seven years he never feels any preoccupation with sense desires, or with ill will, or with harming others, he never feels any eagerness for tastes, or any self-satisfaction. But he thinks: "When does the Bodhisattva Dharmodgata emerge from his trance, [521] so we may spread out a seat for him, and hereon he may demonstrate dharma, and so we may sprinkle well the place he reveals perfection of wisdom and skill in means, anoint this well and bedeck it with manifold flowers?" And the merchant's daughter with her five hundred maidens follow this example, pass their time in two postures only, and accorded with all his works.

One day Bodhisattva Sadaprarudita heard a heavenly voice which said: "On the seventh day from today the Bodhisattva Dharmodgata emerges from his trance, and he at this time, seated in the center of the town, demonstrates dharma." As Sadaprarudita hears the heavenly voice, he is contented, elated, joyous, overjoyed and jubilant. Together with the merchant's daughter and her five hundred maidens he cleans the ground, spreads out the seat made of the seven precious things, takes off his upper garment, and spreads it on top of the seat. The maidens also took off their upper garments, spread their five hundred upper garments on this seat, and thought: "Seated on this seat the Bodhisattva Dharmodgata demonstrates dharma." [522] And these also are contented, elated, joyous, overjoyed and jubilant.

As the Bodhisattva Sadaprarudita wanted to sprinkle the ground he cannot find any water, though he searched all round. For Mara, the Evil One, was thought to and therefore seen to have hidden all the water. And he did this so Sadaprarudita, as he cannot find any water, becomes depressed and sad, or change his mind, with the result his wholesome root may vanish, or the fervor of this worship be dimmed. The Bodhisattva Sadaprarudita now thinks to himself: "Let me pierce my own body, and sprinkle the ground with my blood. The ground is full of rising dust, and I fear some of it may fall on the body of the Bodhisattva Dharmodgata. What else can I do with this body which is of necessity doomed to break up? Better surely this my body be destroyed by such an action rather than by an ineffectual one. For the sake of sense pleasures, as a result of sense pleasures many thousands frames of mine again and again, while I wandered in birth-and-death, break up, but never in conditions as favorable as these, never for the sake of gaining the good law. As these once more be broken up, let these in any case be broken up in a holy cause." He [523] took a sharp sword, pierced his body on every side, and everywhere sprinkled any piece of ground with his own blood. The merchant's daughter with her five hundred maidens followed his example, and did as he did. But here is no alteration of thought in either the Bodhisattva Sadaprarudita, or in all these maidens, which gives what's seen and thought of as Mara, the Evil One, a chance of entering in order to obstruct these wholesome roots.

Sakra, Chief of Gods, thinks to himself: "It is wonderful how this Bodhisattva Sadaprarudita loves dharma, how firm his sense of obligation, how great this armor he has put on, and how he disregards this body, this life, and these pleasures, and how resolutely he sets out with the goal of knowing full enlightenment, in his aspiration to set free any and all beings from measureless sufferings of birth-and-death, once he knows full enlightenment." Sakra now changes by magic all this blood into heavenly sandalwood water. And all round this piece of ground, for one hundred leagues, an inconceivable sublime scent, the scent of the heavenly sandalwood water, filled the air. And Sakra said to Sadaprarudita: "Well done, son of good family! I applaud your inconceivable vigor, your supreme love and search for dharma. The Tathagatas in this past [524] also procure the right to full enlightenment through this kind of earnest intention, vigor, and love for dharma."

The Bodhisattva Sadaprarudita now thinks to himself: "I spread out the seat for the Bodhisattva Dharmodgata, and I swept and sprinkled this piece of ground. Now I must still get flowers with which to cover this peace of ground, and to scatter over the Bodhisattva Dharmodgata as he demonstrates dharma." Sakra now says to Sadaprarudita: "Accept these heavenly Mandarava flowers for this twofold purpose!" And he presented him with a thousand heavenly Khara measures of heavenly flowers. And the Bodhisattva Sadaprarudita accepted these flowers, and used some of them to cover the piece of ground, and, later on, he strewed others over the Bodhisattva Dharmodgata.

Dharmodgata's Demonstration of Dharma

At the lapse of seven years the Bodhisattva Dharmodgata emerges from his trance, goes up to the seat spread out for him, sits down on this, and, surrounded and attended by an assembly of many hundreds of thousands, he demonstrates dharma. The moment the Bodhisattva Sadaprarudita [525] sees the Bodhisattva Dharmodgata, he is filled with a kind of happiness which a monk feels as, with one-pointed attention, he obtains the first trance. And this is the demonstration of the perfection of wisdom by the Bodhisattva Dharmodgata:

"The perfection of wisdom is self-identical and as such, any and all dharmas are same. Perfect wisdom is isolated and as such, any and all dharmas are isolated. Perfect wisdom is immobile and as such, any and all dharmas are immobile. Perfect wisdom is devoid of mental acts and as such, any and all dharmas are devoid of mental acts. Perfect wisdom is unbenumbed and as such, any and all dharmas are unbenumbed. Perfect wisdom has but one single taste and as such, any and all dharmas have one and the same taste. Perfect wisdom is boundless and as such, any and all dharmas are boundless. Perfect wisdom is non-produced and as such, any and all dharmas are non-produced. Perfect wisdom is non-stopping and as such, all dharmas are not stopped. As firmament is boundless, so perfect wisdom. As the ocean is boundless, so perfect wisdom. As Meru shines in multicolored brilliance, so does perfection of wisdom. As firmament is not fashioned, so perfect wisdom is not fashioned. Perfect wisdom is boundless, and as such form, and the other skandhas are boundless. Perfect wisdom is boundless and as such, the element of earth, and the other elements, are boundless. Perfect wisdom is self-identical, and as such, the adamantine dharma is self-identical. Perfect wisdom is undifferentiated and as such, all dharmas are undifferentiated. Non-apprehension of perfect wisdom follows from non-apprehension of all dharmas. Perfect wisdom remains the same regardless of whatever or whoever this may appear to surpass and as such all dharmas remain the same regardless of whatever or whoever these may surpass. [526] Perfect wisdom is powerless to act and as such all dharmas are powerless to act. Perfect wisdom is unthinkable and as such, all dharmas are unthinkable."

Here and now on this occasion is born in the Bodhisattva Sadaprarudita the king of concentrations called "sameness of any and all dharmas," and, consequent on this, the concentrations called "isolation of any and all dharmas," "immobility of any and all dharmas," "absence of any and all mental acts in any and all dharmas," "lack of numbness in any and all dharmas," "the one taste of any and all dharmas," "boundlessness of any and all dharmas," "boundless like firmament," "boundless like the ocean," "brilliant and multicolored like Meru," "not fashioned, like firmament," "boundless like form, etc.," "boundless like the element of earth, etc.," "adamantine," "non-differentiatedness of any and all dharmas," "non-apprehension of any and all dharmas," "sameness of any and all dharmas whatever these may surpass," "any and all dharmas are powerless to act," "any and all dharmas are unthinkable." Beginning with these, the Bodhisattva Sadaprarudita acquired six million concentration doors.

Chapter 32: ~ENTRUSTING~

End of the Story of Sadaprarudita

In conjunction with acquisition of these six million concentration doors, the Bodhisattva Sadaprarudita sees the Buddhas and Lords, - in all ten directions in countless trichiliocosms - surrounded by congregations of monks, accompanied by multitudes of Bodhisattvas, teaching just this perfection of wisdom, through just these methods, in just these words, in just these letters, even as I just now in this great trichiliocosm demonstrate dharma, - surrounded by this congregation of monks, accompanied by multitudes of Bodhisattvas, and teaching just this perfection of wisdom, through just these methods, in just these words, in just these letters. He is endowed with inconceivable learning and a sacred knowledge vast as the ocean. In all his births he never again is deprived of the Buddha. He is reborn only in such places as he is face to face with Buddhas, the Lords. All unfortunate rebirths he abandoned, and he secured circumstances which allowed him to accomplish one auspicious rebirth after another.

The Perfection of Wisdom Entrusted to Ananda

The Lord hereby says to the Venerable Ananda: In this manner also do you know this perfection of wisdom as the one who nurses the cognition of the all-knowing in the Bodhisattvas. Here now, Ananda, a Bodhisattva who aspires to acquire cognition of the all-knowing courses in this perfection of wisdom, [528] hears this, takes this up, studys, spreads, repeats and writes this. Now, through Tathagatas sustaining power this is well written, in very distinct letters, in a great book, one honors, reveres, adores and worships this, with flowers, incense, scents, wreaths, unguents, aromatic powders, strips of cloth, parasols, banners, bells, flags and with rows of lamps all round, and with manifold kinds of worship. This is our admonition to you, Ananda. For in this perfection of wisdom the cognition of all-knowing is brought to perfection. What do you think, Ananda, is Tathagata your teacher?

Ananda: He is, O Lord.

The Lord: The Tathagata is your teacher, Ananda. You minister to me,

Ananda, with friendly acts of body, acts of speech, acts of mind. Here now, Ananda, just as you give affection, faith and respect to me as I am at present in this incarnation, just so, Ananda, act after my decease towards this perfection of wisdom. For the second time, for the third time, I entrust and transmit to you this perfection of wisdom, so this does not disappear. No man is as suitable as you are. As long as this perfection of wisdom is observed in the world, one can be sure for so long does Tathagata abide in this, also for so long does Tathagata demonstrate dharma, and the beings in it are not lacking in vision of the Buddha, hearing of dharma, attendance of the Sangha. One knows these beings are living in presence of Tathagata who hear this perfection of wisdom, take this up, study, spread, repeat and write this, and who honor, revere, adore and worship this.

Thus spoke the Lord. Enraptured, the Bodhisattvas, headed by Maitreya, and the Venerable Subhuti, and the Venerable Ananda, and Sakra, Chief of Gods, and the entire world with its Gods, men, Asuras, Garudas and Gandharvas delighted in the Lord's teaching.

phyag 'tshal lo

SarvaMangalam...

May All Beings Benefit...

In prayer for blessings to all,
Copper ~^~